Essential Music Theory © 2023 by San Marco Publications. All rights reserved.

All right reserved. No part of this book may be reproduced in any form or by electronic or mechanical means including Information storage and retrieval systems without permission in writing from the author.

ISNB: 9798852531308

Contents

Chapter 1: **Fundamentals of Harmonization**   1

Chapter 2: **Seventh Chords**   31

Chapter 3: **Leading Tone 7th Chords**   40

Chapter 4: **Non-dominant 7th Chords**   62

Chapter 5: **Harmonic Sequences**   77

Chapter 6: **Tonicization and Secondary Dominants**   90

Chapter 7: **Modulation**   114

Chapter 8: **Dominant 9th and 13th Chords**   128

Chapter 9: **The Bach Chorales**   139

Chapter 10: **Form and Analysis**   149

Chapter 11: **Melody Writing**   213

1
Fundamentals of Harmonization

Chords Within a Key

Figure 1.1 contains all the chords in a major key that were studied in the first harmony book. Two types of chord symbols are used in this example:

Root Quality Chord Symbols: These are letters placed above the staff to indicate the root of the chord and its quality (major, minor etc). Major chords use the letter only (C). Minor chords use the letter with an "m" (Dm). Minor 7th chords use "m7" (Dm7). Dominant 7th chords use "7" (G7) and diminished chords use "dim" or a degree sign ° next to the letter (Bdim or B°).

Functional Chord Symbols: These symbols are Roman numerals placed beneath the chord and indicate the root of the chord by the scale degree upon which it is built. I is built on $\hat{1}$, ii is built on $\hat{2}$, etc. Uppercase Roman numerals are used for major chords (I), and lowercase are used for minor chords (iii). Diminished chords use a lowercase numeral with a small degree sign (°) placed next to the letters (vii°). 7th chords have a small 7 next to the Roman numeral (V^7).

Figure 1.1

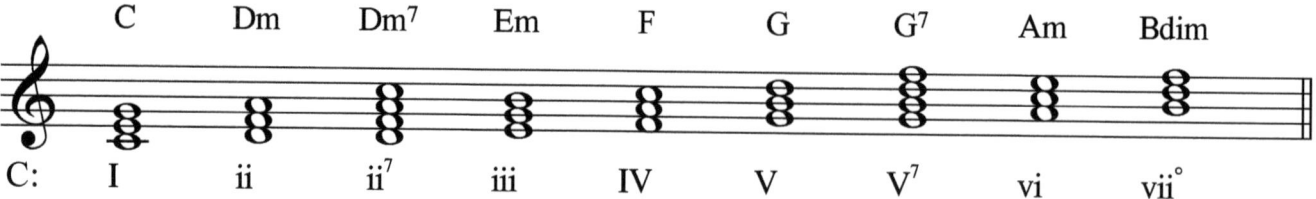

1. Built chords on the following major scale degrees. Include 7th chords built on ii and V. Add the root/quality and the functional chord symbols. Name the keys.

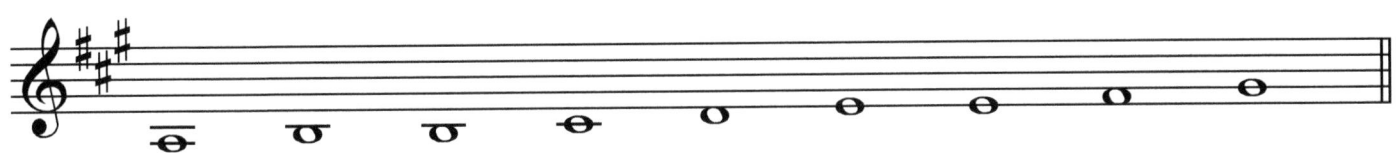

The chords in Figure 1.2 are built on the notes of the minor scale. There are three minor scales, natural, harmonic and melodic. Because of this, there are more notes available, and more chords are possible. The root/quality chord symbol for an augmented chord is an uppercase letter with "aug" as in Faug. The functional chord symbol uses an uppercase Roman numeral with a + sign (III+).

Figure 1.2

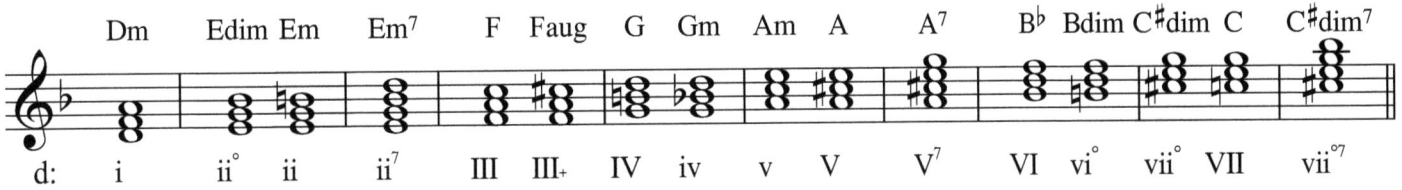

2. Name the keys of the following. Write the root/quality and functional chord symbols for the following chords in minor keys.

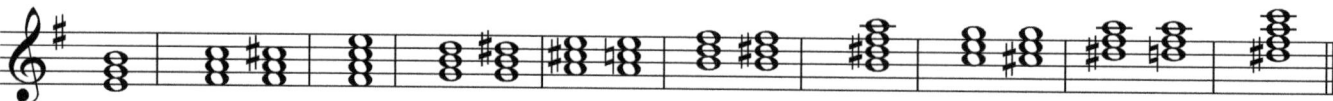

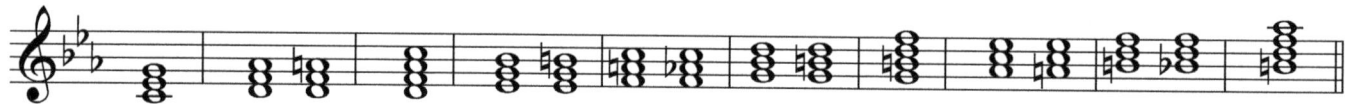

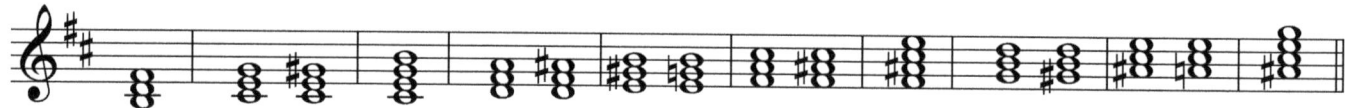

Chord Inversions

First inversion triads have the third in the bass, and are symbolized with a 6 following the Roman numeral (for example, IV⁶).

Figure 1.3

Second inversion triads have the fifth in the bass, and are symbolized with a $^6_4$ next to the Roman numeral (for example IV$^6_4$).

Figure 1.4

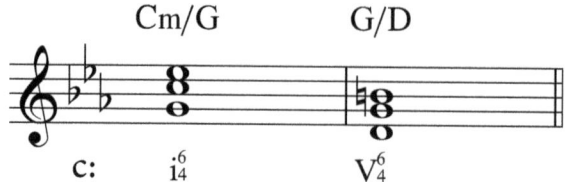

3 Chapter 1: Fundamentals of Harmonization

Figure 1.5 is an illustration of the chord symbols used for 7th chords.

Figure 1.5

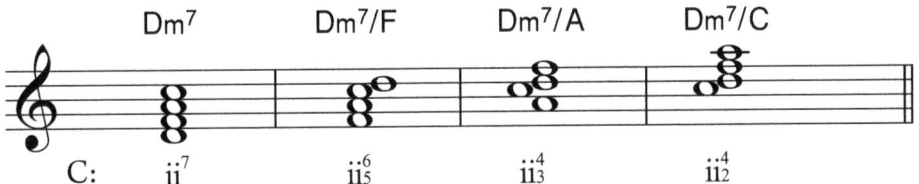

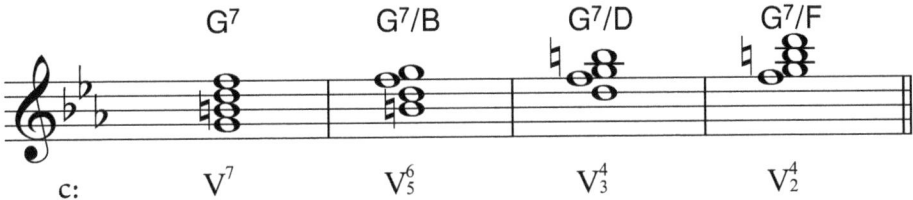

Notation and Voicing

The voice configuration for the four part choir is shown in Figure 1.6. It should be noted that:

- The soprano is the highest voice and is written in the treble clef with the stems going up.
- The alto is the next highest voice and is written in the treble staff with the stems going down.
- The tenor is written in the bass staff with the stems going up.
- The bass is written in the bass staff with the stems going down.

Figure 1.6

When we write for these (human) voices we must consider that there are ranges in which each person can sing. These ranges are shown in Figure 1.7. There are not really absolute limits to voice range. Every singer is different, but you should try to keep within the ranges outlined here.

Figure 1.7

Errors to Avoid in Four Part Writing

In four part writing, the soprano is the highest voice followed in downward order by the alto, tenor and bass. When this order is not followed, a fault called *crossed parts* occurs. In Figure 1.8, the error of crossed parts occurs between the tenor and alto in (a) and between the alto and soprano in (b). (c) and (d) show the corrected versions.

There should not be more than one octave between the top three voices. The spacing between the tenor and bass can exceed an octave as long as it stays within their voice ranges.

Figure 1.8

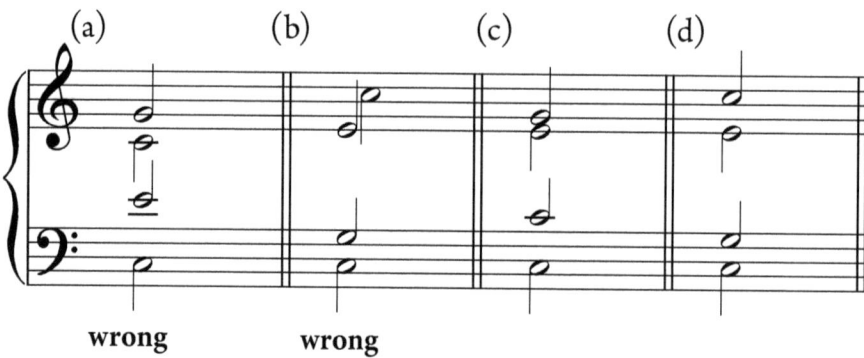

Figure 1.9 (a) and (b) are examples of an error called *voice overlap*. In (a) the alto moves to a pitch (A) higher than the soprano just sang (G). In (b) the tenor moves to a pitch (E) lower than the bass just sang (F). These are incorrect. (c) is acceptable because the overlap is approached by step. Overlaps should be avoided in four part writing.

Figure 1.9

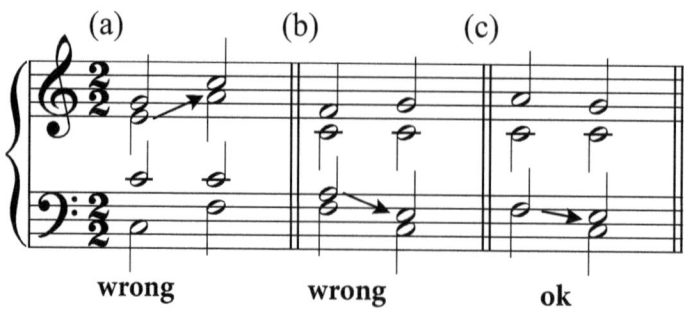

1. Some of the following chords contain errors. Find and mark any errors involving crossed parts or incorrect spacing.

In four part writing certain parallel motion between voices is forbidden. Parallel motion occurs when two voices move in the same direction by the same interval. The following parallel intervals are considered faulty and are forbidden:

- *Parallel unisons* are not allowed between two voices. In Figure 1.10 (a) the alto and tenor move in parallel unison and in (b) the soprano and alto move in parallel unison. When two voices sing the same note, it sounds like one voice has dropped out and there are only three parts remaining.
- *Parallel octaves* are forbidden. 1.10(c) and (d) illustrate parallel perfect octaves. Here, the same pitch and motion is duplicated in a different voice and the individuality and independence of the voices are lost.
- *Parallel perfect fifths* are considered wrong. 1.10(e) and (f) contain faulty parallel perfect fifths. The fifth is a very stable interval. In a texture of individual voices, parallel fifths sound out of character and unstylistic.

Figure 1.10

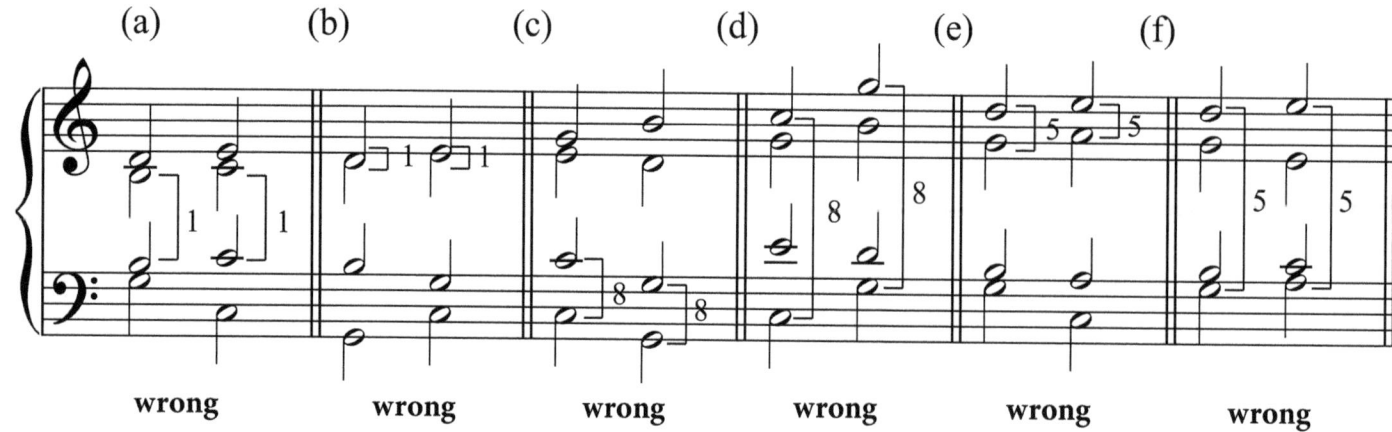

A fault called *hidden* or *direct 8ves* or *5ths* occurs when an octave or perfect fifth between outer voices is approached by similar motion with a leap in the soprano (Figure 1.11 (a) and (b)). The sound of these is similar to a parallel 8ve or 5th. If the soprano is approached by step the 8ve or 5th is fine (Figure 1.11 (c)).

Figure 1.11

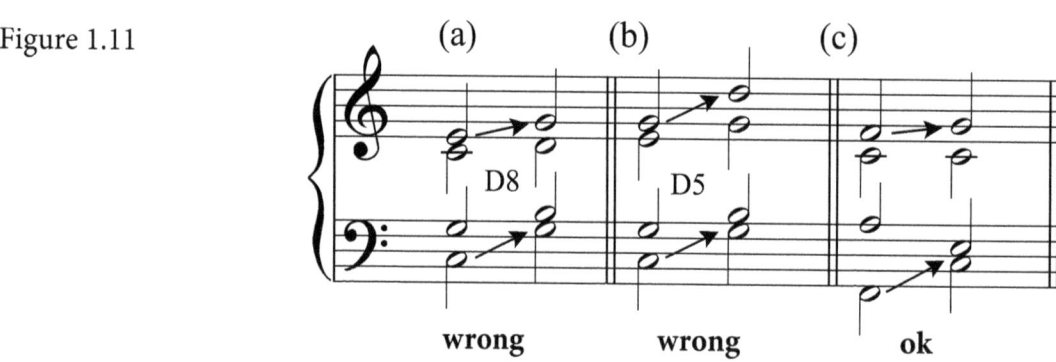

2. Find and mark any faulty parallel, hidden or direct motion, in the following progressions.

The Four Areas of Harmonization

There are four basic areas of harmonic activity: the **beginning tonic**, the **predominant**, the **dominant**, and the **ending tonic**. Most harmonic progressions occur in one of these four areas.

Each of these areas can be expanded so that they sound a longer time. This expansion is called **prolongation**. Figure 1.12 contains the four areas of harmonization and includes a prolongation of the beginning tonic area.

Figure 1.12

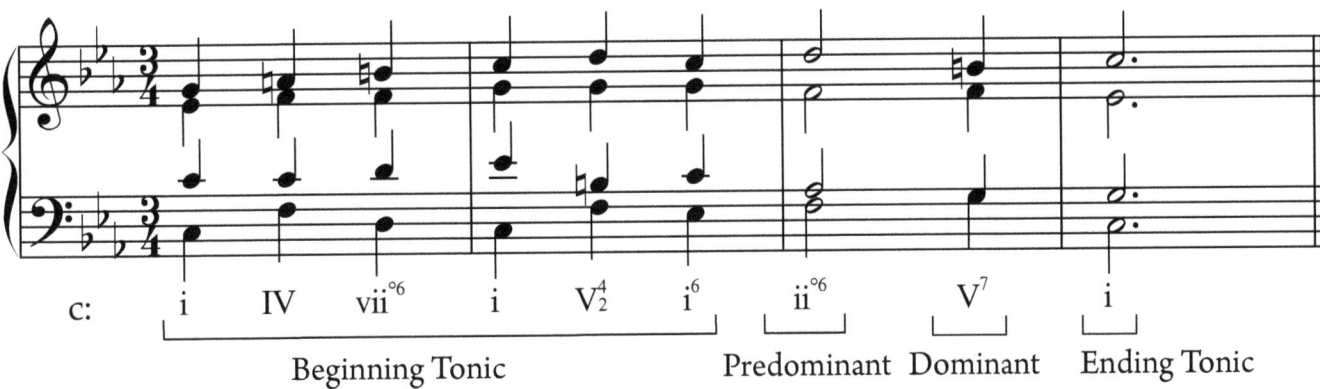

The Tonic Chord

The tonic chord (I or i) functions the same way in both major and minor keys. A tonic chord usually serves as both the opening harmony and the final harmonic goal of a piece of music. In Figure 1.13 Beethoven establishes the key of E♭ by using the I chord for the opening six measures of this movement.

Figure 1.13

The Dominant Chord

A tonic chord is often preceded by a dominant chord (V or V⁷). The major form of V functions in the dominant area in the same way in both major and minor keys, and is used in authentic, half, and deceptive cadences. The opening 2 phrases of Schubert's B minor Waltz in Figure 1.14 consist entirely of tonic and dominant chords.

Figure 1.14

Waltz in B minor
op. 18, no. 5

Franz Schubert
(1797-1828)

The minor form of v, which occurs in minor keys, is not often used, but it may be found in the progression v⁶ - iv⁶. In this progression, the lowered $\hat{7}$ of v⁶ in the bass moves to $\hat{6}$ in chord iv⁶.

Figure 1.15

Johann Sebastian Bach
Chorale no. 208: Als vierzig Tag'nach Ostern

The Supertonic Chord

Chord ii functions in the predominant area, and usually moves to V. Since degree $\hat{6}$ is raised in the melodic form of the minor scale, chord ii can take two forms. In minor scales without an altered $\hat{6}$, ii is most often used in first inversion (ii°6). In minor scales where $\hat{6}$ is raised, ii is a minor chord and may be used in root position or first inversion.

Figure 1.16

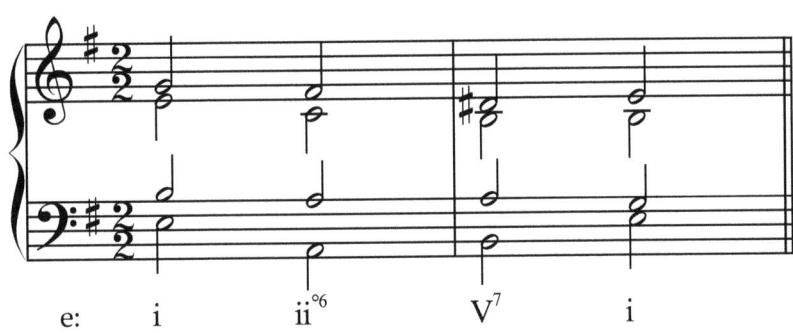

The Subdominant Chord

The subdominant chord is used in the same way in both major and minor keys, and it often functions as a predominant, either alone or linked with ii. In major keys, IV is a major chord. In minor keys the subdominant can be either major or minor, since it contains scale degree $\hat{6}$. Chord IV (or iv) may move to a tonic chord (I or i) creating a plagal cadence.

Figure 1.17

The Submediant Chord

In major keys, chord vi is a minor chord. In minor keys, it can be either major or diminished depending on whether scale degree $\hat{6}$ of the minor scale is raised, but it is rarely used in its diminished form. Chord vi or VI may occur in a deceptive cadence. It may also be used as a predominant, leading to V. The submediant chord can function as a link with other predominant chords, and is particularly effective in a bass line of descending 3rds (I - vi - IV - V - I or I - vi - ii^6 - V).

Figure 1.18

The Mediant Chord

In major keys, iii is a minor chord. In minor keys where degree $\hat{7}$ of the scale is not raised, III is a major chord. The major and minor forms of the mediant chord are used in the same way, and this chord often occurs as a link between I and IV.

Figure 1.19

In minor keys where the harmonic minor scale is used, the triad built on the mediant is augmented (III$^+$). For now we will not use it in root position, but it may be used in first inversion, followed by V or V^7, much like a cadential six four.

Figure 1.20

The Leading Tone and Subtonic Chords

Chord vii° in its diminished form occurs in both major and minor keys, and is most often used in first inversion. It can substitute for V in an authentic cadence, but is used more frequently between two positions of the tonic triad (I - vii°6 - I6 - vii°6 - I).

Figure 1.21

In minor keys, when scale degree $\hat{7}$ is not raised it does not have a leading tone function, and is therefore often referred to as the subtonic rather than the leading tone. If scale degree $\hat{7}$ is not raised, VII is a major chord. This form is found most often in a circle of fifths sequence.

Figure 1.22

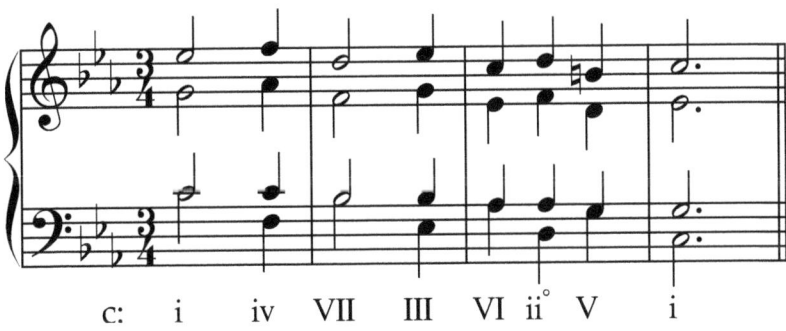

Review of Part Writing Techniques

- When connecting chords whose roots are a fifth apart, (like V and I) repeat the common tone in the same voice and move the remaining voices to the nearest chord tones using correct doubling and spacing. Maintain either open or closed spacing for both chords. Figure 1.23(a)

- Sometimes, because of melodic considerations, it is not possible to repeat the common tone in the same voice. In this case, move all voices to the nearest chord tones using correct doubling and spacing. Maintain either open or closed spacing for both chords. Figure 1.23(b)

- If the leading tone is in an outer voice it must rise to the tonic. Figure 1.23(a)

- Never double the leading tone in a chord.

Figure 1.23

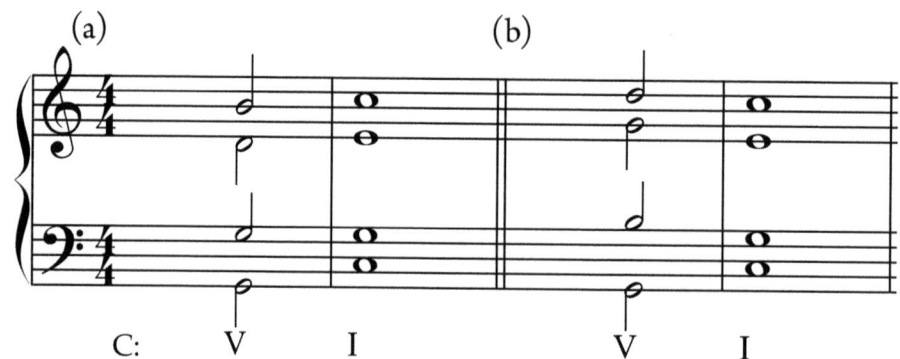

- When connecting some chords whose roots are a second apart like IV to V and I to ii, where there are no common tones, move the three upper notes in contrary motion to the bass (down). This avoids faulty parallel motion.

- Try not to leap more than a 4th in the inner voices (alto and tenor).

Figure 1.24

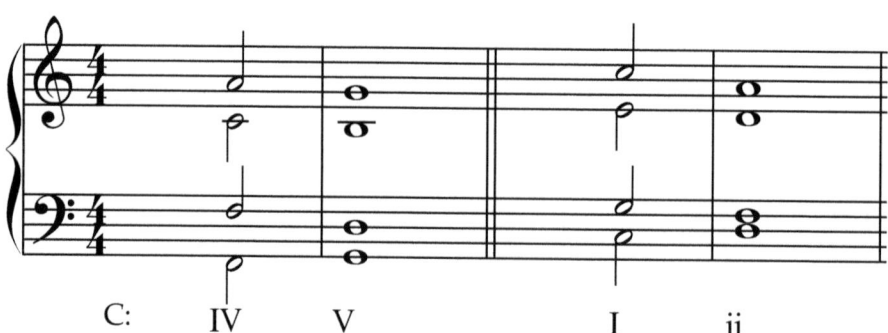

- The progression VI to V or V to VI requires special attention. Here, when connecting these two chords in major keys, one option is to move the three upper voices in contrary motion to the bass as in Figure 1.25(a).

- However, this is not effective in a minor key since an augmented 2nd can occur melodically as shown in Figure 1.25(b).

- In this progression in minor keys it is best to make two voices rise, two voices fall and to double the 3rd in VI as in Figure 1.25(c).
- As a general rule, the voicing as seen in Figure 1.25(c) can be used in both major and minor keys and is effective with this progression.

Figure 1.25

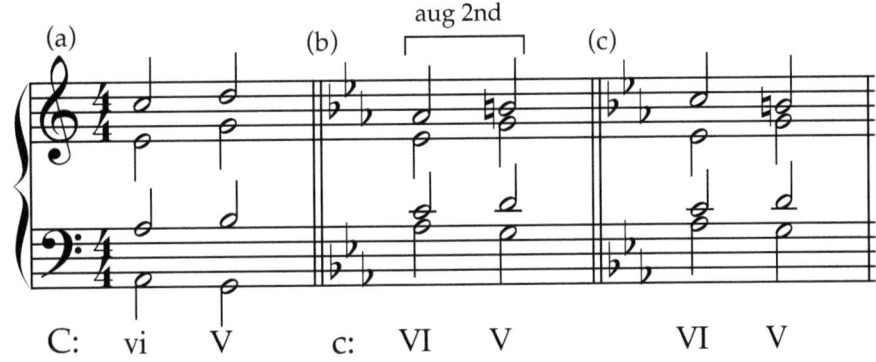

- V⁷ can occur as a complete chord containing the root, 3rd, 5th and 7th (Figure 1.26(a)) or as an incomplete chord containing a doubled root, 3rd and 7th (leaving out the 5th) Figure 1.26(b).
- V⁷ in inversion is always a complete chord containing the root, 3rd, 5th and 7th.
- A complete V⁷ chord can resolve to a I chord consisting of three roots and a 3rd Figure 1.26(a). An incomplete V⁷ always resolves to a complete I chord Figure 1.26(b).

Figure 1.26

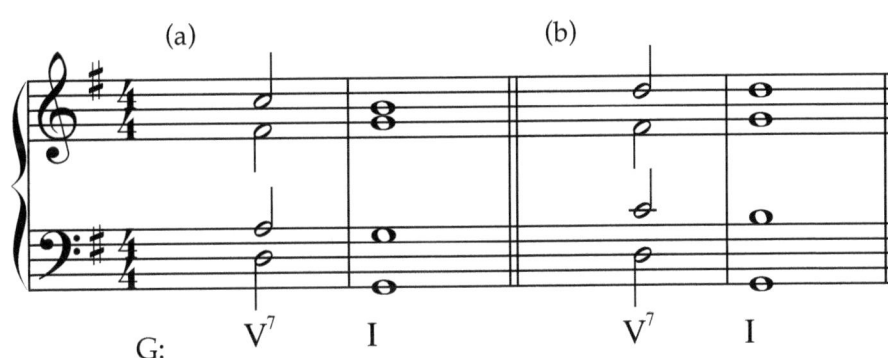

- The 7th of a 7th chord (e.g. V⁷ or ii⁷) always falls in its resolution to the next chord.
- The 7th of ii⁷ should be prepared with common tone motion from the previous chord if possible.
- Unless ii (or ii⁷) is prolonging I, it almost always moves to V or V⁷ or its inversions.

Figure 1.27

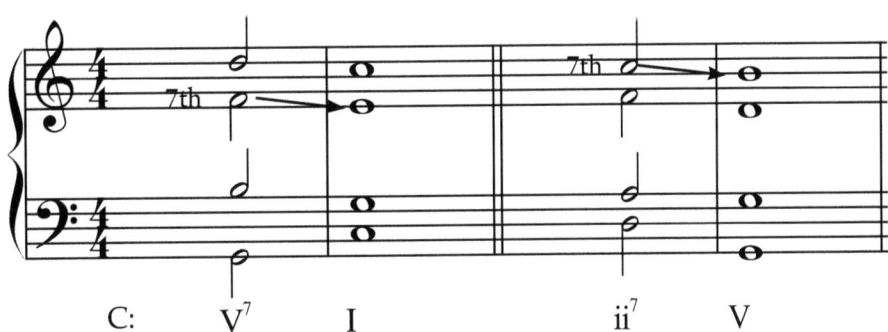

14 Chapter 1: Fundamentals of Harmonization

- When writing vii⁶, always double the bass note which is the 3rd of the chord. Figure 1.28(a)
- Always check every chord for faulty parallel 5ths and octaves. To do this, find the octave and 5th within a chord and check if there is an octave or 5th in the same place in the next chord. For example, if one chord has an octave between the bass and alto, check the bass and alto in the next chord to be sure there is not an octave there. Figure 1.28(b)

Figure 1.28

- Never write an augmented interval melodically, especially augmented 4ths and augmented 2nds, which can occur in a minor scale between $\hat{6}$ and raised $\hat{7}$. Raise both $\hat{6}$ and $\hat{7}$ to avoid an augmented 2nd.

Figure 1.29

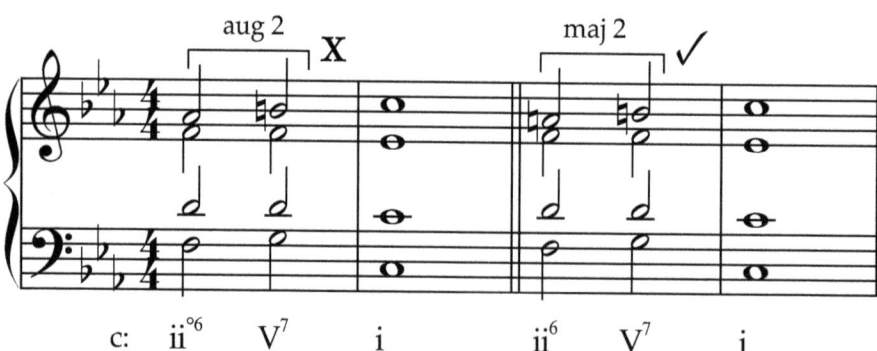

- Six-four chords can only be used in specific progressions. These are ornamental or decorative chords and only function in conjunction with other chords.
- Figure 1.30 illustrates four different six four chords. Cadential, passing, and neighbor six four chords are dissonant and occur as a result of linear motion. Their function is to prolong and decorate other harmonies.
- The arpeggio six four is a consonant six four. Consonant six four chords are heard as the second inversion of a triad and do not have a linear function. *Note that the 5th, which is in the bass, is always doubled in a six four chord.*

Figure 1.30

- Secondary dominants, contain accidentals reflecting the new key. (V/V, V/IV, etc). Always check V/V to see what accidentals are needed.
- In Figure 1.31 the V in m. 3 becomes a temporary tonic because it is preceded by its dominant, V_5^6 of G major. This piece is in C major. The F♯ is not a note of C major and reflects the key of the temporary tonic (G major). We still hear the G chord as V of C major, but it is made a temporary tonic because of the D^7 chord that precedes it. D^7 is not a chord in C major and this example moves to G major for an instant. It then continues with an authentic cadence in C major. The D^7 chord is considered a *secondary dominant*.

Figure 1.31

1. Complete the following progressions in four parts.

2. Harmonize the following melody for four voices. Show all functional chord symbols.

B♭ major

3. Complete the following descending 5ths sequence in four parts. Double the root in each chord.

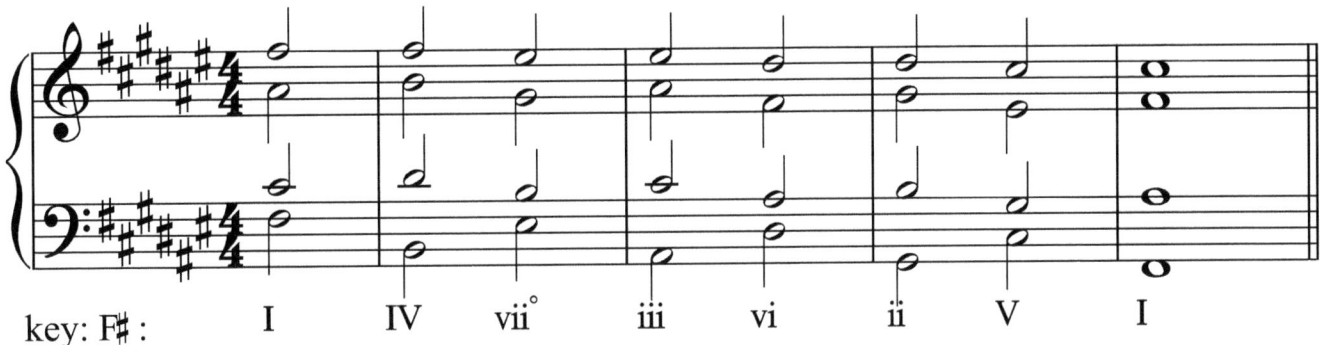

key: F♯ :   I   IV   vii°   iii   vi   ii   V   I

4. Complete the following progressions in four parts.

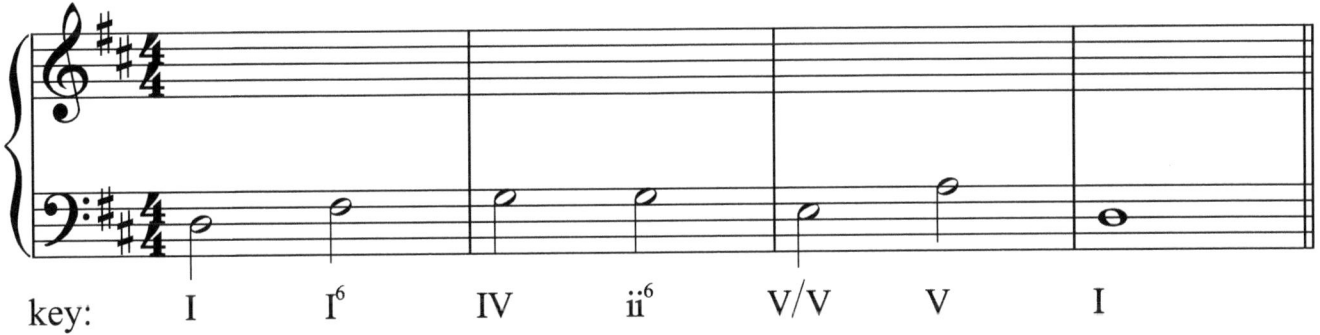

key: I   I⁶   IV   ii⁶   V/V   V   I

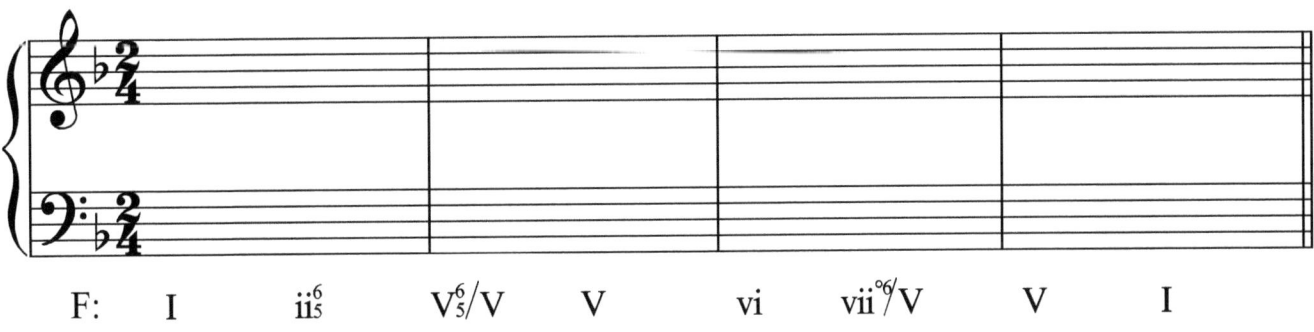

F: I   ii$^6_5$ V$^6_5$/V   V   vi   vii°⁶/V   V   I

Non-chord Tones

Non-chord tones are notes that are not part of the underlying harmony or chord structure. They are used to decorate the melody and provide rhythmic interest and motion. These tones are classified according to their metrical position and the way in which they are approached and left.

The Pedal Point

A **pedal point** is a tone that is held throughout several changes of harmony, but it is not itself part of the harmonies produced by the other voices. This non-chord tone gets its name from the organist's technique of sustaining a single tone with the pedal while playing other harmonies above.

Pedal points can appear in any part but are most often found in the bass. The pedal may be any note but it is usually the tonic or the dominant. If a pedal is in the bass, inversions are not indicated in a harmonic analysis. The sound of the inversions is altered by the pedal and there are no conventional symbols to show this alteration. Figure 1.32 contains a tonic pedal.

Figure 1.32

Johann Sebastian Bach
French Suite no. 1 BWV 812 Allemande

The charts on the following pages contain the most common non-chord tones.

Non-Chord Tone	Approached	Left	Metrical Position	Use in Melody
passing tone (PT)	by step	by step	weak	skip between notes
accented passing tone (APT)	by step	by step	strong	skip between notes
upper neighbor (NN)	by step	by step	weak	between common tones
lower neighbor (NN)	by step	by step	weak	between common tones
accented neighbor (ANN)	by step	by step	strong	between common tones
incomplete neighbor (IN)	by leap	by step	weak	stepwise motion up / stepwise motion down

Chapter 1: Fundamentals of Harmonization

Non-Chord Tone	Approached	Left	Metrical Position	Use in Melody
échappée (Ech)	by step	by leap	weak	stepwise motion down / stepwise motion up
neighbor group (NG)	by step or leap	by step or leap	variable	between common tones
anticipation (Antic)	by step	by repeat	weak	stepwise motion up $\hat{7}$-$\hat{1}$ / stepwise motion down $\hat{2}$-$\hat{1}$
suspension (Susp)	by same note	by step	strong	stepwise motion down
appoggiatura (App)	by leap	by step	strong	leap

Chapter 1: Fundamentals of Harmonization

1. Provide a harmonic analysis of the following excerpts. Identify and label all non-chord tones.

key:

key:

key:

Chapter 1: Fundamentals of Harmonization

Johann Sebastian Bach
WTC I, Prelude in C major, BWV 846

key:

Johann Sebastian Bach
Chorale 74: O Haupt voll Blut und Wunden

key F: vi IV I⁶ ii I ii⁶₅ V I
d. III V⁶ i i⁶ V V⁸⁻⁷ i

Franz Schubert
"Ständchen" from Schwanengesang

Lei se flie - hen mei ne Lie der durch die Nacht zu dir;

key:

Figured Bass Realization

Music written in the baroque era often included a part called the **basso continuo** or **thorough bass**. This consisted of a single bass clef melody with various numbers and accidentals printed beneath the notes.

The part of the basso continuo was played by two instruments: a bass clef instrument like a cello, double bass, or bassoon, and a keyboard instrument like a harpsichord. During performances, the bass clef instrument would play the given melodic line and the keyboard player would improvise a part based on the melodic line and the symbols written below the line.

Figure 1.33 is an example of a this type of melodic line called a **figured bass**.

Figure 1.33

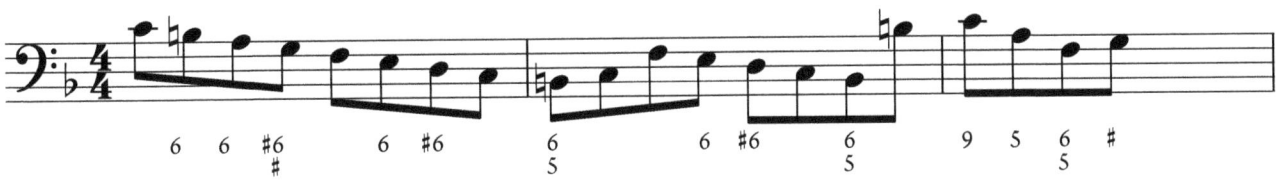

This figured bass line could be played like Figure 1.34. This is called **realizing the bass**.

Figure 1.34

The note given in the bass clef is always the lowest note played. It is the lowest note of the chord but not necessarily the root.

The numbers represent the intervals above the bass, even though some numbers are usually left out. The intervals created by these numbers are always diatonic. Always use notes from the key signature.

Figure 1.35

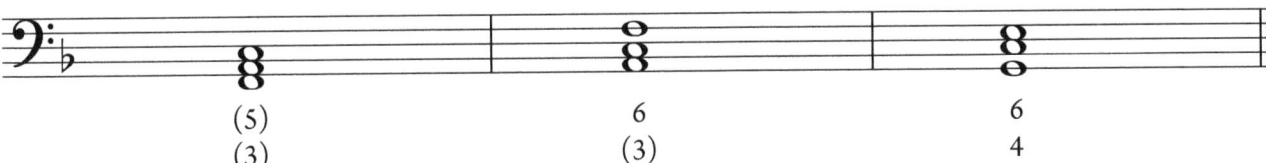

If there are no numbers, add a 3rd and a 5th above the bass to get a *root position triad*

A "6" by itself indicates a 6th and a 3rd above the bass note which creates a *first inversion triad*

A "6" and a "4" indicates a 6th and a 4th above the bass creating a *second inversion triad.*

Figure 1.36

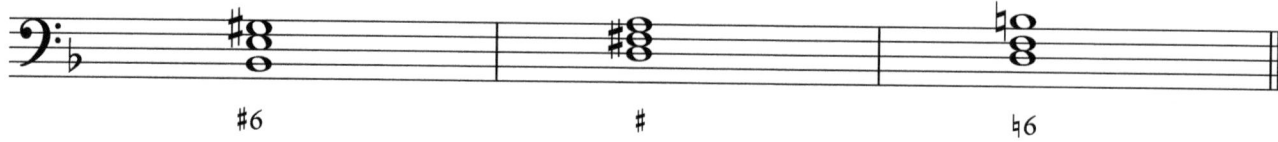

♯6	♯	♮6
In this chord the sharp applies to the 6th above the bass. We add a sharp to the G	If there is no number next to the sharp it always means to apply the accidental to the 3rd above the bass	This example uses a natural not a sharp. B is flat and a natural is used to raise it.

Accidentals are applied to the interval number that they appear with. An accidental by itself always applies to the third above the bass. If a composer wants a natural note raised by a half step, a sharp will be used. If the note is flat, a natural will be used in the figuration.

Study the following chart indicating figures used for triads and 7th chords and their inversions.

Chord		Complete Figure	Figures Used
Triad in root position		5 3	No figures used
Triad in first inversion		6 3	6
Triad in second inversion		6 4	6 4
Seventh chord in root position		7 5 3	7
Seventh chord in first inversion		6 5 3	6 5
Seventh chord in second inversion		6 4 3	4 3
Seventh chord in third inversion		6 4 2	4 2

To **realize** a figured bass we play or write out the figured bass keyboard part. For written out figured bass parts in keyboard style, the bass note is placed in the bass clef and played by the left hand. The upper notes (soprano, alto, and tenor) are placed in the treble clef and are played by the right hand. The notes are written in close position with the distance between the three upper parts not more than one octave.

The voice leading rules are the same as those for chorale settings. No inappropriate doubling, voice crossing, or parallel motion is allowed.

In Figure 1.37 (a), all chords are in root position so no figuration is needed. Figure 1.37(b) illustrates the acceptable ranges is for the notes in each clef.

Figure 1.37

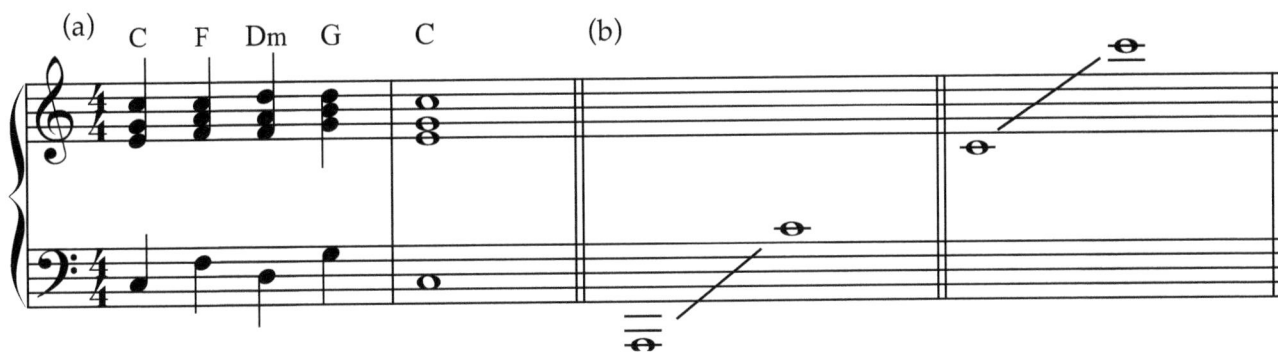

When notes are doubled, care must be taken with the placement of stems and doubled whole notes. Review the notation in Figure 1.38 (a).

A slash across the number, or a + after a number, means that the note is raised a half step. All three symbols in Figure 1.38 (b) have the same meaning.

Figure 1.38

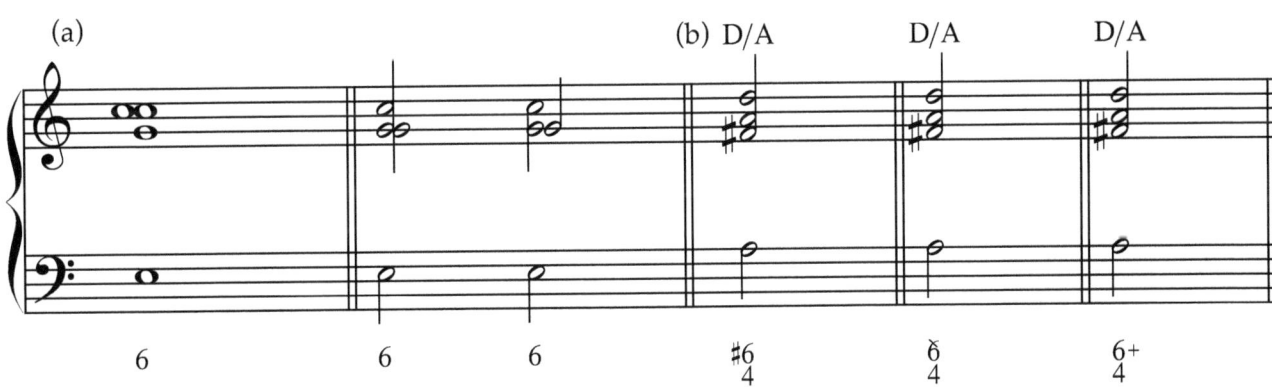

26 Chapter 1: Fundamentals of Harmonization

Octave doubling may occur if the composer wants a certain note to be doubled, but they are not usually indicated in the figures. In Figure 1.39 (a), the line after the 8 means that the note an octave above the bass(G) must be repeated or sustained in the same voice.

Dashes between figures indicate movement in the upper parts. The 6th and the 5th above G must be placed in the same voice (6-5 = E-D)and the same applies to the 4th and 3rd above G (4-3 = C-B). In Figure 1.39 (b), with a dash over a stationary bass, the actual chord occurs with the figure at the end; here, a C major chord in first inversion.

Dashes placed below a moving bass indicate that the notes in the upper voices remains stationary (Figure 1.39 (c)).

Figure 1.39

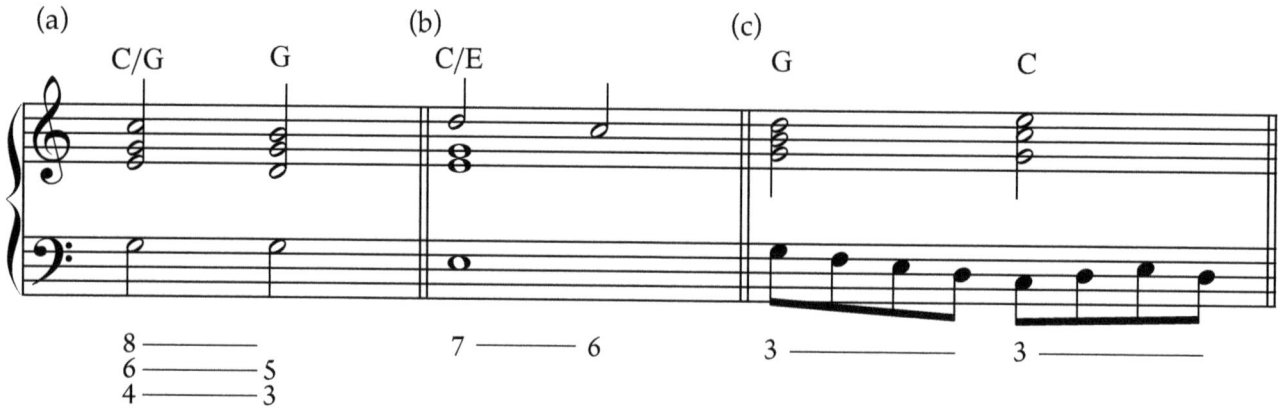

Occasionally, some segments of a figured bass may be realized in three part texture. In this case, two voices are placed in the treble clef above a single note in the bass. This voicing may be used when a series of first inversion chords occur in scale-wise succession (Figure 1.40).

Figure 1.40

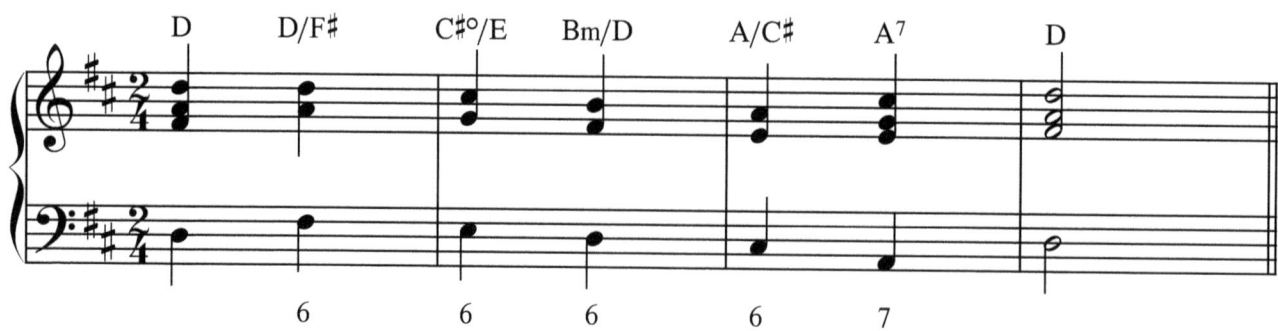

Chapter 1: Fundamentals of Harmonization

1. Give the root/quality chord symbols implied by the following figured bass symbols.

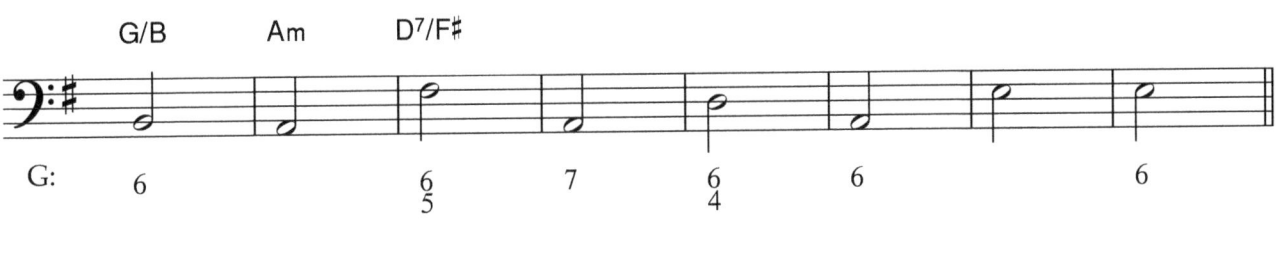

2. Provide the figured bass and root/quality chord symbols for the following chords.

3. Complete the following chords in keyboard style according to the given figures. Add root/quality chord symbols.

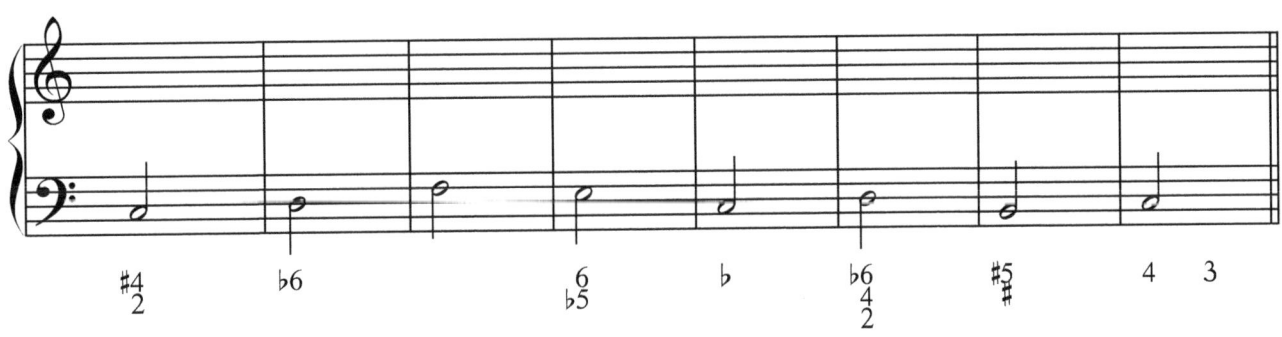

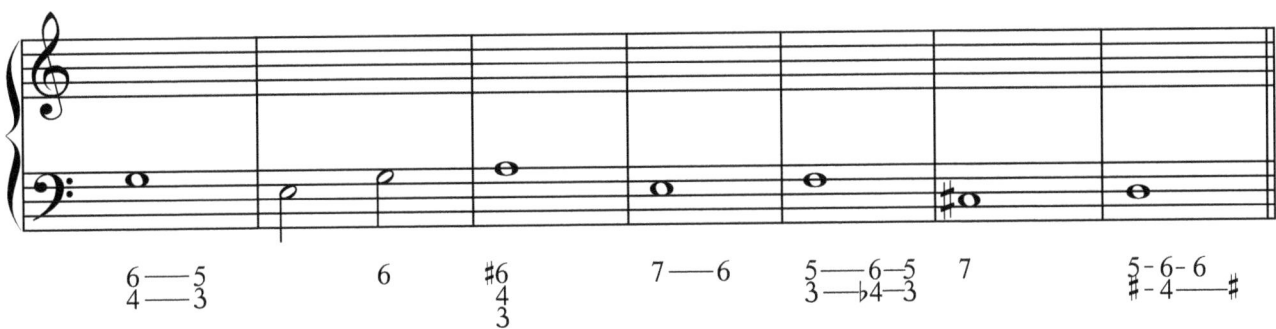

28   Chapter 1: Fundamentals of Harmonization

If you were a keyboard player in the 17th or 18th century, your part may have looked like the bass clef line below. Two instrumentalists usually played this part. One played the bass line as written on a cello, double bass, or bassoon and the other realized the bass by filling in the harmonies from the given figures on a keyboard instrument. Together they formed a group called the *continuo* or *basso continuo*.

Figure 1.41

1. Here is a simple realization of the above figured bass in keyboard style. Play the keyboard part and provide a harmonic analysis of the continuo using root/quality chord symbols.

2. Realize the given figured basses in keyboard style.

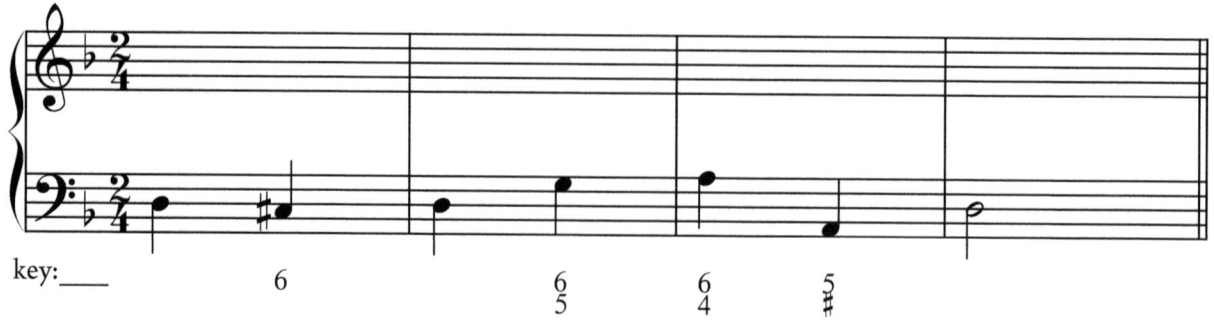

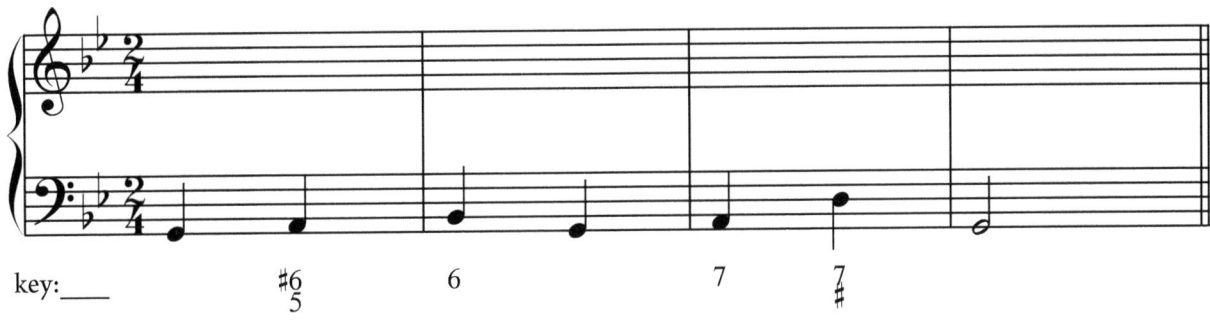

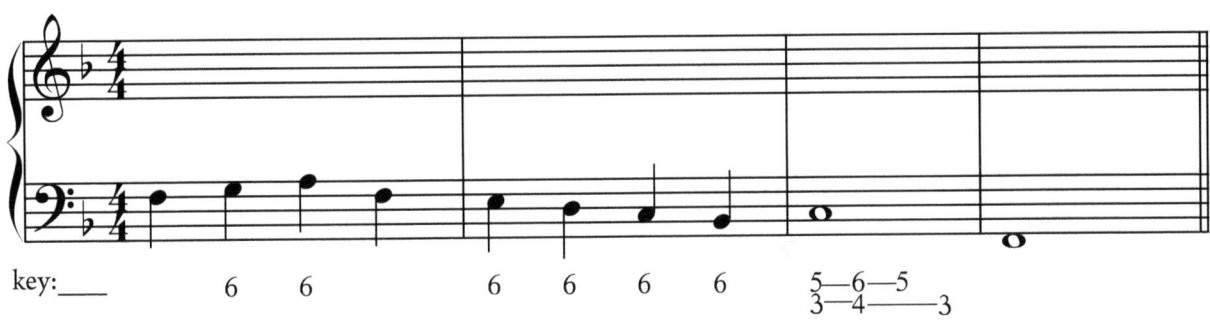

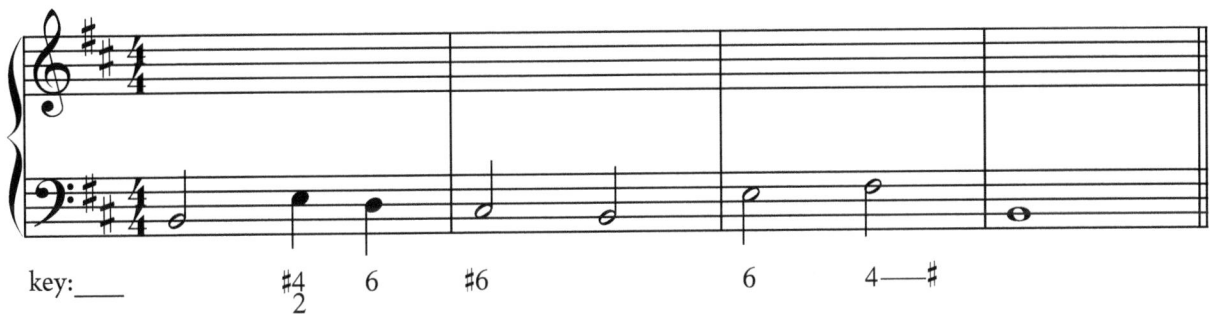

3. Realize the following figured bass in keyboard style. Label the continuo with root/quality chord symbols.

Sonata no. 3 for Flute and Continuo
BWV 1035 (2nd mvt)

Johann Sebastian Bach
(1685-1750)

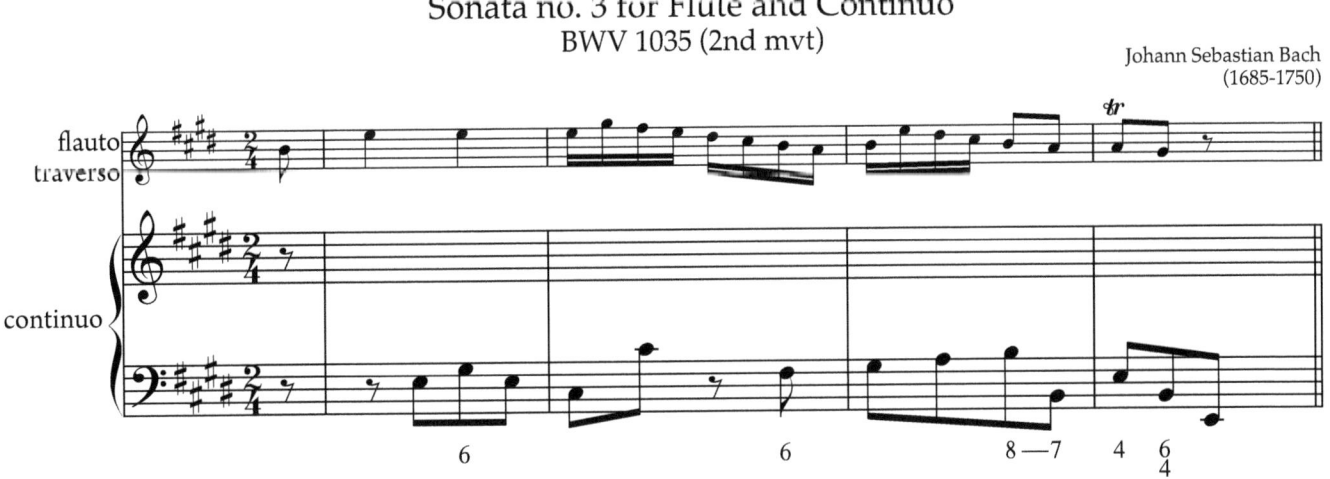

2
Seventh Chords

Seventh chords have been used in music for centuries. After the triad, seventh chords are the next step to a complete understanding of the language of tonal harmony. As a general overview to diatonic 7th chords, this chapter will touch on most of them.

Diatonic 7th Chords in Major Keys

The triad is the basic building block of harmony. Stacking thirds on the notes of a scale creates various qualities of triads. This harmony, based on third relationships, is called *tertian harmony* and is the basis for the tonal harmony that we are studying here.

If we add another third to a triad we form a *7th chord*. This chord gets its name from the fact that the top note is the interval of a 7th from the root of the chord (Figure 2.1).

Figure 2.1

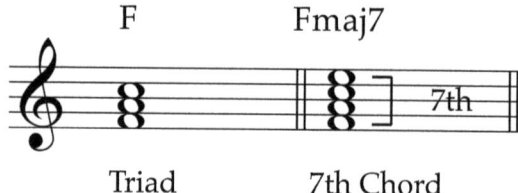

Figure 2.2 shows the *diatonic 7th chords* in C major. We build 7th chords by stacking three thirds on each scale degree. This creates a four note chord with the interval of a 7th between the root and the top note. In order to keep these chords diatonic, we can only use the notes of the scale with which we are working. Here, we are building 7ths in C major. We can only use the notes that make up the C major scale (C D E F G A B C).

Figure 2.2

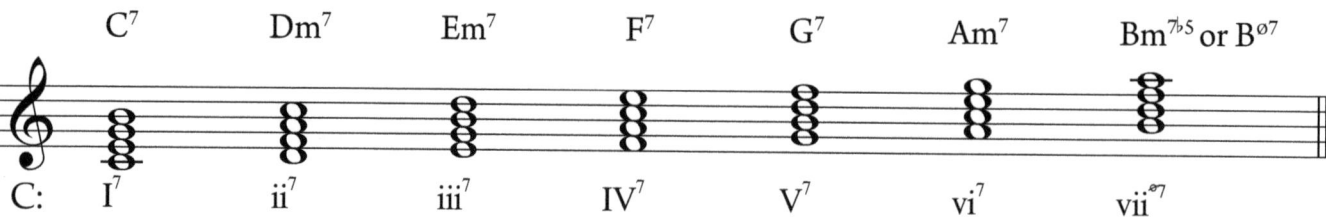

The example in Figure 2.2 results in four different types of 7th chords. In these examples, the root/quality chord symbols tell us more about the 7th chords than the functional chord symbols. We will discuss each type of 7th in detail.

Major 7th Chords

A major triad with a major 7th is considered a *major 7th chord*. Figure 2.3 is a major 7th chord. Its main features are: It is a major triad (C-E-G), and is contains the interval of a major 7th between the root (C) and the 7th (B). Technically, this chord is a major/major 7th. The first major refers to the major triad and the second major refers to the major 7th interval. However, we abbreviate this and simply call it a major 7th chord.

The verbal expression of the chord in Figure 2.3 is: "C major 7th." Major 7th chords occur when you build 7th chords on $\hat{1}$ and $\hat{4}$ of the major scale.

A 7th chord built on $\hat{1}$ is considered a *tonic 7th*, and on $\hat{4}$ a *subdominant 7th*.

Figure 2.3

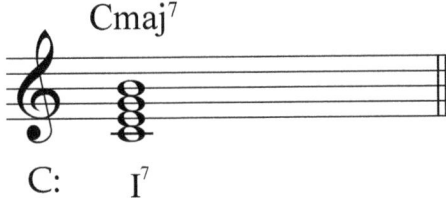

Major/Minor 7th Chords

The chord in Figure 2.4 is a major/minor 7th chord. It is a major triad (G-B-D) with the interval of a minor 7th between the root (G) and the 7th (F). Although this is a major/minor 7th chord it is know as a *dominant 7th*. This is the chord that occurs when you build a 7th chord on $\hat{5}$ (the dominant).

The verbal expression for the chord in Figure 2.4 is: "G7" or "G dominant 7th."

This chord occurs diatonically only on $\hat{5}$ of the major and harmonic and melodic minor scales. This is a very common chord and was covered extensively in the previous book.

Figure 2.4

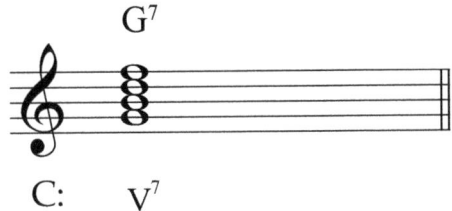

Chapter 2: Seventh Chords

Minor 7th Chords

A *minor 7th chord* is really a minor triad with the interval of a minor 7th above the root. The chord in Figure 2.5 is a minor triad (D-F-A) with a minor 7th between the root (D) and the 7th (C). This could be considered a minor/minor 7th because both the triad and the 7th are minor, but we simply call it a minor 7th chord.

The verbal expression of the chord in Figure 2.5 is: "D minor 7th." Minor 7th chords occur on $\hat{2}$, $\hat{3}$, and $\hat{6}$ of the major scale.

Figure 2.5

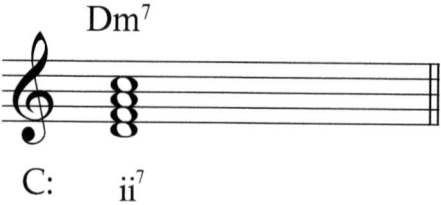

Diminished/Minor 7th Chords

If we build a 7th chord on $\hat{7}$ in a major key we get a chord with a diminished triad and a minor 7th. This diminished/minor 7th chord is commonly known as an *half diminished 7th chord*. The chord in Figure 2.6 contains a diminished triad (B-D-F) with the interval of a minor 7th between the root (B) and the 7th (A). It occurs diatonically on $\hat{7}$ of the major scale.

The symbol for this chord contains a degree sign with a slash through it (ø). This sign is used in both the root/quality and functional chord symbols.

The verbal expression for the chord in Figure 2.6 is: "B half diminished 7th."

Figure 2.6

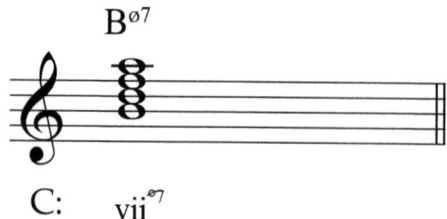

1. Identify the following 7th chords as *major 7th, minor 7th, dominant 7th or half diminished 7th*. Write the root/quality chord symbols above each.

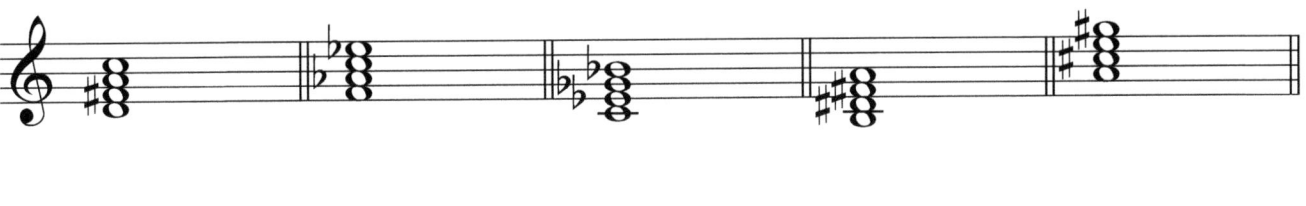

_____   _____   _____   _____   _____

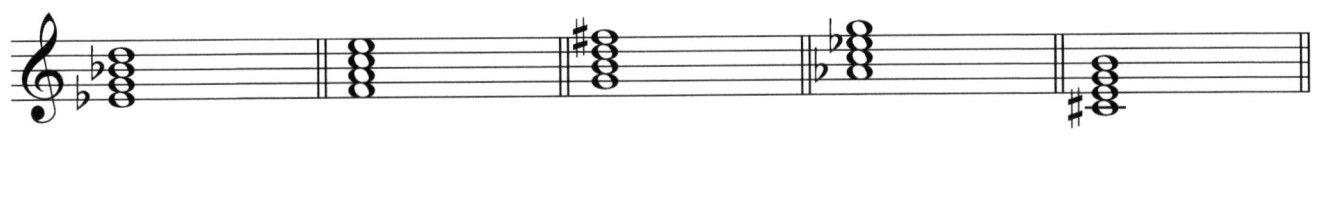

_____   _____   _____   _____   _____

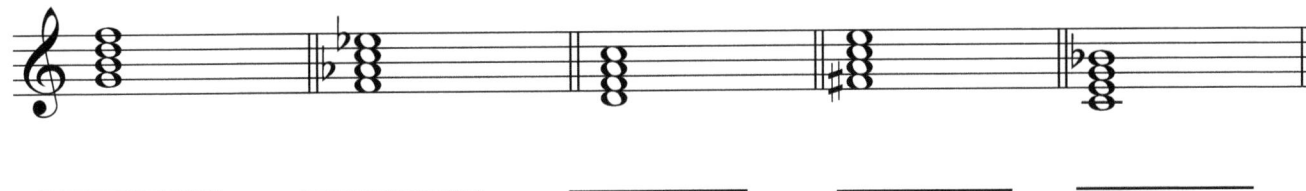

_____   _____   _____   _____   _____

2. Write the following 7th chords according to the root/quality chord symbols.

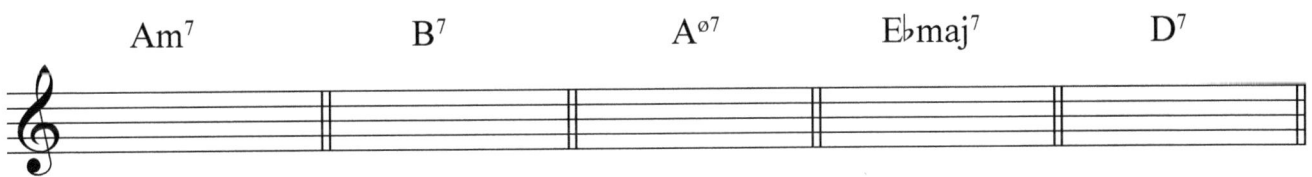

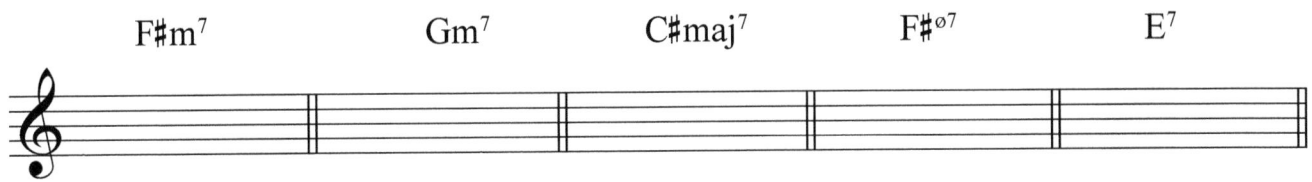

Diatonic 7th Chords in Minor Keys

Figure 2.7 illustrates the 7th chords that occur on the notes of the harmonic minor scale.

There are three 7th chords here that we do not see in a major key. They are the *minor/major 7th* (i^7), the *augmented/major 7th* (III^{+7}) and the *diminished/diminished 7th* (vii^{o7}). We will discuss each one in detail.

Figure 2.7

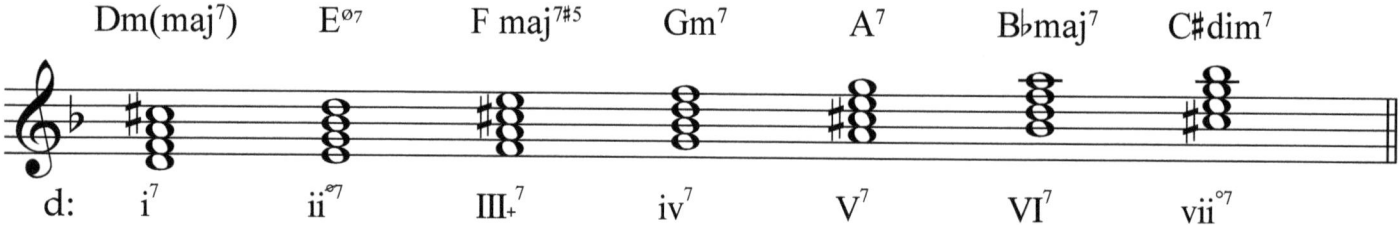

Minor/Major 7th Chords

The minor/major 7th chord has an unusual sound. Figure 2.8 illustrates this chord. It is a minor triad (D-F-A) with a major 7th from the root (D) to the 7th (C#). There is no shortening of its name. Here, it is called D minor/major 7th.

In root/quality chord symbols it may be shown as Dm(maj7), Dmin(maj7), or D-(maj7).

This chord only occurs tonally in the harmonic or melodic minor scale. It is sometimes used in pop and jazz music most notably by Pink Floyd.

Figure 2.8

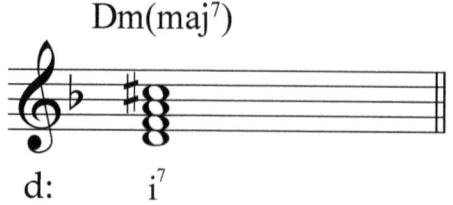

Chapter 2: Seventh Chords

Augmented/Major 7th Chords

The *augmented 7th chord/major 7th* is not used frequently. It can be heard in modern music. It is common in jazz, and also the music of the late 19th and the 20th centuries.

This chord occurs on III in the minor key with raised $\hat{7}$. Figure 2.9 illustrates this chord in d minor. In d minor, III is an augmented triad (F-A-C#) and there is a major 7th between the root(F) and the 7th (G).

The root/quality symbol may appear as Fmaj7#5, F+7, or Faug7. The functional chord symbol is an uppercase III with the + sign and a 7.

Figure 2.9

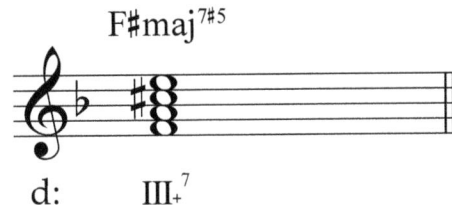

Diminished 7th Chords

The *diminished 7th* chord occurs diatonically on raised $\hat{7}$ in the harmonic and melodic minor scale. It consists of a diminished triad and the interval of a diminished 7th above the root.

The half diminished is a diminished triad with a minor 7th. However, in the diminished 7th chord, both the triad and the 7th are diminished, and it is considered a *fully* diminished 7th chord. It's really a diminshed/diminished 7th, but we simply call it a "diminished 7th."

Figure 2.10 is a diminished 7th in d minor. It is built on raised $\hat{7}$ (C#). The diminshed triad is (C#-E-G) and the diminished 7th occurs between the root (C#) and the 7th (B♭).

The functional chord symbol is a lower case vii with a degree sign (°) and a 7. The verbal expression for the this is: "seven diminished 7th." The root/quality chord symbol is C#dim7 or C#°7. This is expressed as: "C# diminished 7th."

Figure 2.10

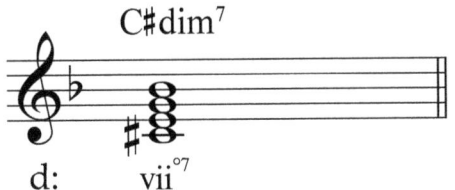

3. Supply the correct functional chord symbol for each chord.

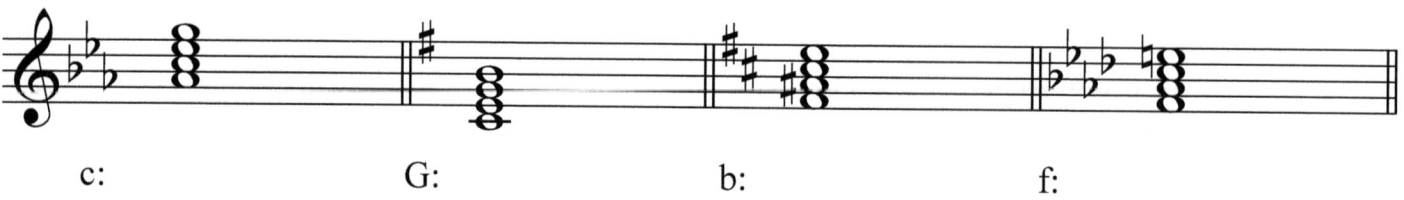

c: G: b: f:

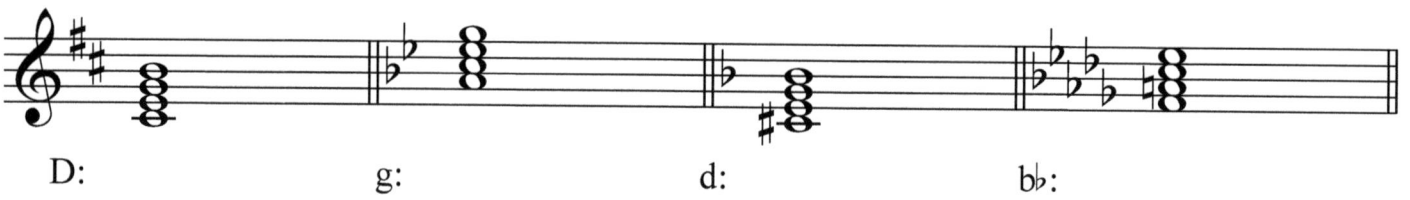

D: g: d: b♭:

4. Write the following chords according to the given chord symbols.

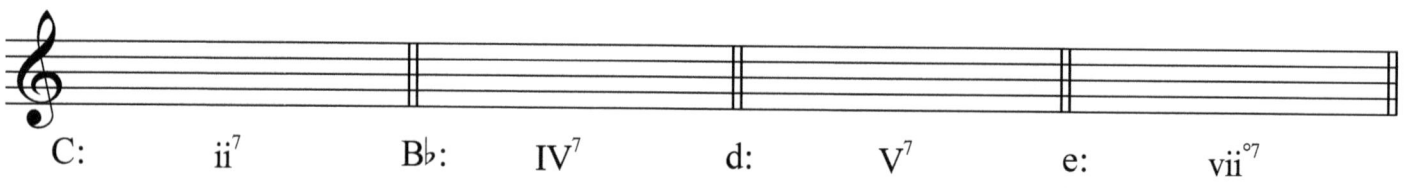

C: ii⁷   B♭: IV⁷   d: V⁷   e: vii°⁷

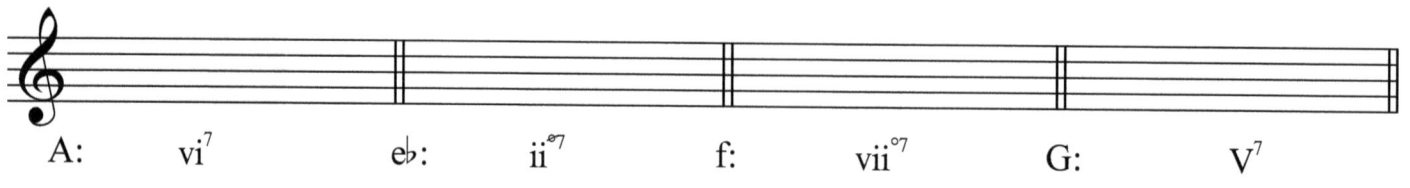

A: vi⁷   e♭: ii°⁷   f: vii°⁷   G: V⁷

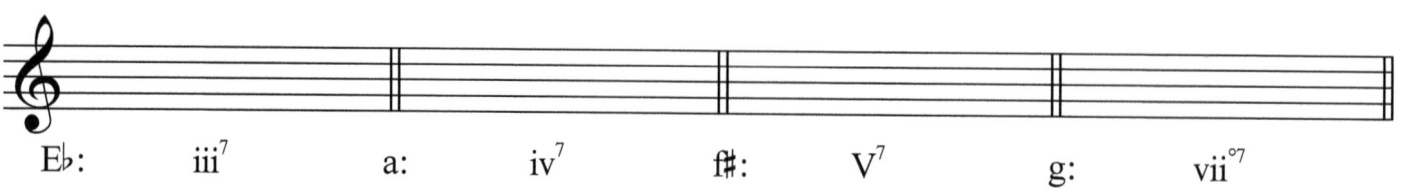

E♭: iii⁷   a: iv⁷   f#: V⁷   g: vii°⁷

Analyzing 7th Chords

As a result of rhythmic activity, many 7th chords can appear to result from non-chord tones.

It can be difficult to determine if the dissonant 7th note is a part of the harmony, or a result of melodic activity. This may be determined by duration of the note, or by determining the importance of the dissonance in relation to the harmony.

Figure 2.11 is an example of such a case. The circled note at the end of m.3 could be anaylzed as a passing tone or as the 7th of V^7. Due to duration and metrical position, in this progression it is probably a passing tone. This note is the 7th of V^7 and could correctly be analyzed as such. However, its function here is more melodic than harmonic.

Figure 2.11

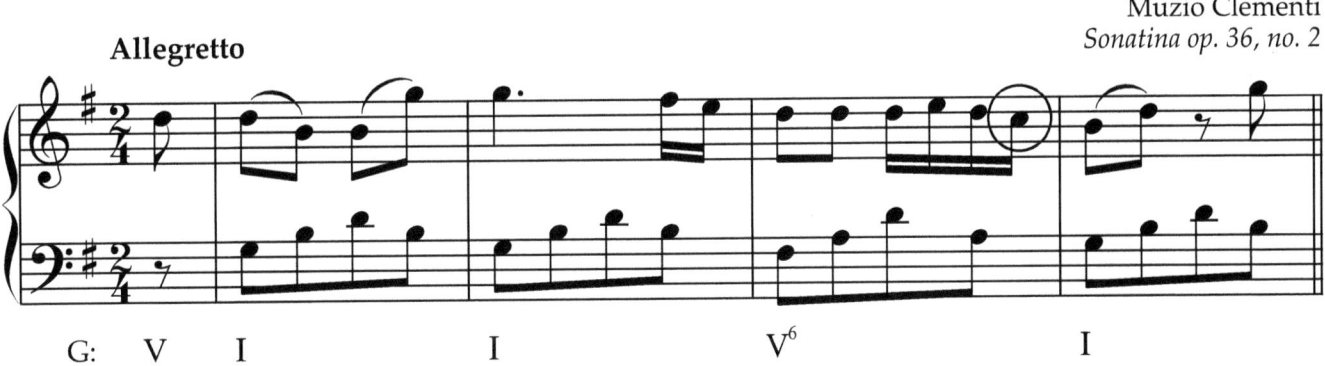

It is clear that the dominant 7th in m.22 of Figure 2.12 has a harmonic function and cannot be explained as a result of non-chord tones.

Figure 2.12

Treatment of the Seventh

The seventh of 7th chords must resolve downward. Some sevenths also need preparation. It is not necessary to prepare the seventh of V^7, vii^{o7}, or $vii^{ø7}$, but the seventh in other diatonic 7th chords is often prepared as a common tone of the previous chord. This is especially important in chords that contain a major seventh (I^7 and IV^7 in major keys and III^7 and VI^7 in minor keys). Notice the preparation and the downward resolution of the sevenths in Figure 2.13.

Figure 2.13

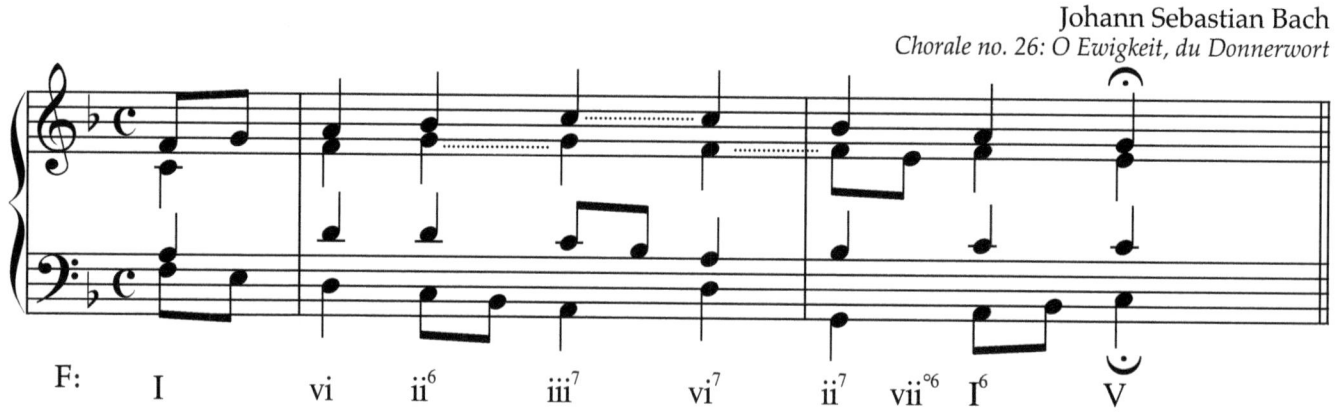

5. Provide a harmonic analysis of the following examples using functional chord symbols.

3
Leading Tone 7th Chords

A seventh chord built on the leading tone in a major key results in a half diminished 7th chord (vii^{ø7}). That is, a chord consisting of a diminished triad with a minor seventh above the root.

In minor keys with raised $\hat{7}$, this chord is a fully diminshed 7th (vii^{o7}) consisting of a diminished triad and a diminished 7th above the root of the chord. Although this fully diminished 7th chord is not diatonic in major keys, since it requires a lowered scale degree $\hat{6}$, it is often used in the major mode. In fact it is used in major keys more often that vii^{ø7}, which is a fairly infrequent chord. In major keys, when we use vii^{o7}, we consider the lowered scale degree $\hat{6}$, which is not a member of the major key, to be borrowed from the tonic minor.

vii^{ø7} and vii^{o7} both resolve to the tonic and most often have a dominant function. These chords are closely related to V^7 since they each contain three notes in common with V^7. Because of this close relationship, leading tone 7th chords often substitute for, or move to V^7 before resolving to the tonic.

Play the two examples in Figure 3.1 and notice how vii^{o7} can substitute for V^7.

Figure 3.1

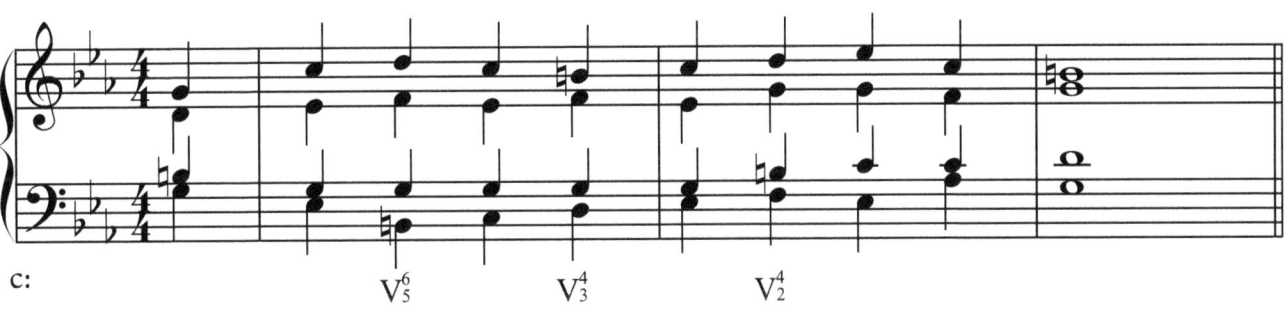

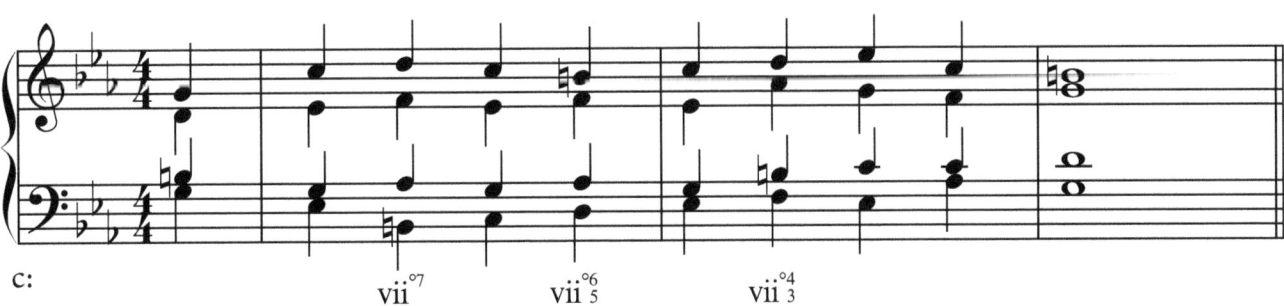

1. Using key signatures, write leading tone 7th chords in the following keys.

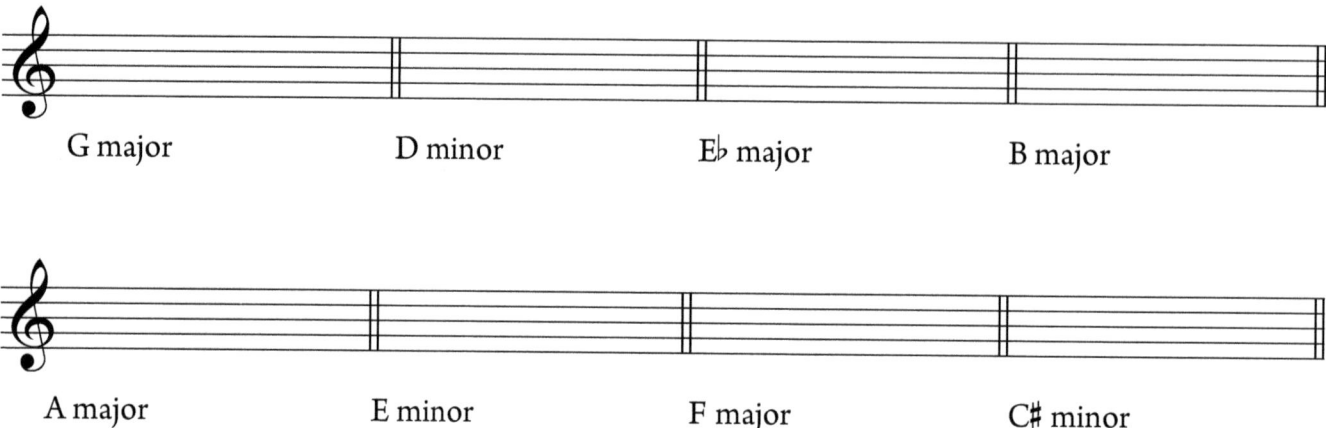

G major   D minor   E♭ major   B major

A major   E minor   F major   C♯ minor

The Diminished 7th Chord

Unlike the diminished triad, the diminished seventh chord occurs frequently in root position. This chord is found diatonically in minor keys, and is based on the harmonic form of the minor scale (which has a raised leading tone). It occurs as a complete chord, containing scale degrees $\sharp\hat{7}$, $\hat{2}$, $\hat{4}$, and $\hat{6}$, and is most often used to prolong tonic harmony. The diminished 7th is closely related to the dominant 7th, since the two chords differ by only one note; both chords contain scale degrees $\hat{2}$, $\hat{4}$, and $\sharp\hat{7}$. Because of this, in addition to prolonging the tonic, vii°7 may also have a dominant function.

Figure 3.2

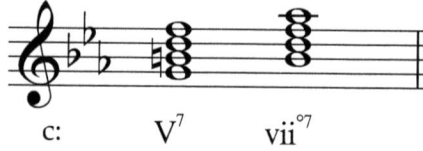

c: V⁷   vii°⁷

Because the diminished 7th contains a number of dissonant intervals, it must be resolved carefully. The diminished 7th that occurs betweeen the root and the seventh is an extremely unstable interval that should be resolved to a perfect 5th: the leading tone ($\hat{7}$) rises to the tonic, and the 7th (scale degree $\hat{6}$) falls to $\hat{5}$.

Figure 3.3

c: vii°⁷   i

The diminished 7th chord also contains two diminished 5ths. Generally, these intervals resolve inward to an interval of a 3rd.

Figure 3.4

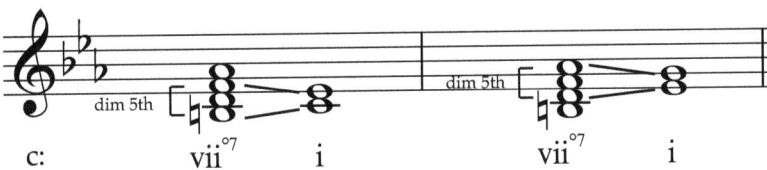

In some arrangements, a vii°7 chord may also contain other dissonant intervals. An augmented 2nd should resolve outward by step to a perfect 4th. An augmented 4th usually, but not always, resolves outward to the interval of a 6th.

Figure 3.5

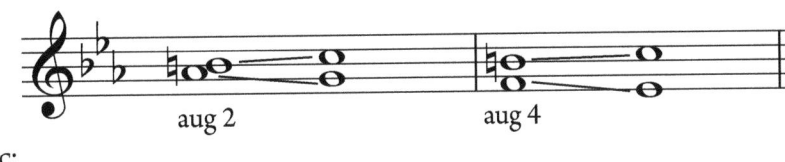

Figure 3.6 contains two resolutions of diminished 7th chords in root position. In these examples, $\hat{6}$ resolves to $\hat{5}$, $\hat{4}$ resolves to $\hat{3}$, $\hat{2}$ resolves to $\hat{3}$, and $\hat{7}$ resolves to $\hat{1}$.

Figure 3.6

2. Name the keys and resolve the following diminished 7th chords.

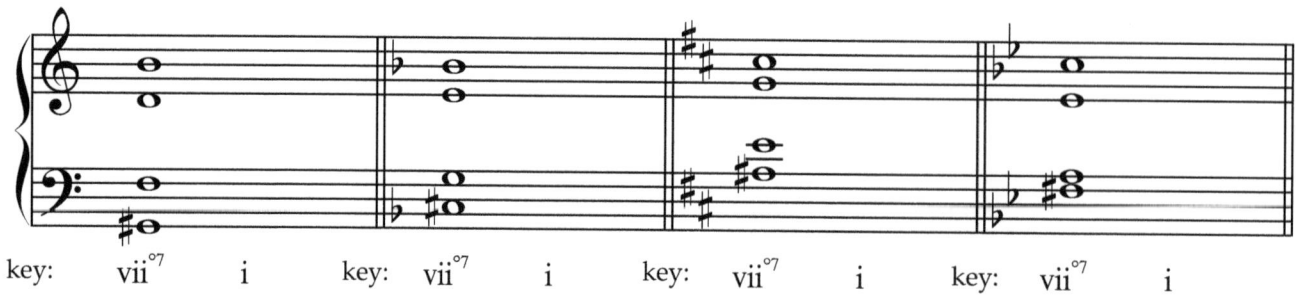

key: vii°7 i key: vii°7 i key: vii°7 i key: vii°7 i

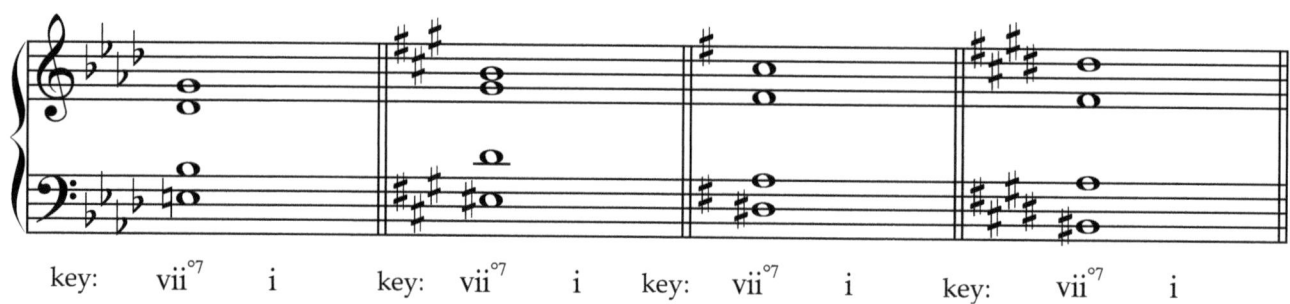

key: vii°7 i key: vii°7 i key: vii°7 i key: vii°7 i

There are other ways to resolve vii°7. In Figure 3.7, the augmented 4th between the soprano and the alto moves to a perfect 4th, with both voices moving in similar motion. This resolution is especially effective when the soprano falls from $\hat{2}$ to $\hat{1}$, resulting in a chord with a doubled root. Here, $\hat{6}$ resolves to $\hat{5}$, $\hat{4}$ resolves to $\hat{3}$, $\hat{2}$ resolves to $\hat{1}$, and #$\hat{7}$ resolves to $\hat{1}$.

Figure 3.7

e: vii°7 i

Such a resolution is possible when $\hat{2}$ is placed above $\hat{6}$ in the vii°7 chord (creating a 4th or a compound 4th). However, if $\hat{2}$ is below $\hat{6}$, as shown in Figure 3.8, this progression should be avoided. The two notes form a dim 5th (rather than an aug 4th) and similar motion which would result in hidden 5ths.

Figure 3.8

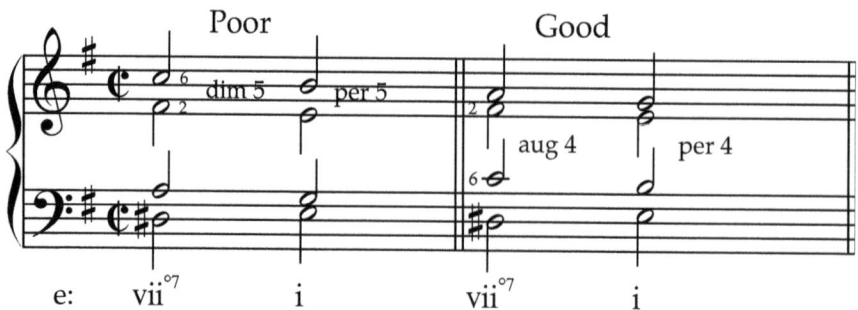

e: vii°7 i vii°7 i

Chapter 3: Leading Tone 7th Chords

$vii°{}^6_5 - i^6$

The first inversion of the diminished 7th chord, $vii°{}^6_5$, may resolve to i^6. $\hat{6}$ resolves to $\hat{5}$, $\hat{4}$ resolves to $\hat{3}$, $\hat{2}$ resolves to $\hat{3}$, and $\hat{7}$ resolves to $\hat{1}$. Notice the doubled third in i^6.

Figure 3.9

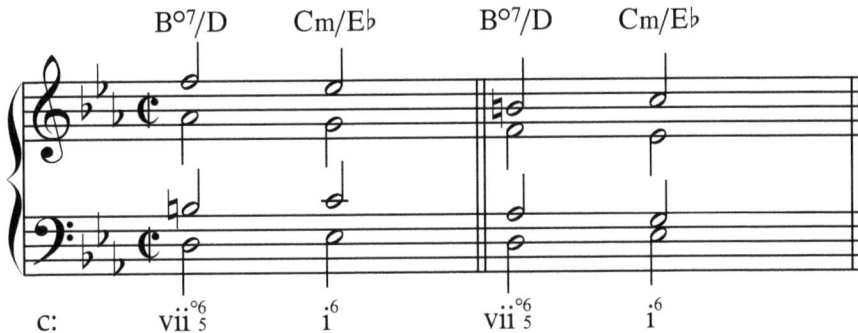

3. Name the keys and resolve the following $vii°{}^6_5$ chords to i^6. Provide functional chord symbols.

$vii°{}^6_5 - i$

$vii°{}^6_5$ may resolve to a root position tonic chord. This progression is acceptable if the shift from a dim 5th to a per 5th occurs between the bass and the tenor, or between the bass and the alto. Do not use this progression if the 5ths occur between the two outer voices.

Figure 3.10

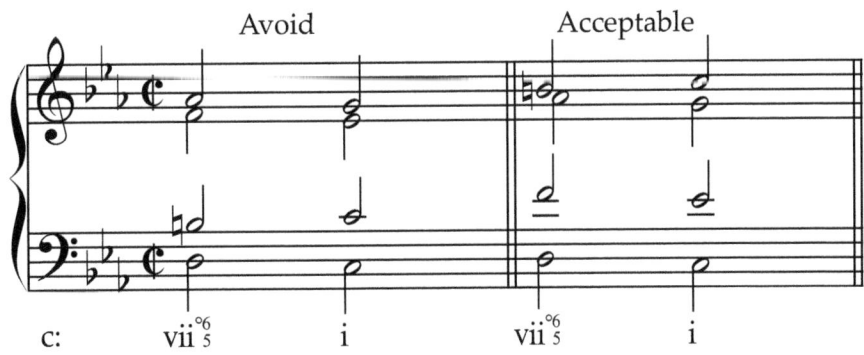

4. Name the keys and complete the following progressions for four voices.

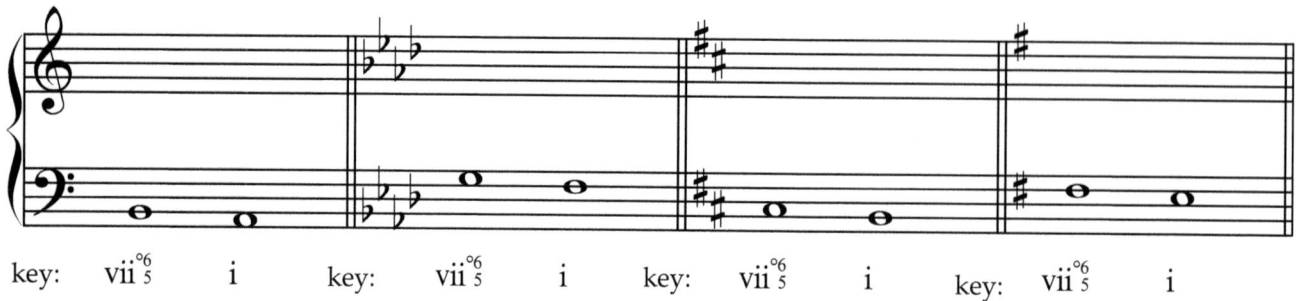

key: vii°$^6_5$ i   key: vii°$^6_5$ i   key: vii°$^6_5$ i   key: vii°$^6_5$ i

vii°$^4_3$ - i^6

In a second inversion diminished 7th chord (vii°$^4_3$), scale degree $\hat{4}$ is in the bass. Since this note resolves to $\hat{3}$, the chord of resolution is i^6.

Figure 3.11

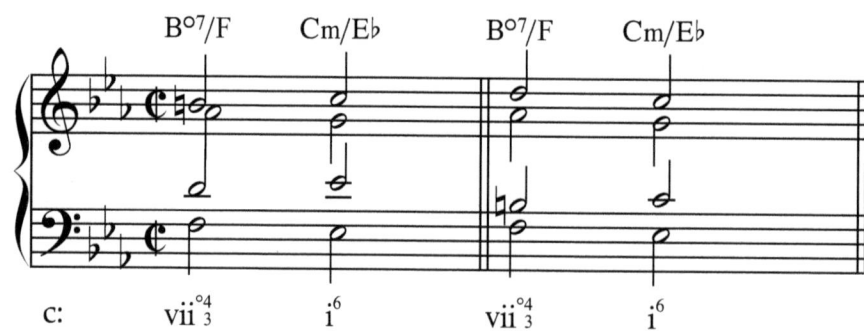

c: vii°$^4_3$ i^6 vii°$^4_3$ i^6

5. Name the keys and resolve the following vii°$^4_3$ chords to i^6. Add functional chord symbols.

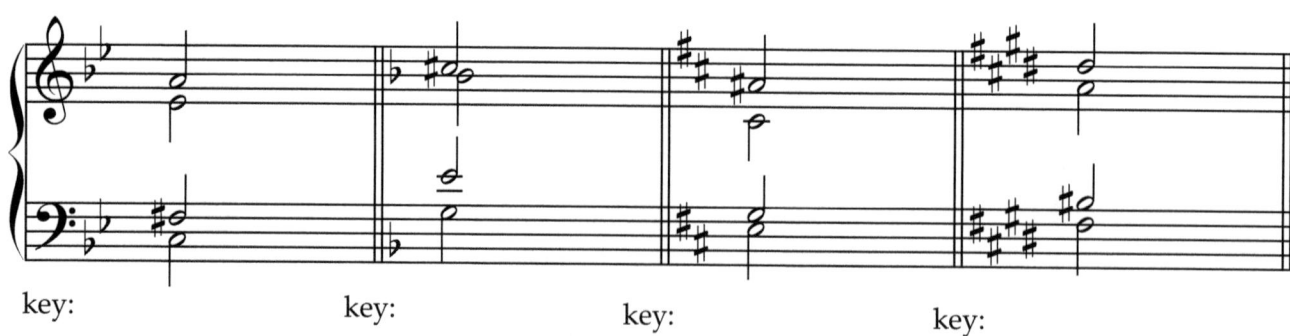

key: key: key: key:

45

Chapter 3: Leading Tone 7th Chords

$\text{vii}^{\circ}{}^{4}_{2}$ - V^7 or $\text{vii}^{\circ}{}^{4}_{2}$ - $V^{6\ 5}_{4\ 3}$

The third inversion of the diminished 7th chord $(\text{vii}^{\circ}{}^{4}_{2})$, is the least commonly used. The seventh is in the bass and must resolve downward to scale degree $\hat{5}$, the root of V^7 or a cadential six-four.

Figure 3.12

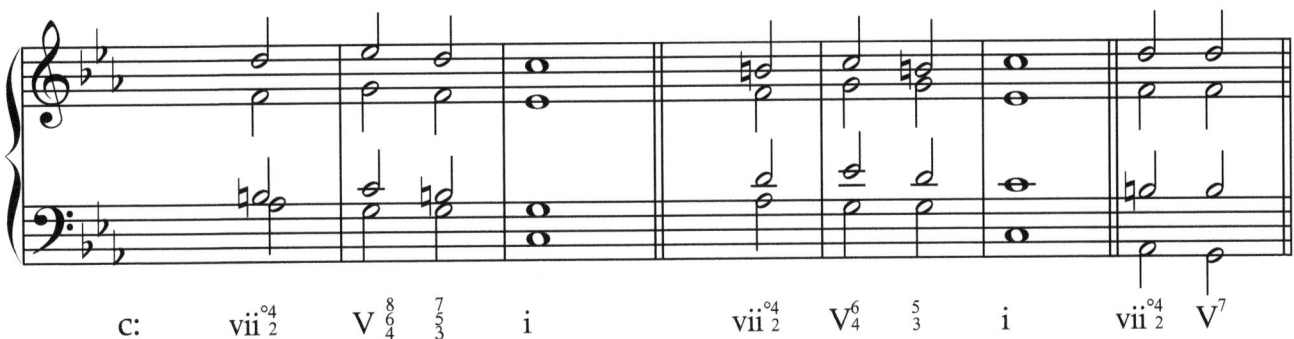

6. Name the keys and resolve the following $\text{vii}^{\circ}{}^{4}_{2}$ chords according to the chord symbols.

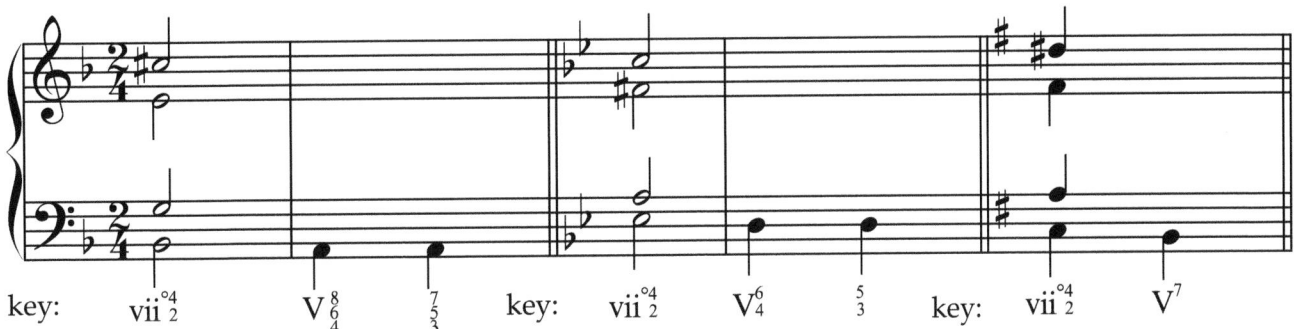

7. Name the keys and resolve the following diminished 7th chords. Add functional chord symbols.

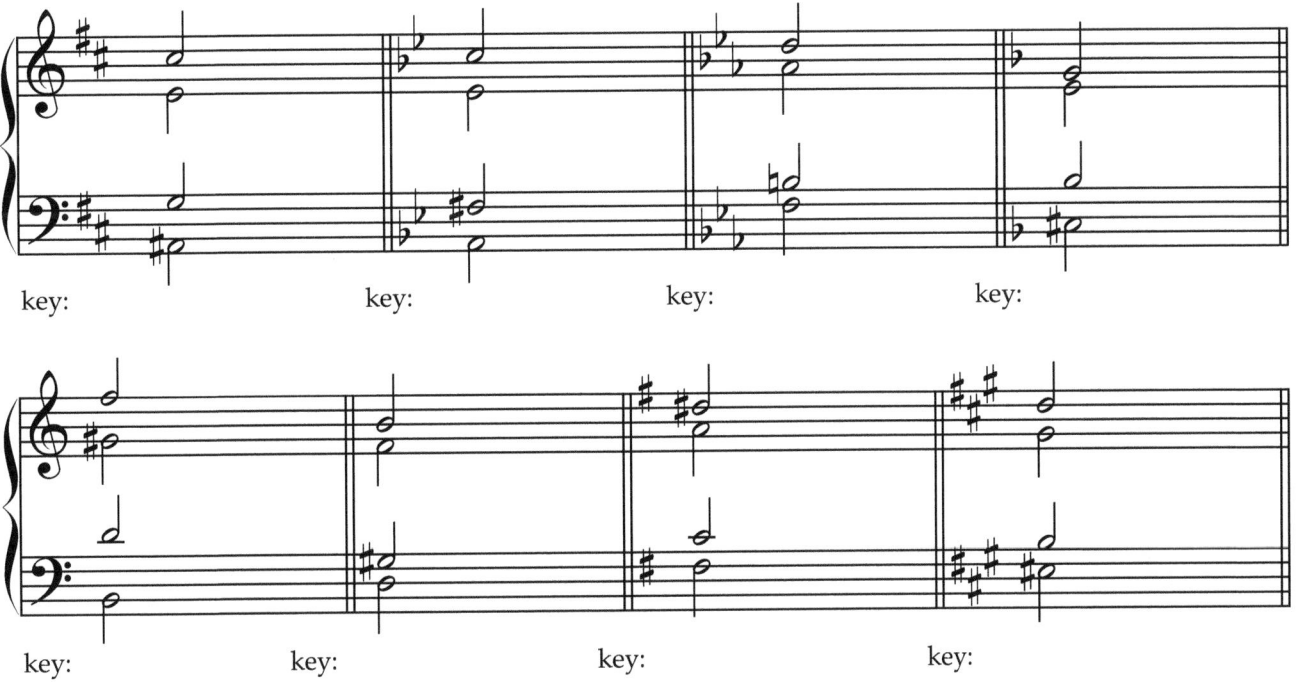

The Half Diminished 7th Chord

The half diminished seventh chord (viiø7) is found diatonically in major keys. This chord may be resolved to I, I⁶, V, V⁷, V⁶, or to cadential six four. The resolutions for the half diminished 7th and it's inversions are the same as those for the diminished 7th chord. Figure 3.13 contains two resolutions of root position viiø7. In Figure.13 a), $\hat{2}$ resolves to $\hat{3}$, resulting in a tonic chord with a doubled third. In Figure 3.13 b), $\hat{2}$ resolves to $\hat{1}$, resulting in a tonic chord with a doubled root. If the arrangement of the upper voices of viiø7 creates a 5th, parallel 5ths can occur in the resolution. To solve this, let $\hat{2}$ go to $\hat{3}$, or arrange the viiø7 chord with $\hat{2}$ above $\hat{6}$.

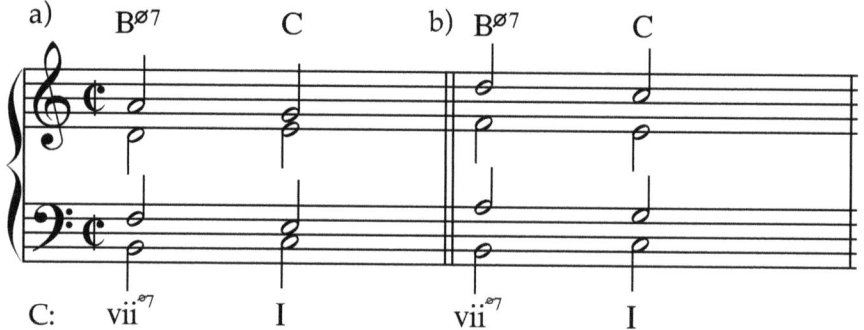

Figure 3.13

8. Name the keys and resolve the following half diminished 7th chords.

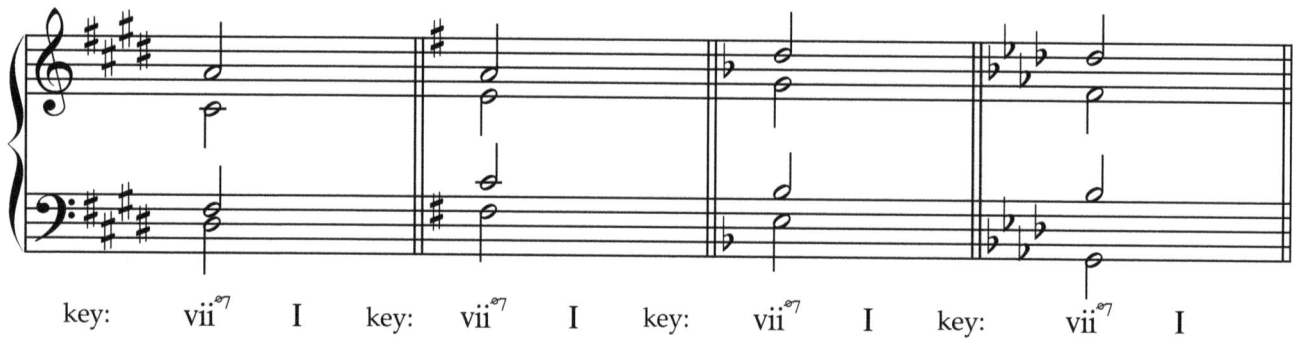

When viiø7 resolves to V⁶₅, three voices remain as common tones and the seventh of viiø7 falls from $\hat{6}$ to $\hat{5}$ as seen in Figure 3.14 a).

A viiø⁶₅ may resolve to I⁶. In this progression, $\hat{6}$ moves to $\hat{5}$, $\hat{4}$ moves to $\hat{3}$, $\hat{2}$ moves to $\hat{3}$, and $\hat{7}$ moves to $\hat{1}$ as seen in Figure 3.14 b).

Figure 3.14

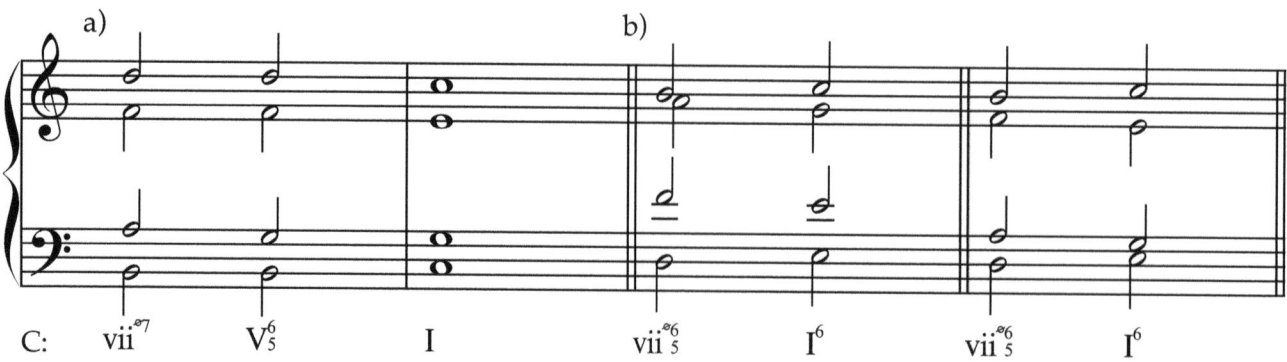

9. Name the keys and complete the following progressions for four voices.

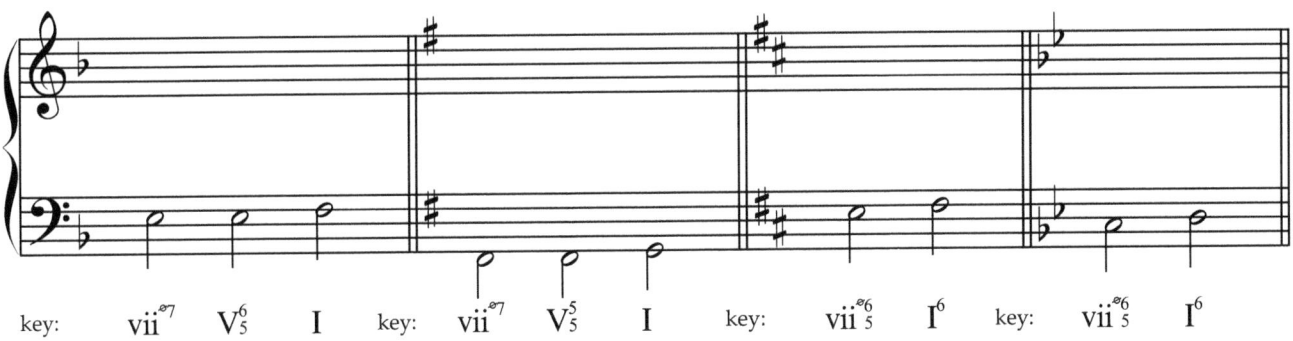

key: _____ vii°7 V⁶₅ I   key: _____ vii°7 V⁵₅ I   key: _____ vii⌀⁶₅ I⁶   key: _____ vii⌀⁶₅ I⁶

Other than root position, the half diminished 7th occurs most often in second inversion. This chord (vii⌀⁴₃) usually resolves to I⁶.

Figure 3.15

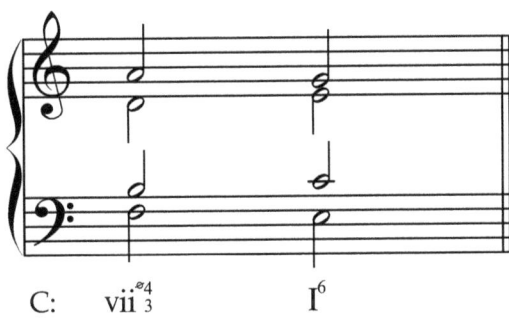

C: vii⌀⁴₃   I⁶

10. Name the keys and resolve the following vii⌀⁴₃ chords. Provide functional chord symbols.

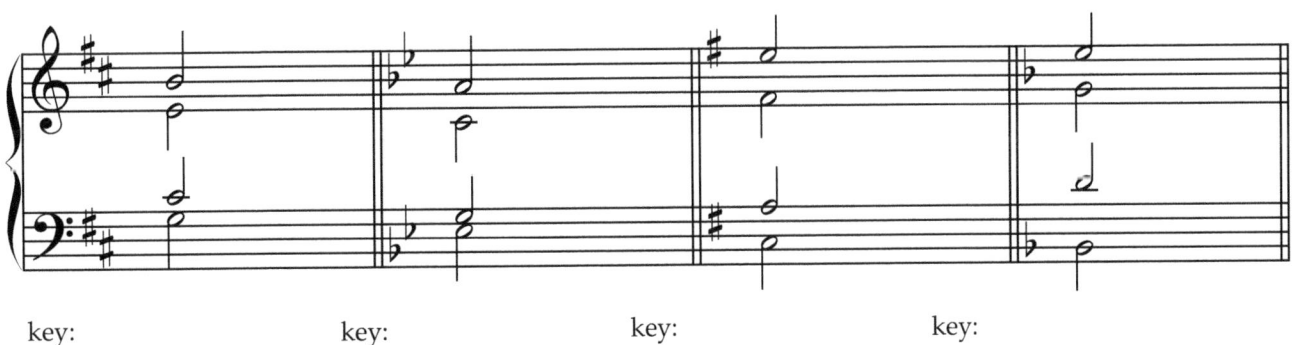

key: _____   key: _____   key: _____   key: _____

48   Chapter 3: Leading Tone 7th Chords

When vii°⁴₂ resolves to V⁷, there are three common tones. The seventh in the bass falls a step (from $\hat{6}$ to $\hat{5}$) to the root of V⁷. This chord may also resolve to a cadential six four. In this progression, $\hat{7}$ resolves to $\hat{1}$, $\hat{6}$ resolves to $\hat{5}$, $\hat{4}$ resolves to $\hat{3}$, and $\hat{2}$ resolves to $\hat{3}$.

Figure 3.16

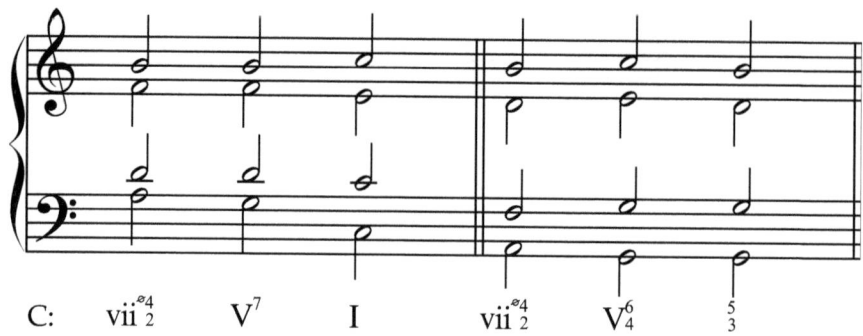

11. Name the keys and complete the following progressions for four voices.

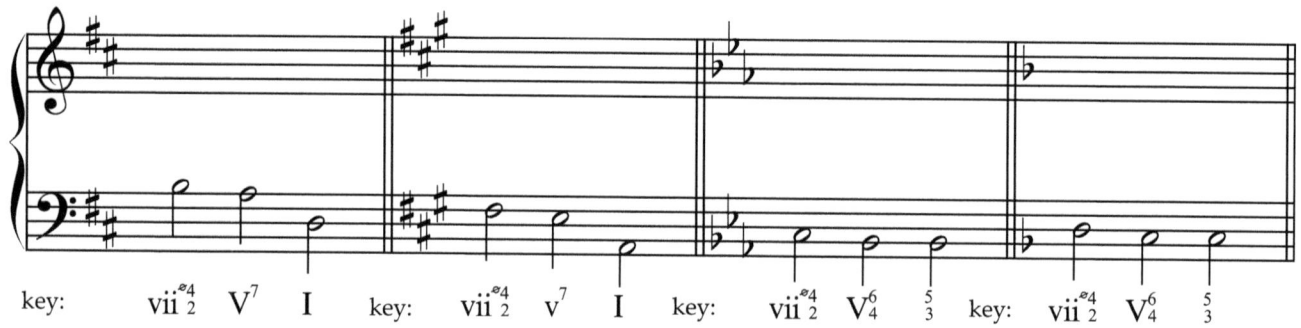

The Diminished 7th in Tonic Prolongation

The diminished 7th and its inversions function much like the dominant 7th when used in tonic prolongation. Compare the function of V⁷ and vii°⁷ in Figure 3.17.

Like V⁶₅, vii°⁷ may be used as a neighbor chord between two statements of i to prolonging tonic harmony. vii°⁷ and V⁶₅ differ by only one note.

Figure 3.17

Chapter 3: Leading Tone 7th Chords

Like V$^6_5$, vii^{o7} may also be used as an incomplete neighbor between i^6 and i to prolong tonic harmony. Either the root or the fifth of i^6 may be doubled. The doubling in the i chord will be affected by the voice leading used in the resolution of vii^{o7}.

Figure 3.18

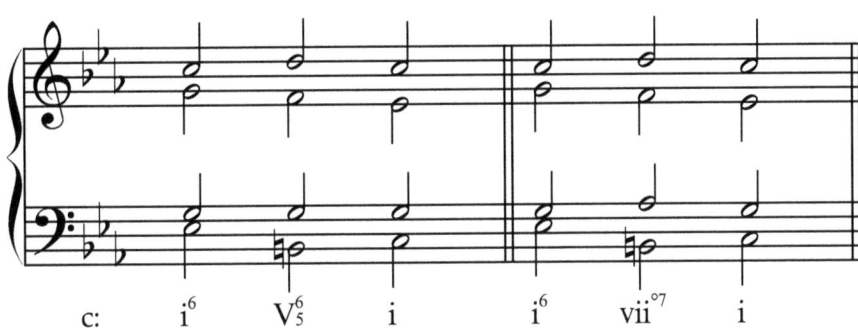

A diminished 7th chord is often preceded by iv or iv^6 in a tonic prolongation. In these effective progressions, the seventh of vii^{o7} is approached as a common tone from iv or iv^6 and resolves downward by step.

The bass movement from the subdominant chord to vii^{o7} (Figure 3.19: F - B♮ with iv, or A♭ - B♮ with iv^6) produces a melodic diminished 5th or diminished 7th. These diminished intervals are acceptable as long as they are resolved correctly. For example, the B♮ cannot be approached from below because this movement would create an augmented 4th or an augmented 2nd, both of which should be avoided.

Figure 3.19

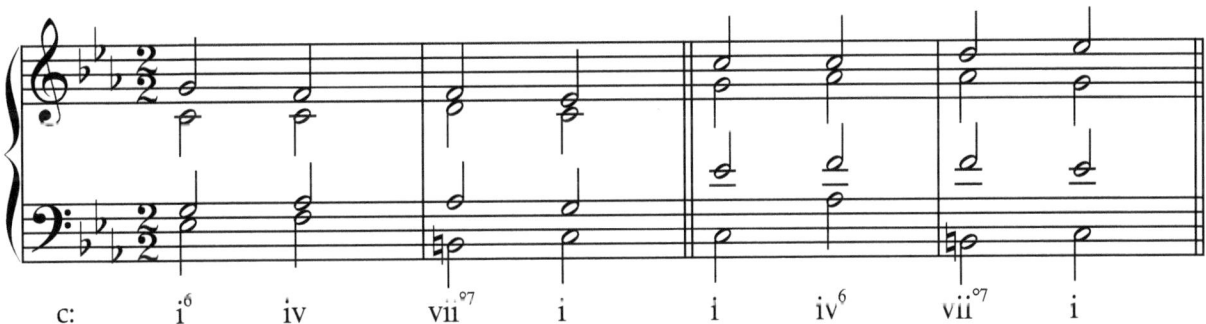

12. Name the keys and complete the following progressions for four voices.

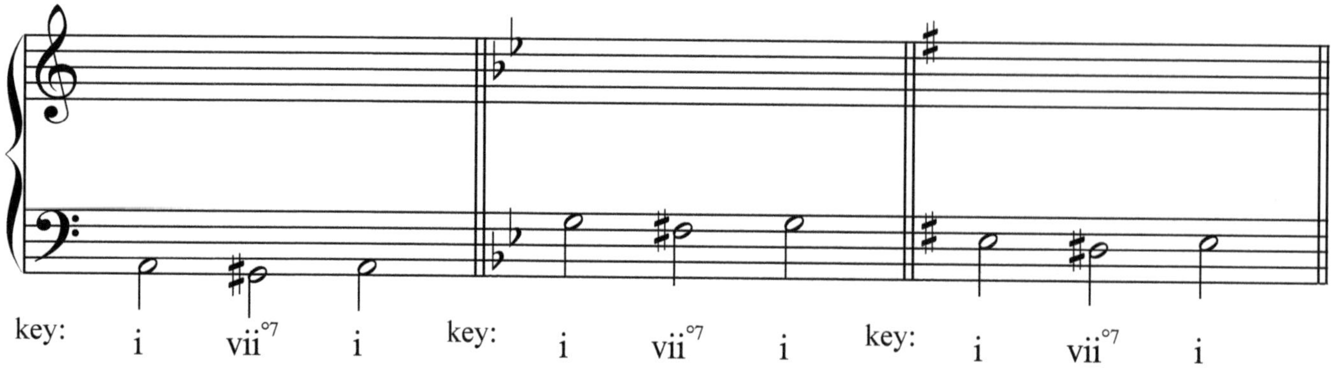

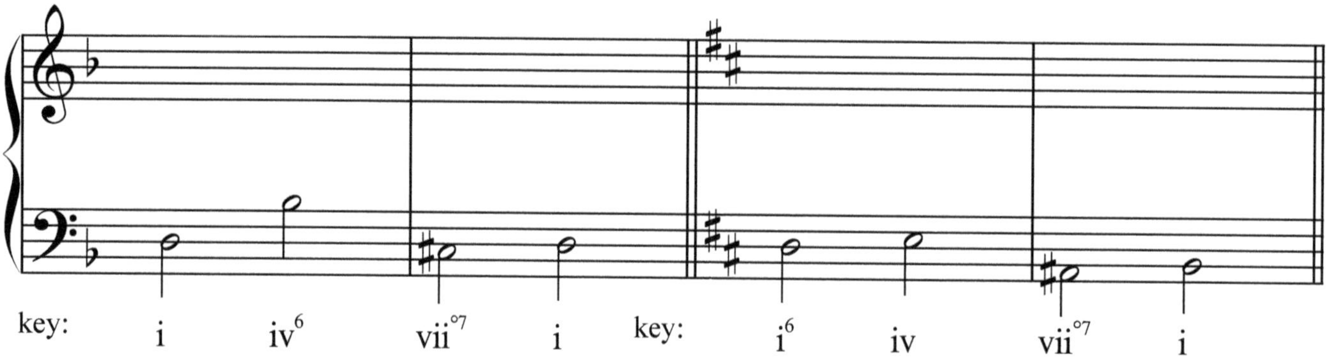

key:　i　vii°⁷　i　　key:　i　vii°⁷　i　　key:　i　vii°⁷　i

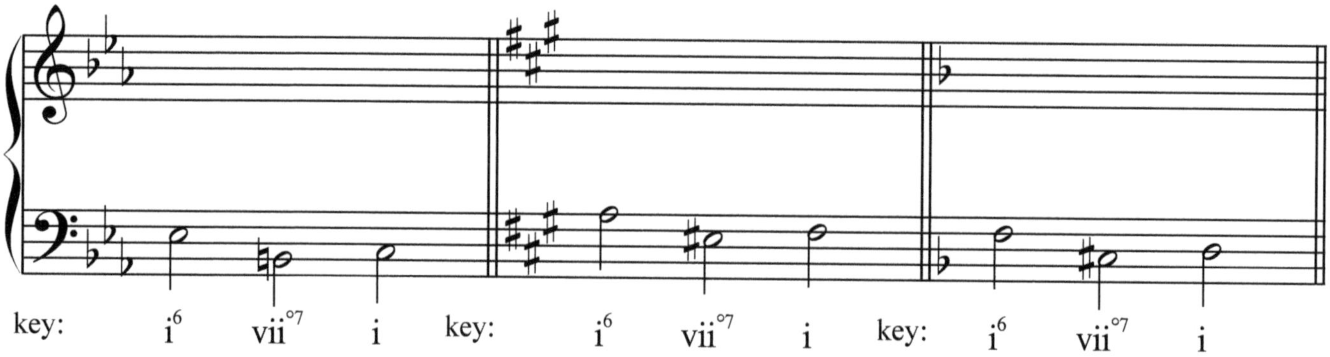

key:　i⁶　vii°⁷　i　　key:　i⁶　vii°⁷　i　　key:　i⁶　vii°⁷　i

key:　i　iv⁶　vii°⁷　i　　key:　i⁶　iv　vii°⁷　i

The first inversion of a diminished 7th (vii°⁶₅) may be used as a passing chord between i and i⁶ to prolong tonic harmony as seen in Figure 3.20 a).

This chord may also act as a neighbor chord between two statements of i⁶ as seen in Figure 3.20 b).

Figure 3.20

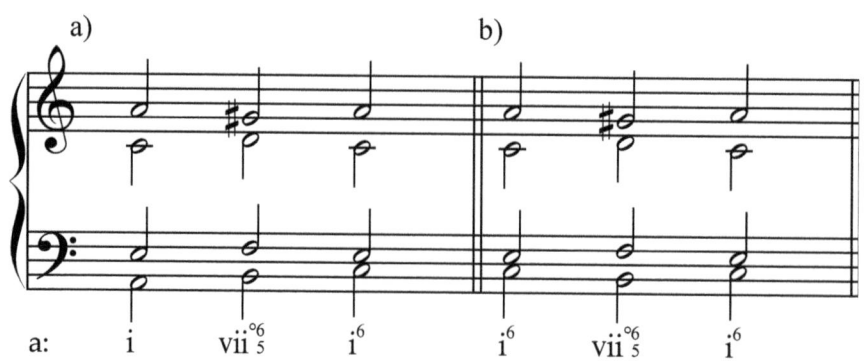

a:　i　vii°⁶₅　i⁶　　i⁶　vii°⁶₅　i⁶

Chapter 3: Leading Tone 7th Chords

The second inversion of a diminished 7th chord (vii°$^4_3$) may occur as a neighbor chord between two statements of i⁶ to prolong tonic harmony as seen in Figure 3.21 a).

This chord may also act as an incomplete neighbor between i and i⁶ in tonic prolongation as shown in Figure 3.21 b).

Figure 3.21

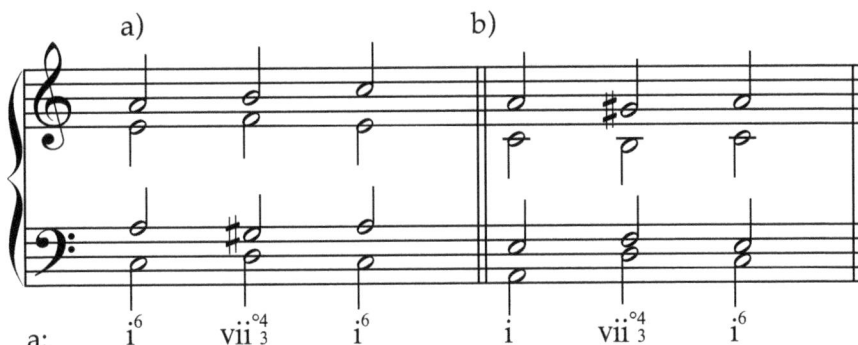

A vii°$^4_3$ may be preceded by iv in a prolongation of tonic harmony. In this progression, both iv and vii°$^4_3$ have scale degree four in the bass. Thus, the seventh of vii° is introduced as a common tone and it behaves like a suspension from iv. The repetition of the bass note (here, G) over the bar line is acceptable because this note is a dissonance on the downbeat (Figure 3.22 a).

A vii°$^4_3$ may also occur as a passing chord following a six four chord Figure 3.22 b).

Figure 3.22

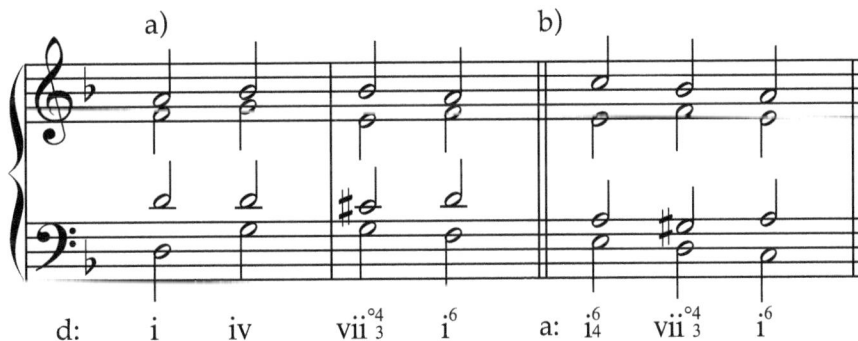

The previous prolongations of tonic harmony using vii°7 are also effective with vii⌀7 in major keys. Care must be taken when approaching and leaving vii⌀7 or its inversions in order to avoid parallel 5ths (see Figure 3.23 a and b). Parallel 5ths can be avoided either by doubling the third in chord I (see Figure 3.23 c) or by revoicing the chord (see Figure 3.23 d). Note that vii⌀ should resolve to I6 rather than to I.

Figure 3.23

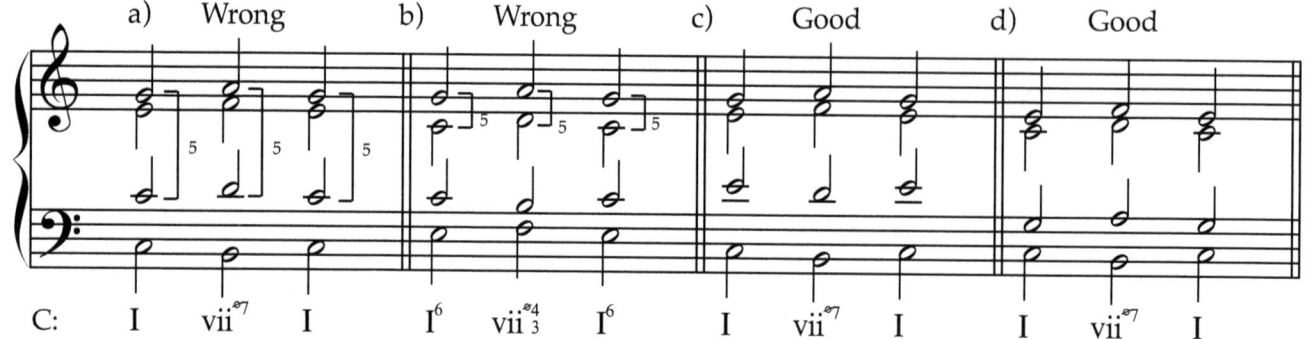

13. Name the keys and complete the following progressions for SATB.

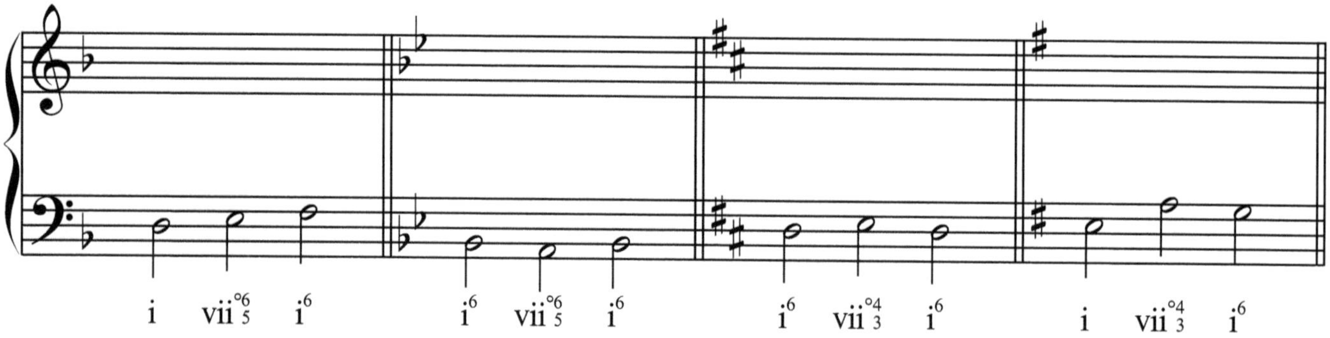

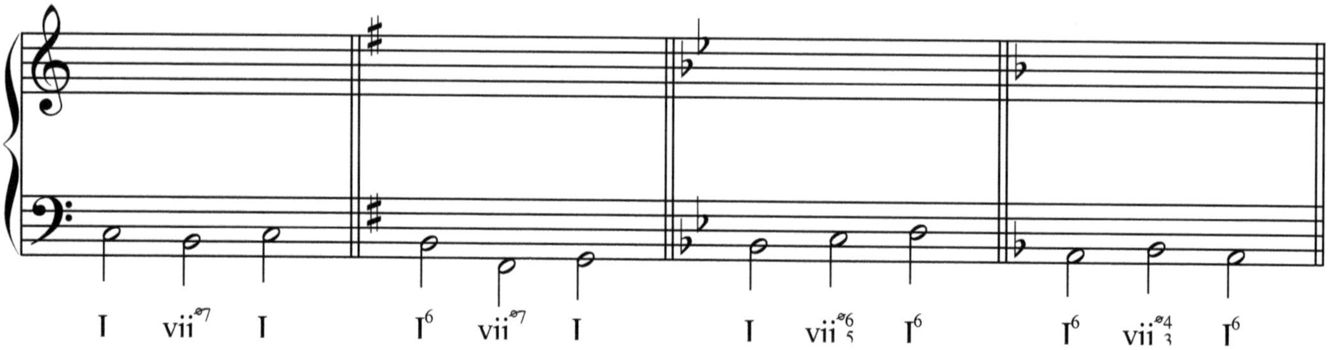

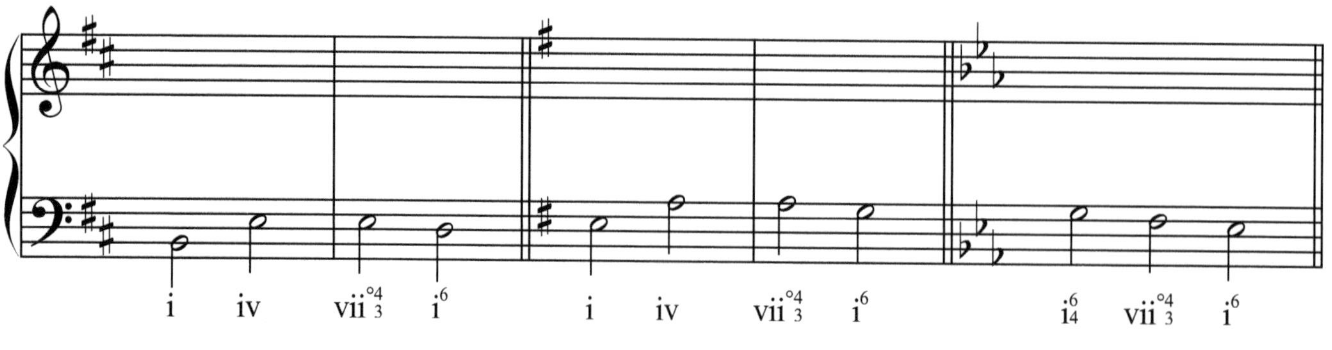

14. Name the keys and complete the following progressions for SATB.

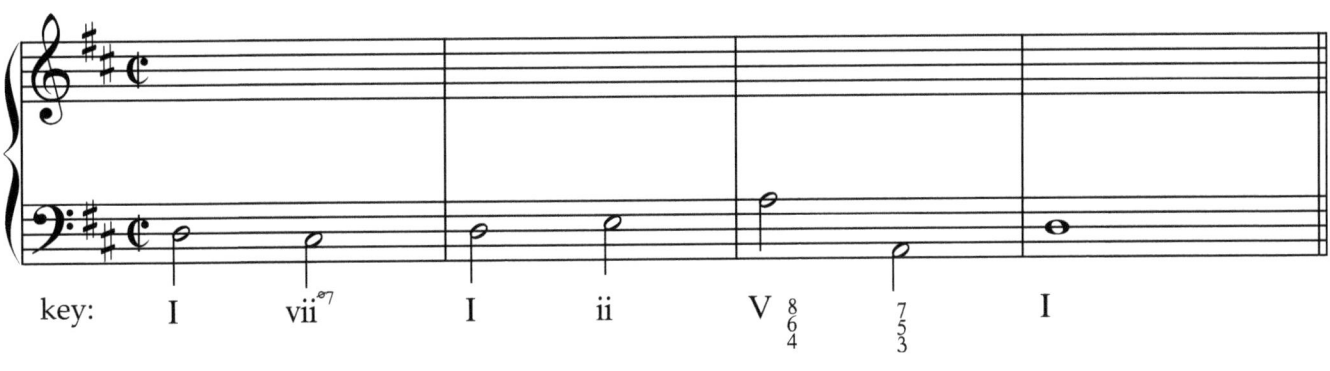

key: I   vii°7   I   ii   V $^8_{6\,4}$ $^7_{5\,3}$ I

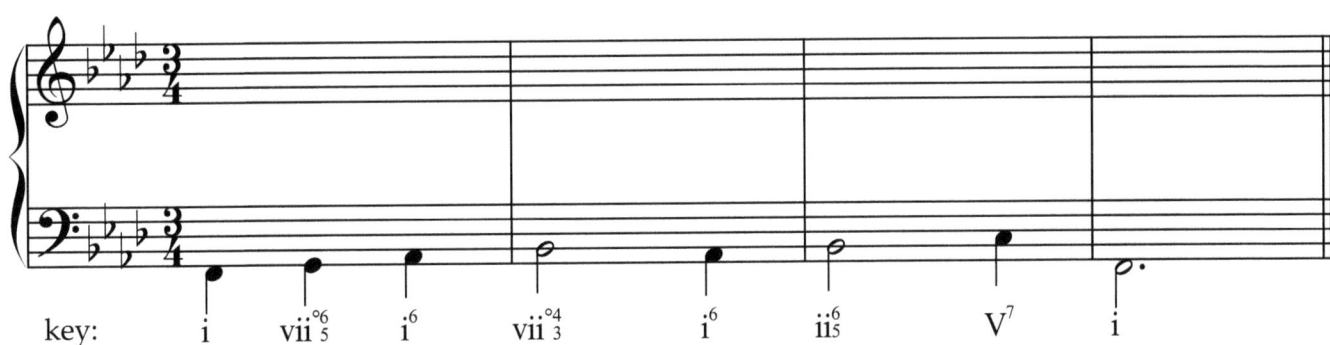

key: i   vii°$^6_5$ i^6 vii°$^4_3$ i^6 ii°$^6_5$ V^7 i

It is possible to use vii°7 in major keys if the seventh of the chord (scale degree $\hat{6}$) is lowered. Composers often use the diminished seventh in major keys to provide colour and interest. In Figure 3.24, the A flat is not part of the C major scale. Notice also that the diminished 7th chord is the same in both C major and C minor (B-D-F-A♭). We say that this chord is borrowed from the tonic minor. In C major, vii°7 does not occur diatonically, but is borrowed from the tonic minor, C minor.

Figure 3.24

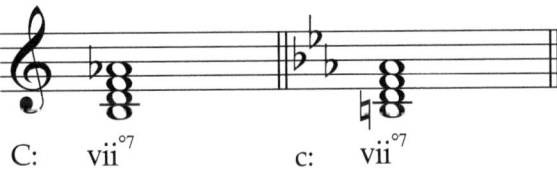

C: vii°7   c: vii°7

15. Write the following diminished 7th chords and name the major keys for each.

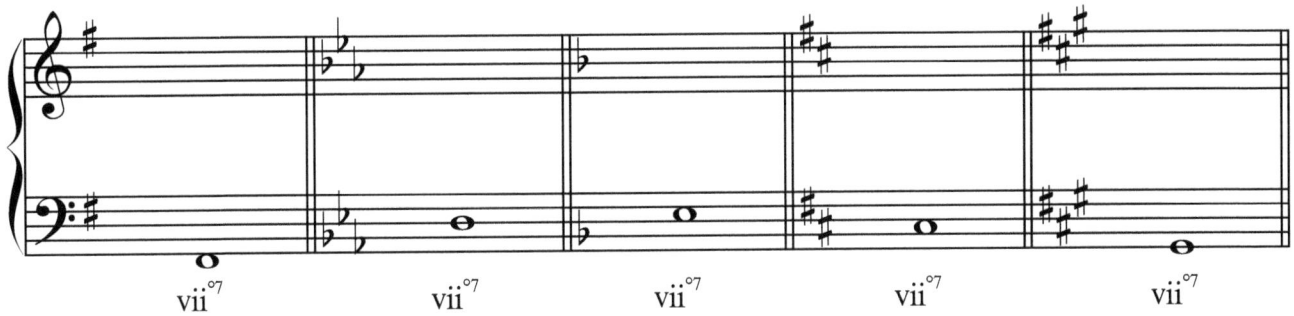

vii°7   vii°7   vii°7   vii°7   vii°7

16. Name the keys and complete the following progressions for SATB.

The Diminished 7th as a Dominant Function Chord

Leading tone 7th chords can function as dominant chords and take the place of V or V^7 in a basic harmonic progression. When approached by the predominant chords ii^6, iv, or VI, the seventh of vii^{o7} is often prepared as a common tone.

Figure 3.25

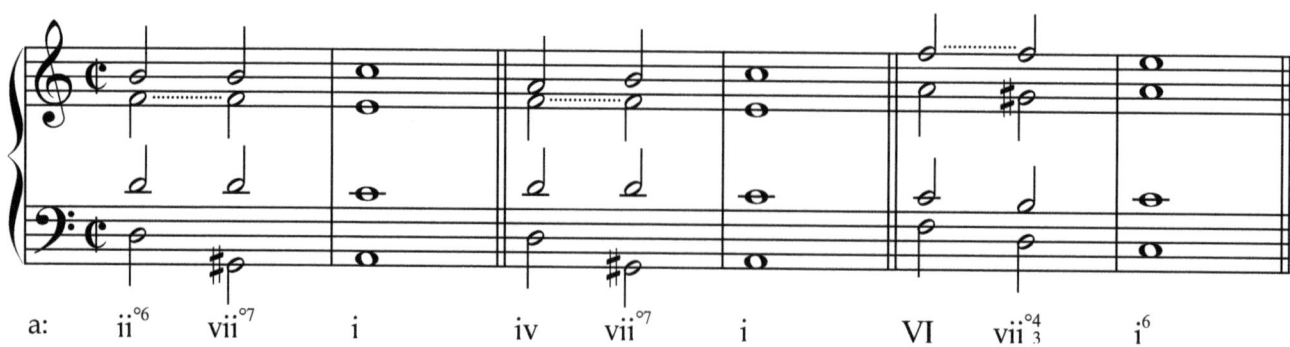

The Diminished 7th in Dominant Prolongation

In Figure 3.26, a leading tone 7th chord is used to prolong dominant harmony. Progressions that move from V to vii°7 can be effective. Aim for the smoothest voice leading.

Figure 3.26

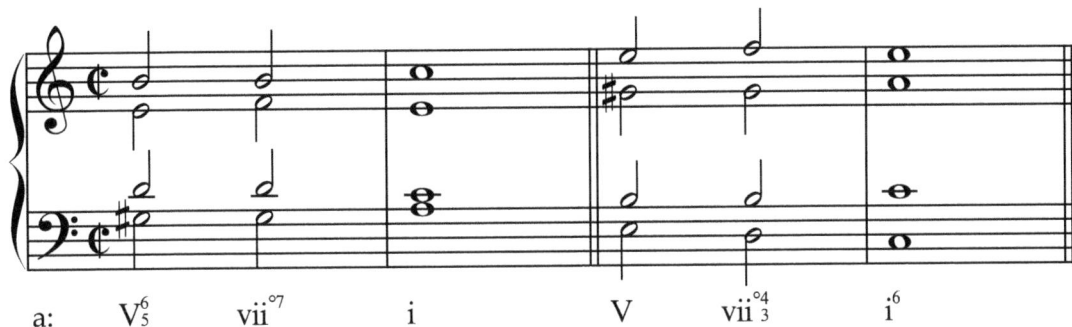

a: V_5^6 vii°7   i   V   vii°$_3^4$ i^6

17. Name the keys and complete the following progressions for SATB.

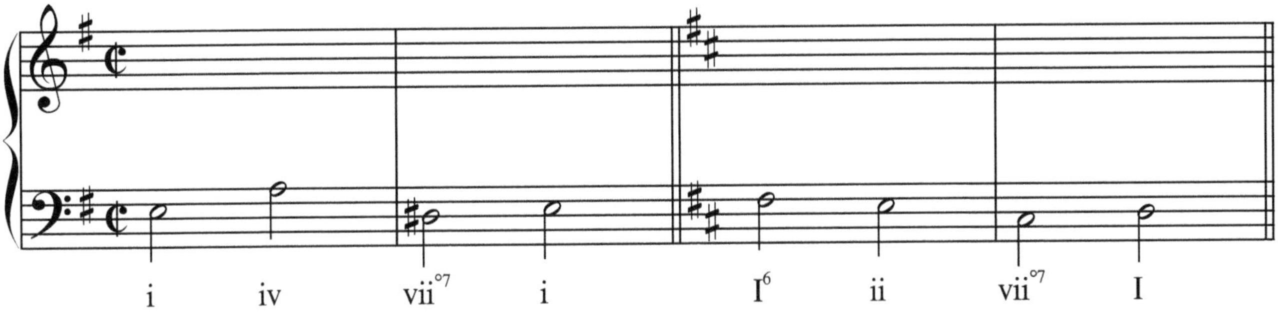

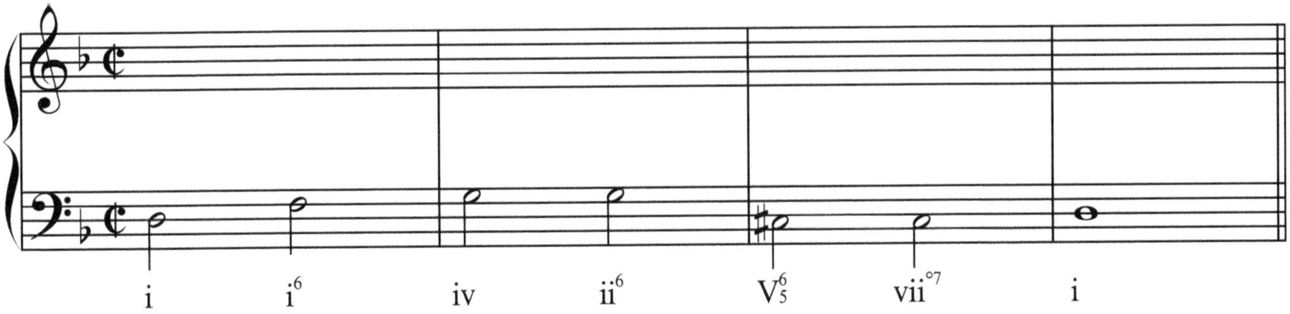

i   iv   vii°7   i   I^6 ii   vii°7   I

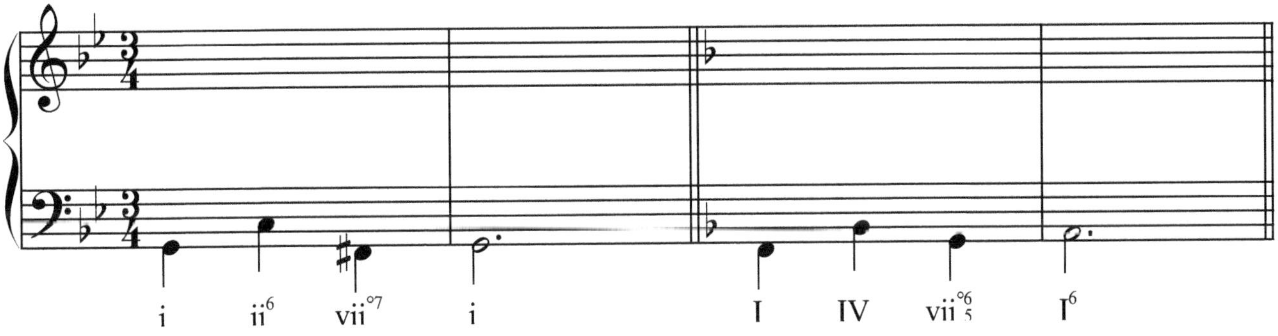

i   ii^6 vii°7   i   I   IV   vii°$_5^6$ I^6

i   i^6 iv   ii^6 V_5^6 vii°7   i

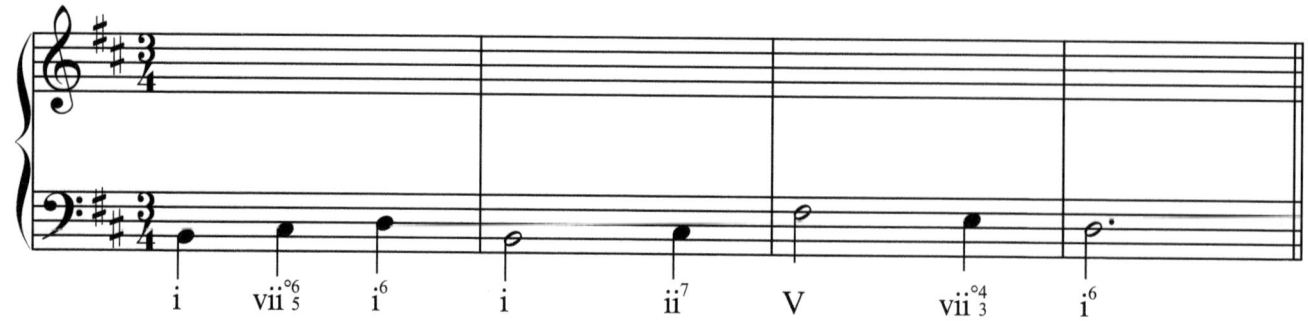

18. Provide a harmonic analysis of the following excerpts. Name the keys, provide functional chord symbols, and circle and identify any non-chord tones.

String Quartet in G major
op.17, no. 5, Hob:29 (Adagio)

Franz Joseph Haydn

Sonata for Violin and Piano
K 379

Wolfgang Amadeus Mozart

Ballade
op. 10, no. 4

Johannes Brahms

Piano Sonata
op. 10, no. 1 (1st movement)

Ludwig van Beethoven

continued

Chapter 3: Leading Tone 7th Chords

Sonata no. 3 Violin and Clavier
BWV 1016

Johann Sebastian Bach

Chapter 3: Leading Tone 7th Chords

Summary

1. The vii°7 chord is built on the leading tone and is called a leading tone 7th chord.

2. There are two types of leading tone 7th chords.

   - The half diminished seventh (vii°⁷), which consists of a diminished triad and minor seventh, occurs diatonically in major keys.

   - The fully diminished seventh (vii°⁷), which consists of a diminished triad and a diminished seventh, occurs diatonically in minor keys.

3. There are two options for resolving leading tone 7th chords. The first, in which $\hat{6}$ resolves to $\hat{5}$, $\hat{4}$ to $\hat{3}$, $\hat{2}$ to $\hat{3}$, and $\hat{7}$ to $\hat{1}$, results in a tonic chord with a doubled third. The second option may only be used if scale degree $\hat{2}$ occurs above $\hat{6}$. This resolution, in which $\hat{6}$ resolves to $\hat{5}$, $\hat{4}$ to $\hat{3}$, $\hat{2}$ to $\hat{1}$, and $\hat{7}$ to $\hat{1}$, results in a tonic chord with doubled root.

4. The chords vii°⁷, vii°$^6_5$, and vii°$^4_3$, may be used to prolong tonic harmony.

5. Leading tone seventh chords must be resolved carefully: vii°⁷ resolves to i and vii°$^6_5$ and vii°$^4_3$ resolve to i⁶; vii°$^4_2$ may resolve to V⁷ or to a cadential six four.

6. The half diminished 7th (vii°⁷) chord is used only in major keys. The diminished seventh chord (vii°⁷) may be used in major keys, especially to add colour and interest. The resulting lowered seventh is considered to be borrowed from the tonic minor.

7. Leading tone 7th chords can replace V and V⁷ in the dominant area of a basic harmonic progression (tonic - predominant - dominant - final tonic). In such progressions, the 7th chords are approached in the same way as other dominant function chords.

4

Non-dominant 7th Chords

Compared to the dominant 7th, and perhaps the leading tone 7th, other seventh chords are used less frequently. The reason for this is that dominant harmony provides structural importance next to the tonic. Non-dominant 7th chords are effective when used sparingly and saved for important places in the phrase where their activity and color can really contribute to the music and create expressive harmony. However, overuse of these chords makes them lose their effectiveness.

In all of these chords, the seventh introduces harmonic dissonance to the music and as a result must be prepared and resolved correctly. The seventh should never be doubled. In most of these non-dominant 7ths, the seventh should be prepared with common tone motion and resolved downward by step.

The Tonic 7th Chord

The addition of a 7th to a tonic chord creates a chord that is not tonally stable. Thus, I^7 is harmonically an active chord. Instead of being a place of rest, it has a strong tendency to move to IV, ii, or vi, or their corresponding 7th chords. The chord to which I^7 resolves must contain $\hat{6}$ in order to allow the seventh to resolve downwards, and this downward motion takes precedence in the resolution. Figure 4.1 shows three approaches and resolutions for tonic 7th chords. In Figure 4.1 b), notice that the seventh is approached as a descending passing tone within the tonic chord.

Figure 4.1

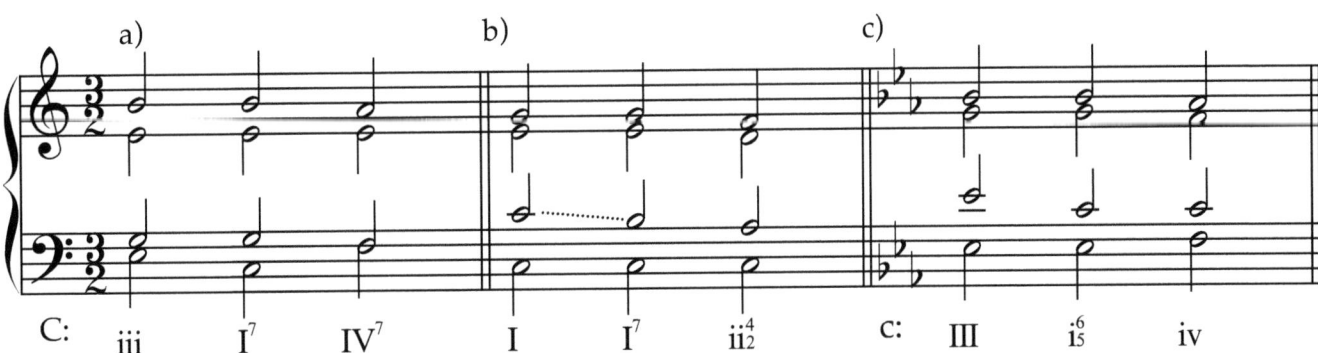

1. Provide a functional harmonic analysis for the following excerpt.

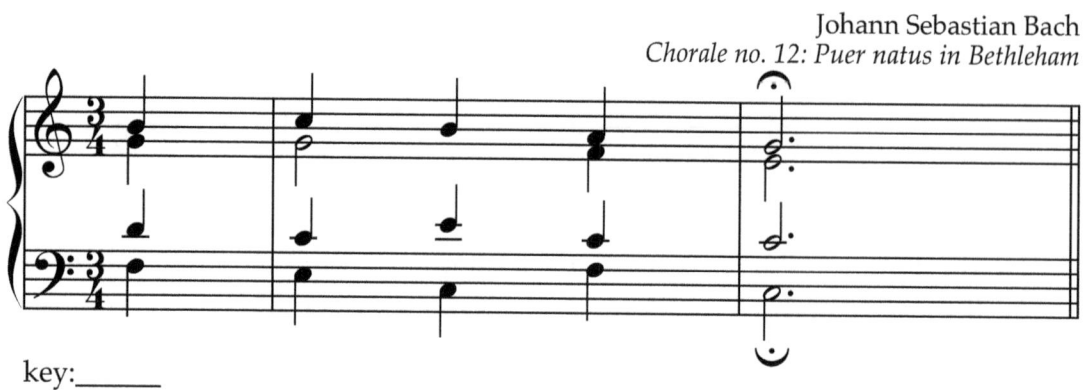

key:_____

The Supertonic 7th Chord

The supertonic 7th (ii^7) often acts as a predominant chord proceeding an authentic cadence. In major keys, it is used in root position and all inversions. In minor keys it occurs more frequently in first or third inversion. Also, in minor keys, ii^{ø7} is a half diminished seventh chord. If possible, the seventh should be prepared as a common tone, or should arrive as a descending passing tone (Figure 4.2 a)).

Note that in ii$^{ø4}_{2}$ the seventh is in the bass and must resolve downward by step. Thus, this chord precedes a first inversion dominant chord (V^6 or V$^6_5$). This progression is often used as a prolongation of tonic harmony (Figure 4.2 b)).

Figure 4.2

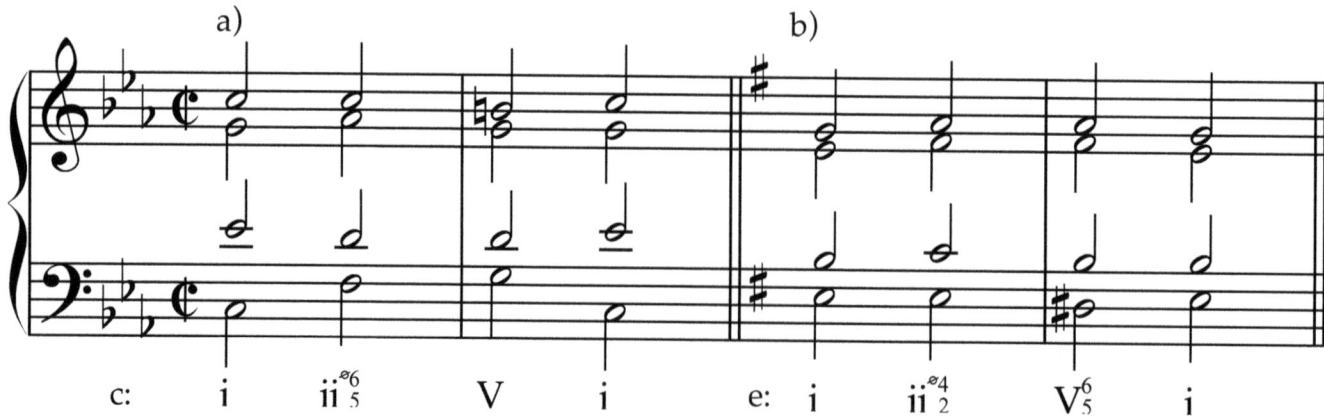

Chapter 4: Nondominant 7th Chords

2. Provide a harmonic analysis of the following excerpts. Include both functional and root/quality chord symbols.

Frederic Chopin
Prelude op. 28, no. 22

key:_____

Wolfgang Amadeus Mozart
Symphony no. 41 K 551 (IV)

key:____

Johann Sebastian Bach
Prelude I BWV 846

key:____

Johann Sebastian Bach
Partita no. 2 for solo violin BWV 1002

key:____

The Mediant 7th Chord

The mediant 7th chord is not often used. It usually resolves to the submediant chord, and is sometimes found as part of a harmonic sequence. In minor keys, it is rarely used in its augmented form (with a raised leading tone), but it may occur with a subtonic. In Figure 4.3 the seventh is prepared as a common tone.

Figure 4.3

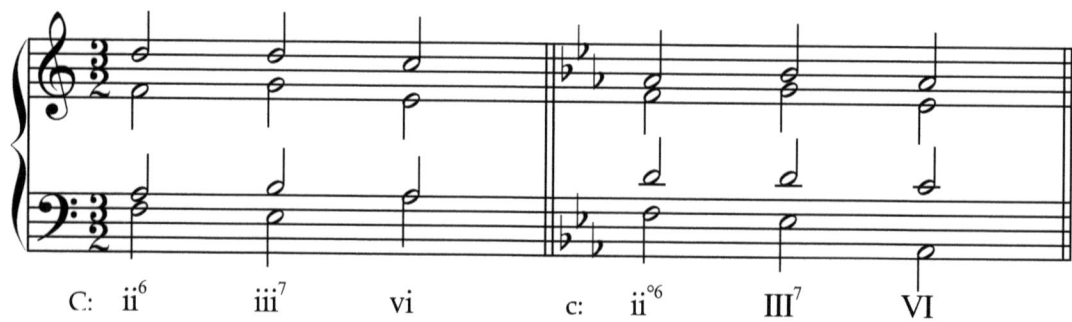

The mediant 7th chord may have the same function as a mediant triad, and it can be used as a link between opening tonic and predominant chords. In Figure 4.4, it links I with the predominant iv. The seventh of III⁷ is approached as a descending passing tone.

Figure 4.4

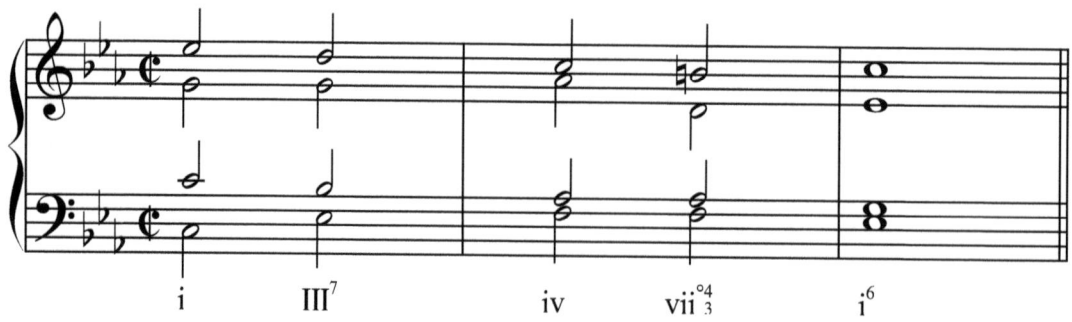

III⁷ often appears in a sequence of 7th chords. Here is a typical example of such a sequence, using a pattern of descending fifths in the bass.

Figure 4.5

Wolfgang Amadeus Mozart
Sonata in F major K 332 (I)

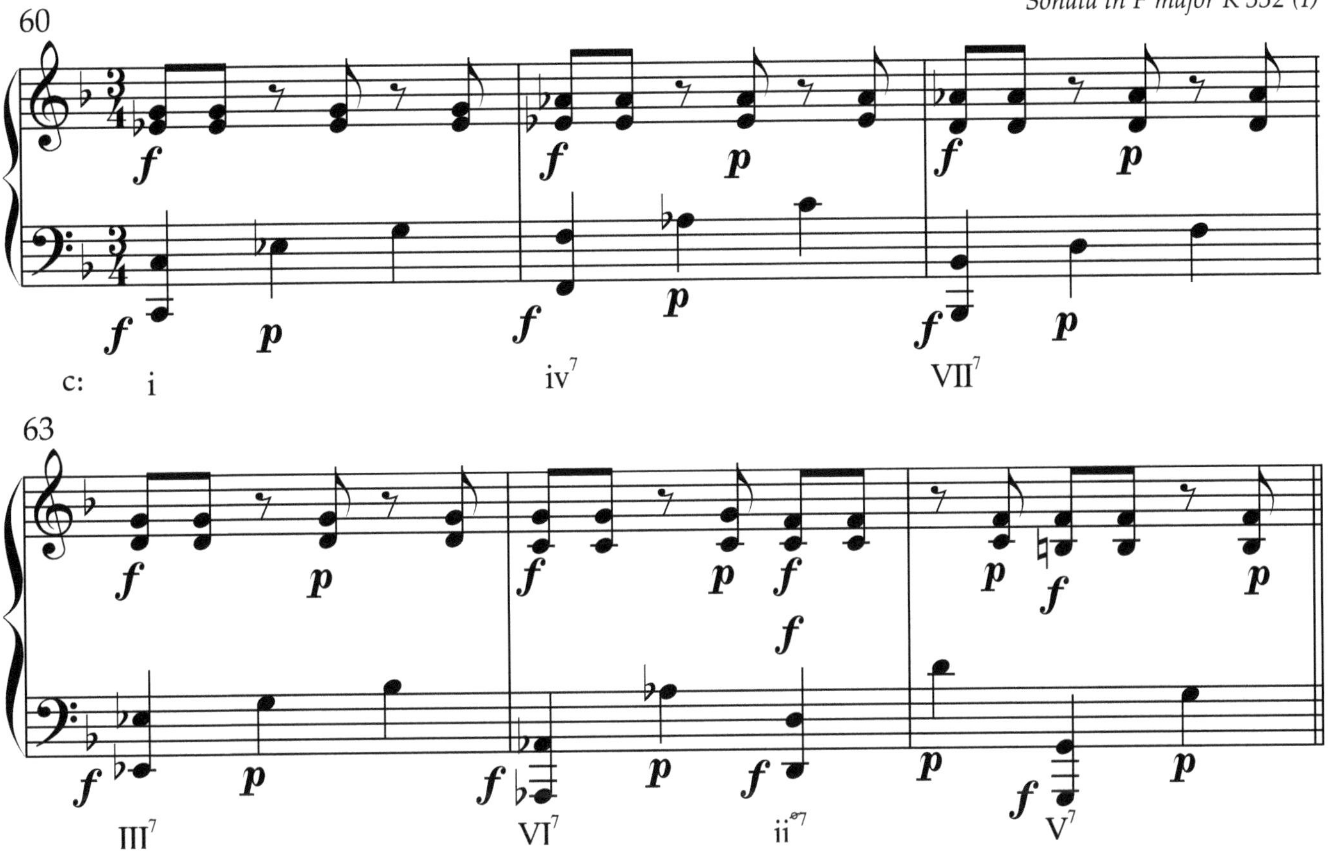

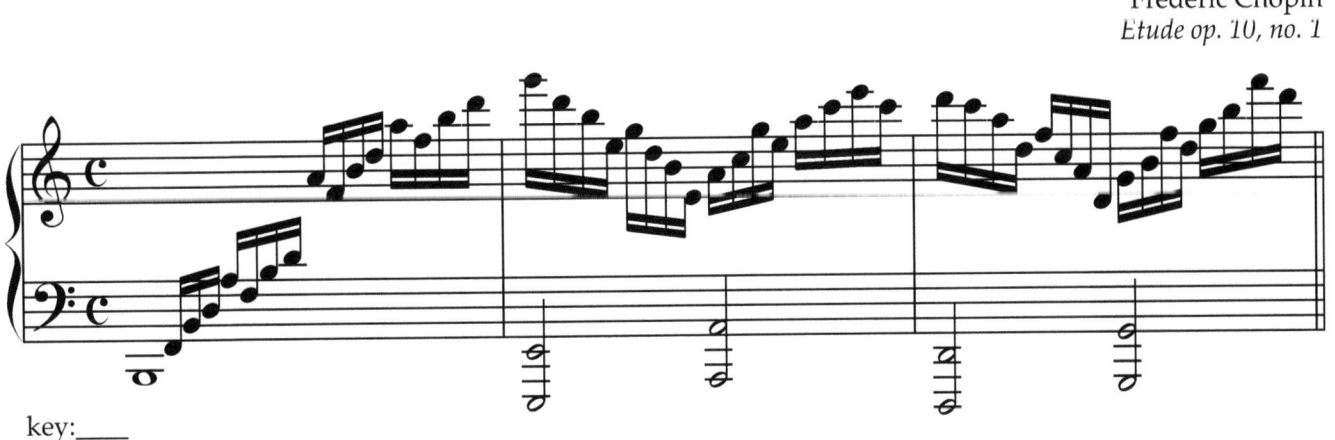

3. Provide a harmonic analysis of the following excerpts using functional chord symbols.

Frederic Chopin
Etude op. 10, no. 1

The Subdominant 7th Chord

The subdominant 7th chord acts as a predominant, moving directly to V or V^7. The progression may also pass through ii or ii^7 (or their inversions) on the way. The tonic chord is a good chord of approach to iv^7 since the seventh (scale degree $\hat{3}$) can be prepared as a common tone. In a shift from iv^7 to ii^7, only the seventh needs to move. All the other notes are common tones between the two chords.

Figure 4.6

In the progression IV^7 - V, parallel fifths may result if the seventh of IV^7 is placed above the third (see Figure 4.7 a). This can be avoided by doubling the fifth of chord V (See Figure 4.7 b), by using a cadential six-four (Figure 4.7 c), or by placing the third above the seventh in IV^7 (Figure 4.7 d).

Figure 4.7

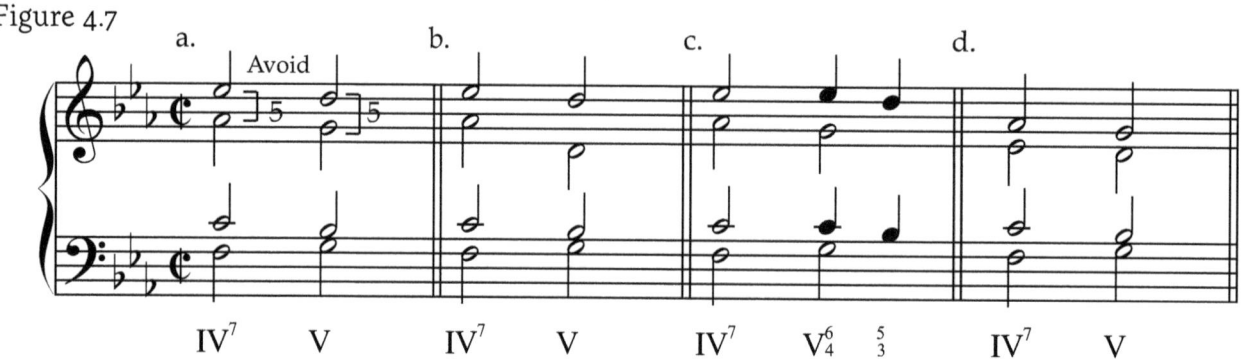

In minor keys, the subdominant 7th maybe used in root position and inversion. These chords usually resolve to dominant functioning harmony (V, V^7, VII, or VII^7). In Figure 4.8 b, IV$^6_5$ is used in its major form (with a raised $\hat{6}$) in order to avoid the melodic augmented 2nd in the bass between scale degrees $\hat{6}$ and $\sharp\hat{7}$. In both examples, the seventh is prepared as a common tone. Note also that in Figure 4.8 a, the fifth of V is doubled to avoid faulty parallels.

Figure 4.8

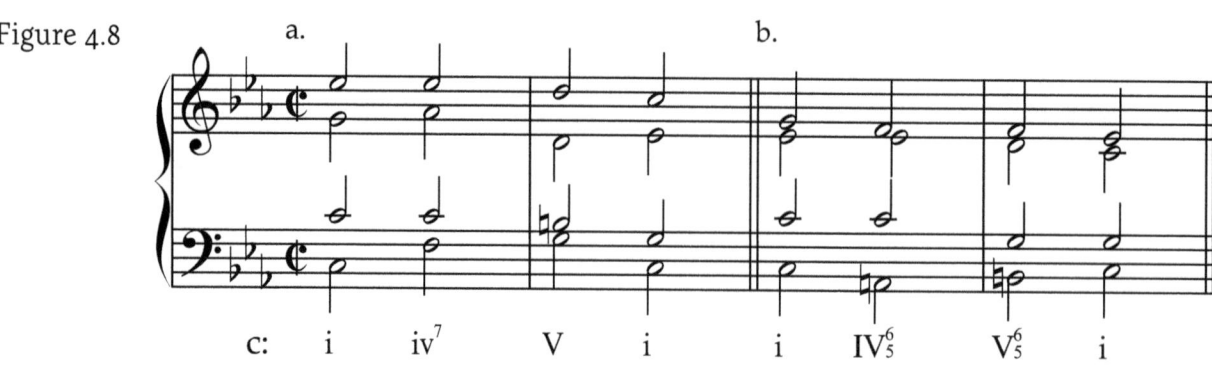

Chapter 4: Nondominant 7th Chords

1. Provide a harmonic analysis of the following excerpts using functional chord symbols.

key:

d:

key:

key:

The Submediant 7th Chord

The submediant 7th chord occurs most frequently in root position. It may resolve to supertonic, subdominant, dominant, or leading tone triads or 7th chords. In Figure 4.9, vi⁷ functions in a prolongation of predominant harmony.

Figure 4.9

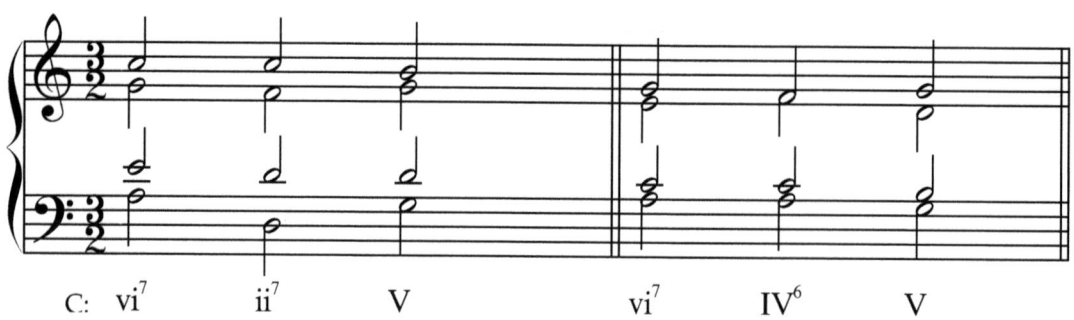

C: vi⁷   ii⁷   V   vi⁷   IV⁶   V

When vi⁷ moves directly to V or V⁷, the seventh may remain as a common tone rather than falling. This type of resolution, which is called a **passive resolution**, is rare. It's usually preferable to release the tension created by the dissonant 7th by resolving it downward by step. In order to avoid parallel fifths in a progression to the dominant, use V⁶, V⁷, or V$^6_5$ instead of root position V. Note that the seventh of VI⁷ is prepared as a common tone from I.

Figure 4.10

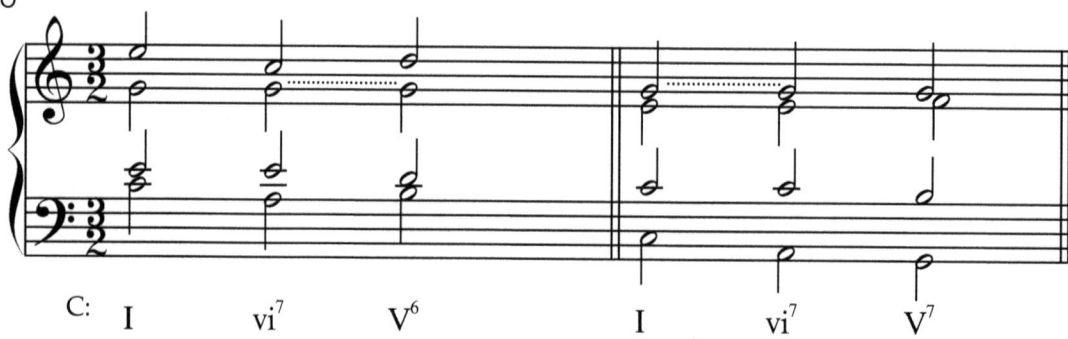

C: I   vi⁷   V⁶   I   vi⁷   V⁷

In minor keys, the submediant 7th occurs in two forms. The more usual version is the major VI⁷. The other form is a half diminished chord in which scale degree $\hat{6}$ is raised. The reason for this alteration is to avoid the melodic augmented second formed when the root of vi⁷ moves up by step to scale degree $\hat{7}$. This half diminished chord (vi⁰⁷ or ♮vi⁰⁷) is rarely seen.

Figure 4.11

VI⁷   iv⁶   vi⁰⁷   vii°   vi⁰⁷   V$^6_5$

1. Provide a harmonic analysis of the following excerpts.

Ludwig van Beethoven
Piano Sonata op.2, no. 1

key:

Johann Sebastian Bach
Chorale 145: Warum betrubst du nich, mein Herz

key:

The Subtonic 7th Chord

The 7th chord built on the subtonic (VII^7) is a major-minor 7th chord that occurs in minor keys. This chord is most often used either in a sequence or as a secondary dominant (V^7/III). Both of these functions will be discussed later.

Figure 4.12

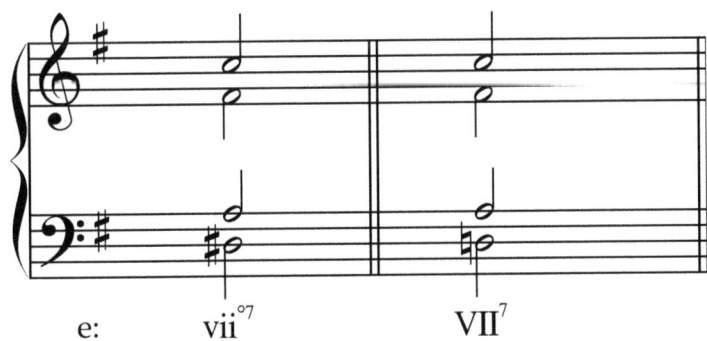

e: vii$^{\circ 7}$ VII^7

Harmonic Functions of 7th Chords

Compared to the dominant 7th, other 7th chords occur less frequently. This is because in tonal music, dominant harmony has a strong structural importance occuring next to the tonic.

With the exception of the tonic 7th, all 7th chords have the same harmonic function as their corresponding triads in the basic area of harmonization (beginning tonic, predominant, dominant, ending tonic). Note, however, that V^7 rarely replaces V in a half cadence.

It is important to remember that 7th chords have a wider field of harmonic activity. This is because the 7th is a strong **tendency tone**. A tendency tone is unstable and tends to move to a stable tone (as the leading tone leans towards the tonic). For example, a chord with a dominant function has a tendency to move toward the tonic, and the addition of a 7th to that chord will increase this tendency. Indeed, most 7th chords resolve to a chord with a root that is a fifth below.

The two most commonly use seventh chords in major keys are the dominant 7th (V^7) and the super tonic 7th (ii^7).

$$\text{most commonly used} \longrightarrow \text{least commonly used}$$
$$V^7 \quad ii^7 \quad vii^{o7} \quad IV^7 \quad vi^7 \quad I^7 \quad iii^7$$

As a general rule, a triad may be replaced by its corresponding 7th chord. In Figure 4.13, the predominant chords vi and ii and the dominant chord V are replaced by their corresponding 7th chords.

The addition of the 7th adds color, variety, and harmonic activity, but overuse of these chords will make them less effective.

Figure 4.13

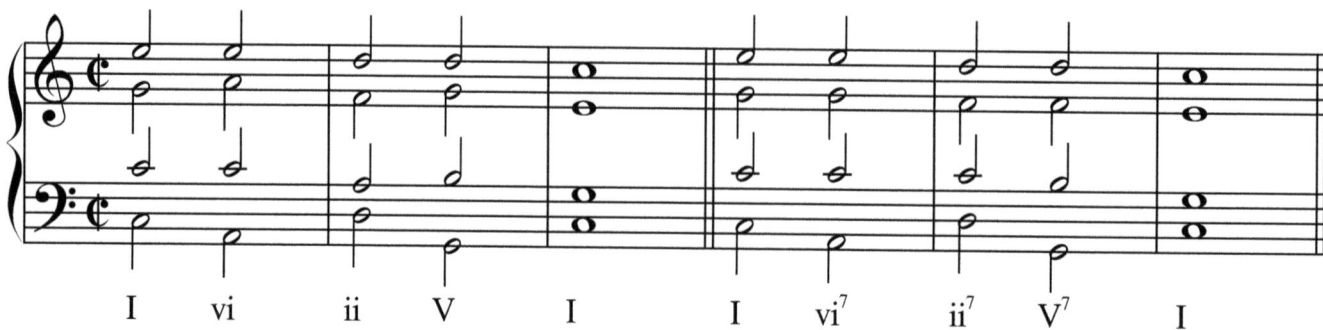

1. Rewrite the alto and tenor in the following example, changing one note in ii⁶ chord so that it becomes a supertonic 7th chord.

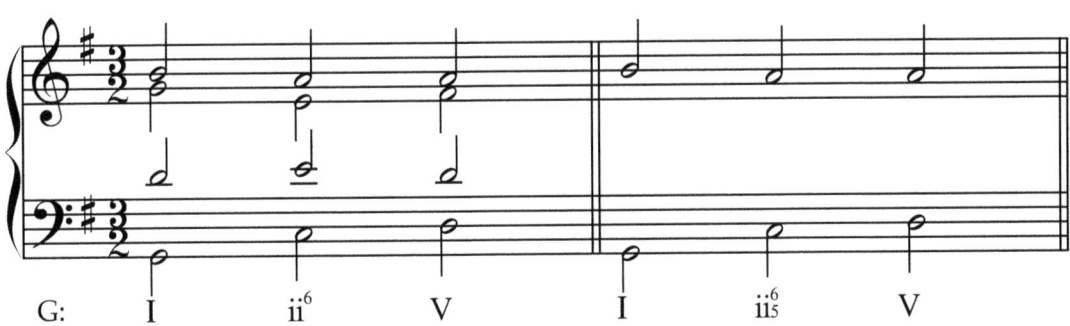

2. Rewrite the alto and tenor in the following example, changing one note in chords vi, ii and V so they become 7th chords.

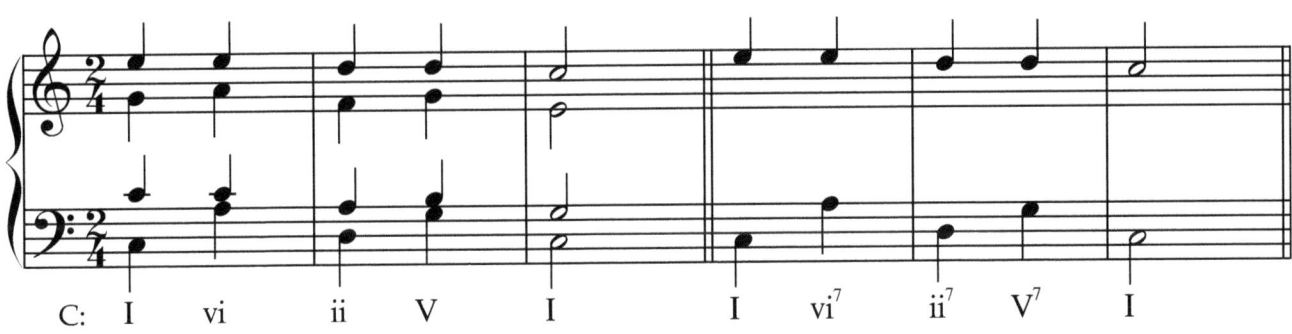

3. Rewrite the alto, tenor, and bass in the following example so that chords iv and V become 7th chords.

4. Name the keys and harmonize the following progressions in four parts according to the given chord symbols.

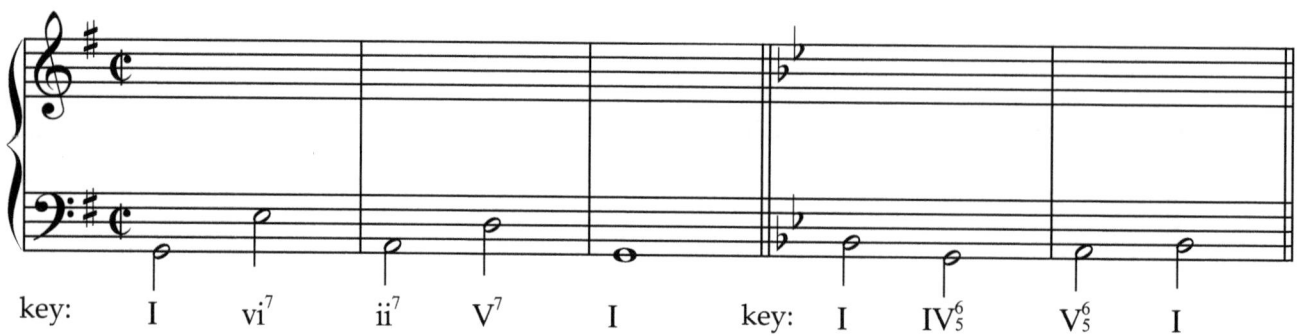

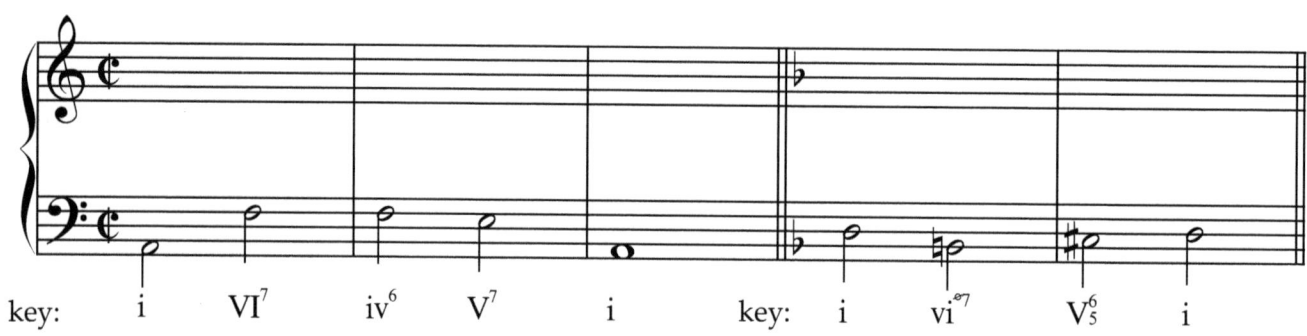

Johann Sebastian Bach
Chorale no. 105, Herliebster Jesu, was hast du verbrochen

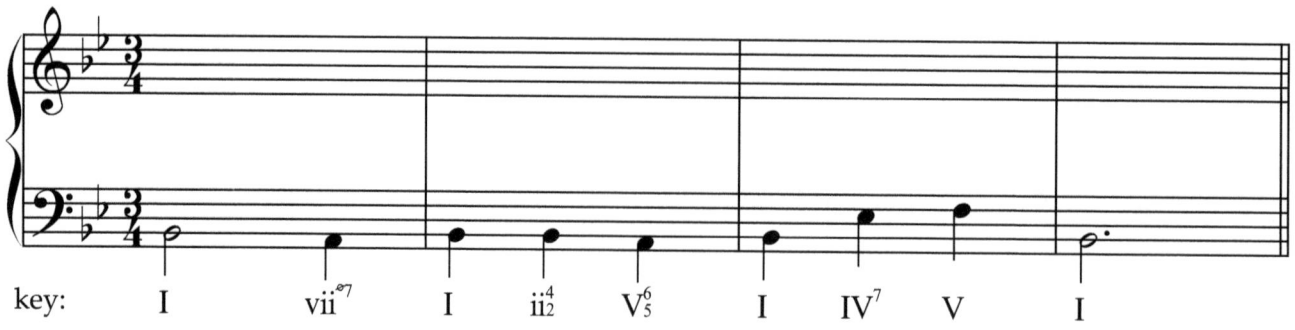

Harmonizing a Melody with 7th Chords

Any melody note can be considered the root, third, fifth, or seventh of a chord. In the following example, the tonic of G major can be harmonized by four different chords: G is the root of I, the third of vi, the fifth of IV, and the seventh of ii⁷. Although all these chord choices are possible, it is of primary importance to consider the overall harmonic progression when examining the possible chord choices for a given melody note.

Figure 4.14

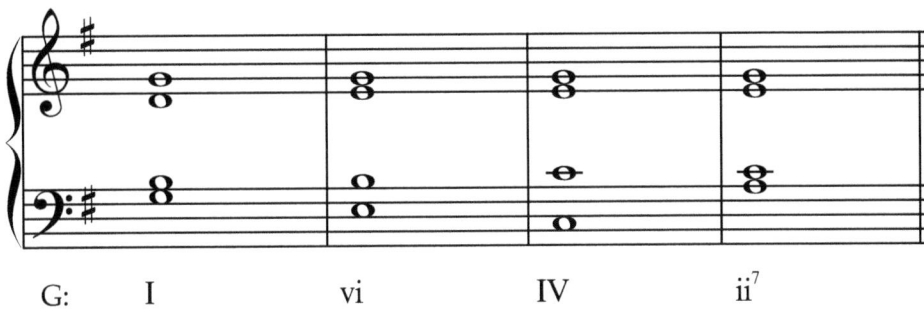

The sevenths of V⁷, vii°⁷, and viiø⁷ do not need preparation, but the sevenths of all other 7th chords should be prepared by common tone motion from the previous chord, and they should also resolve downward by step. If a melody note is to serve as the seventh of a 7th chord, it should be preceded by a common tone, and it should fall a 2nd to allow for a proper resolution.

In Figure 4.15 there are only two notes that could function as sevenths: the E and the F in m. 2. The E can serve as the seventh of IV⁷ because it is prepared by common tone motion and it moves downward by step to D, allowing a resolution. The F on the third beat can function as the seventh of V⁷. The seventh of the dominant 7th does not need preparation, but it should resolve downward by step (here, moving downward to E).

Figure 4.15

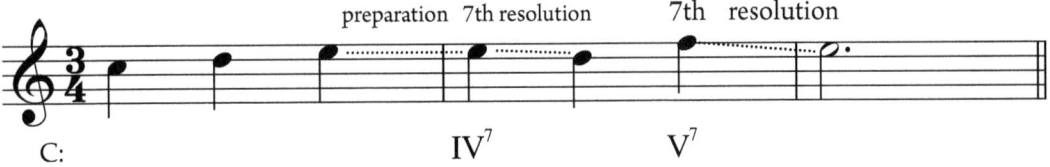

In Figure 4.16, the C on the third beat might function as the seventh of a ii^7 chord because it is prepared as a common tone and it could resolve downward by step. A second option is to place ii on the second beat and delay the resolution of the seventh until the fourth beat where it can resolve downward by step. Notice also that the seventh of V^7 (F) enters by step from within the same chord as a passing seventh (8-7).

Figure 4.16

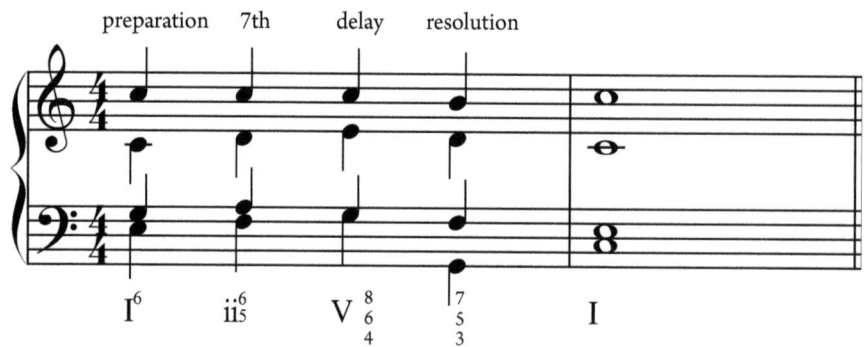

1. For the following melodies, state which notes could be harmonized as the seventh of a 7th chord.

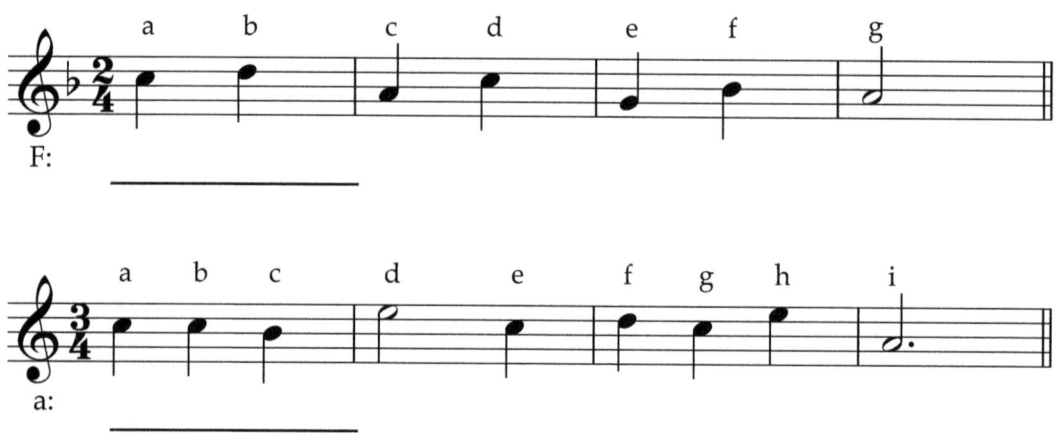

2. Harmonize the following melodies in four parts using seventh chords were appropriate. Add functional chord symbols.

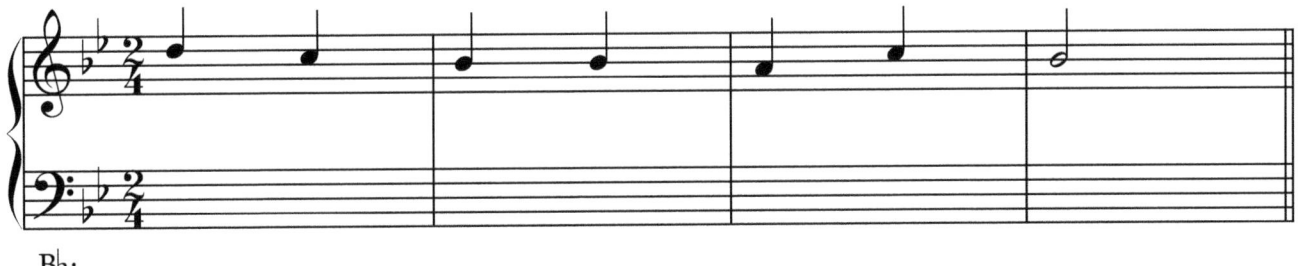

B♭:

Summary

1. A 7th chord can be built on any note of a major or minor scale.

2. Most 7th chords have the same functions as their corresponding triads. For example, ii^7 and IV^7 have the same predominant function as ii and IV. The important exception to this rule is the tonic 7th. When a seventh is added to a tonic triad, the resulting chord is unstable and cannot function as a harmonic goal. Thus, the tonic 7th is an active chord because the seventh of a I^7 chord must resolve downward.

3. It is not necessary to prepare the seventh of V^7, vii°^{7}, or vii^{ø7}, but the sevenths of all other diatonic 7th chords are usually prepared by common tone motion from the previous chord.

4. The seventh usually resolves downward by step.

5. There is a greater variety of available 7th chords in minor keys because of the three different forms of the minor scale.

5
Harmonic Sequences

A sequence is the repetition of a musical pattern at a higher or lower level of pitch. If the repetition is of a melody, it is called a **melodic sequence**. If the repetition is made up of a series of chords it is a **harmonic sequence**.

The Descending Circle of 5ths Sequence

The **descending circle-of-fifths sequence** is the most common sequence in tonal music. It is very strong harmonically because of its root relationship by a 5th. Each chord's root is a fifth lower than the previous chord's root. This sequence may sound familiar, not only because it is a common sequence in tonal music, but also because its second half is a common functional progression (vi - ii - V - I). It sounds especially good in minor keys, but appears frequently in major keys as well. Study the descending circle of 5ths sequences in Figure 5.1 and make note of the following:

1. The bass alternates descending 5ths and ascending 4ths. This helps to keep the range for the bass. If it continued to descend in 5ths it would quickly move out of singing range.

2. The voice leading patterns in each part remain the same throughout: the soprano steps up, the alto holds a common tone, and the tenor steps up. The voice leading in the three upper parts alternates at every second chord, just as the direction of the bass changes. It is important to follow this voice leading since a sequence is based on the repetition of different patterns of scale degrees in melodic lines.

3. In this progression in major keys, vii°7 moves to iii. The root of each chord is doubled. This leads to a doubled leading tone in chord vii°, which is allowed since it does not move to I and the leading tone does not resolve to scale degree $\hat{1}$.

4. In minor keys, scale degree $\hat{7}$ is not raised in chords VII and III since it does not function as a leading tone. In chord V, however, $\hat{7}$ is raised for the authentic cadence at the end of the sequence.

5. Chord vii° in the major sequence and chord ii° in the minor sequence are diminished chords in root position and are used in these progressions.

Figure 5.1

The descending fifths sequence can be used in its complete form but sometimes it is seen in a shortened version consisting of I - iii - vi - ii - V - I. In this version, the chord built on $\hat{7}$ is omitted and the other chords maintain their normal harmonic function. Occasionally, strict sequential motion is broken at the cadence to create a stronger ending with a fully closed cadence.

Figure 5.2

The root-position ii° triad is acceptable in this progression. We normally avoid root-position diminished triads, but in this common sequence we don't mind the sound because it fits into the overall pattern. However, many composers avoid this problem by adding a seventh to alternate chords (Figure 5.3 a) or to every chord other than the tonic (Figure 5.3 b). It is necessary to alternate between complete and incomplete chords if you use sevenths throughout. Another common solution is inverting alternate chords (Figure 5.3 c), possibly adding a seventh to the inverted chords (Figure 5.3 d).

Figure 5.3

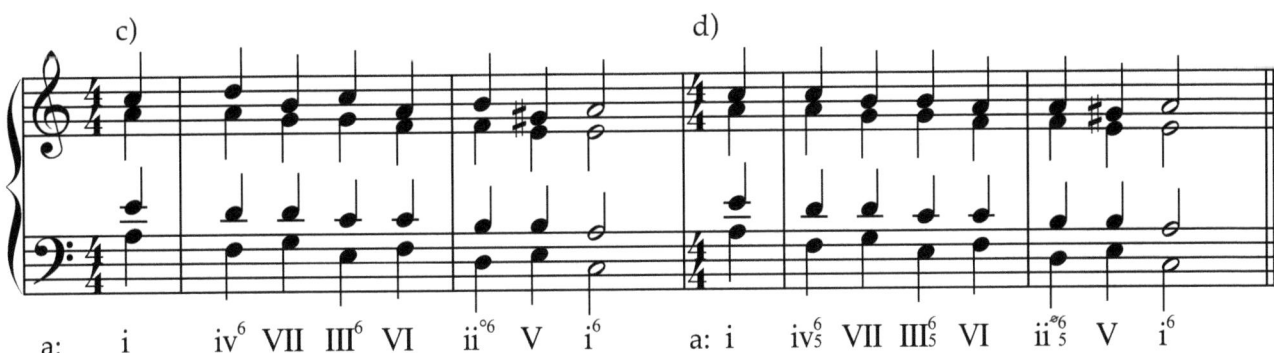

1. Provide a harmonic analysis using functional chord symbols for the following musical excerpts.

Piano Sonata
K 545 (1st mvt.)

Wolfgang Amadeus Mozart (1756-1791)

G:

Suite no. 7 in G minor
HWV 432 (Passacaglia)

George Frideric Handel (1685-1759)

Chapter 5: Harmonic Sequences

2. Complete the following sequences in four parts for SATB.

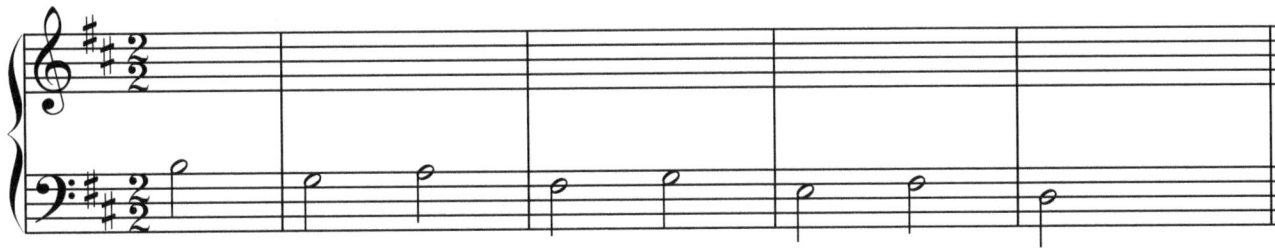

Rhythmic Placement of a Sequence

The metrical placement of the sequences shown so far places the final tonic on a strong beat. This isn't always required, especially if the final goal of the sequence is a chord other than the tonic. The most important rhythmic element to consider in writing a sequence is that alternate chords should fall on comparably strong beats.

Figure 5.4

☑ Good. This pattern corresponds to the rhythm   ☒ Bad. This pattern conflicts with the rhythm

The Descending 5-6 Sequence

The **descending 5-6 sequence** is sometimes known as the descending 3rds sequence because the pattern moves down a third with each repetition. In its most common form the bass line moves down by step and is harmonized with alternating root position and first inversion chords. This pattern of inversions gives it the name descending 5 - 6 sequence, 5 referring to the root position chords, and 6 to the first inversion chords.

Notice in these sequences in Figure 5.5 the leading tone ($\hat{7}$) that occurs in V^6 in the major key, descends to the root of vi instead of rising to the tonic ($\hat{1}$). This voice leading is necessary in order to keep the sequential motion of the voices consistent. In minor keys v^6 does not have a raised leading tone in order to avoid an augmented 2nd. However, the final V chord has the raised leading tone for the half cadence. Here $\hat{6}$ is raised along with $\hat{7}$ in order to avoid an augmented 2nd melodically.

Figure 5.5

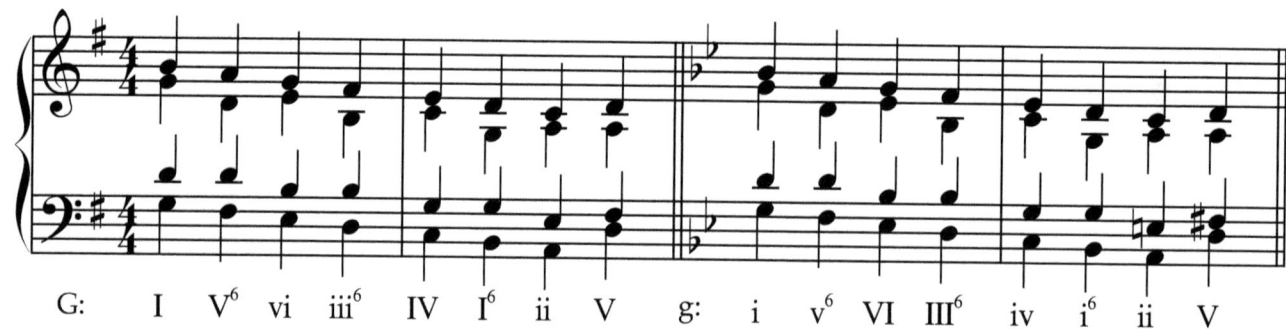

Another option for this sequence is to insert root position chords between the descending 3rds, creating a sequence with a bass pattern of a descending 4th followed by an ascending 2nd. This sequence occurs in the well-known *Canon in D major* by Johann Pachelbel. In Pachelbel's canon, the sequential chords are in root position. The leading tone ($\hat{7}$), in chord V descends to the doubled root of vi instead of rising to the tonic ($\hat{1}$), maintaining the sequential motion. When writing the sequence in minor keys, the minor v chord must not have a raised leading tone so as to avoid a melodic augmented 2nd. It is not necessary here, because it is leading away from the tonic. This sequence almost always begins on the tonic and places the odd-numbered chords (I - vi - IV - ii) on strong beats. It is very effective when harmonizing a melody descending in steps.

Figure 5.6

3. Provide a harmonic analysis using a functional chord symbols for the following musical excerpts.

Piano Sonata no. 4

Carl Philipp Emmanuel Bach
(1714-1788)

Sonata for Violin and Piano

K 372 (1st mvt.)

Wolfgang Amadeus Mozart
(1756-1791)

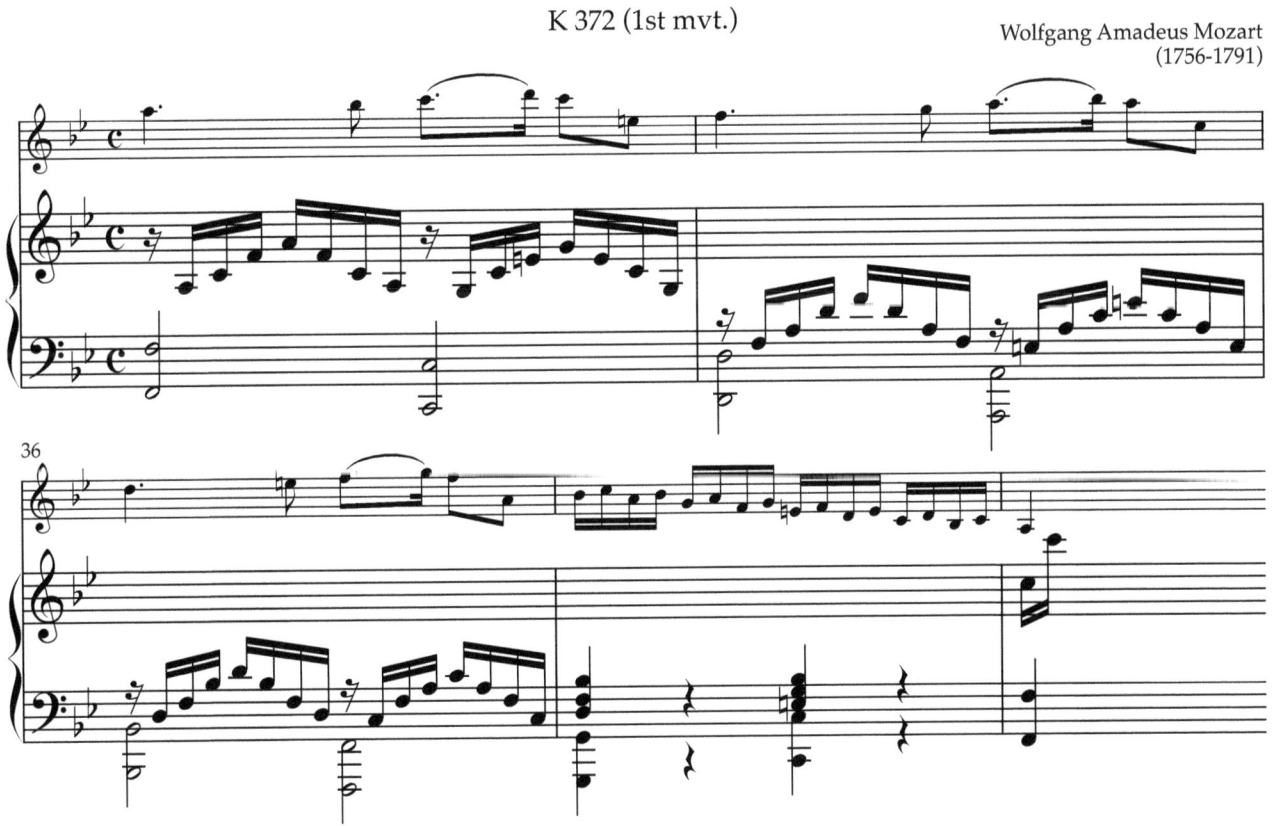

4. Name the keys. Complete the following sequences for four voices show both the functional and the root quality chord symbols.

The Ascending 5-6 Sequence

Most sequences descend in pitch. However, it is possible to have an ascending sequence. The **ascending 5-6** sequence gets its name from the interval motion of 5-6 in an upper voice over an ascending bass. In the most common form of this sequence, the bass line ascends and it is harmonized with alternating root and first inversion chords. This may also be written with a bass that is held for two chords, depending on the type of writing and musical texture. The bass ascends by step so sometimes it can be described as an ascending second sequence. This pattern can be difficult to write in four voices. It is easier to write in three voices as seen in Figure 5.7 b.

Figure 5.7

The ascending 5 - 6 sequence may be written using root position chords rather than the usual alternating root position and first inversion pattern. This version makes it easier to write in four parts.

Root position diminished triads may be used in this sequence but they should not be placed on strong beats. It is common to avoid them altogether. If the sequence is used in a minor key it should not start on the tonic since it will place ii° on a strong beat. However, this sequence can start on any other stable chord.

Figure 5.8

5. Provide a harmonic analysis using a functional chord symbols for the following musical excerpts.

Palestrina
Agnus Dei II, Missa Sanctorum Meritis

Violin Concerto in F minor (Inverno)
II, Largo

Antonio Vivaldi

Chapter 5: Harmonic Sequences

The Ascending Circle of 5ths Sequence

The **ascending circle-of-fifths sequence** is not a very common sequence since it directs motion way from tonic harmony. Essentially it reverses the descending circle of fifths sequence. Each chords root is a 5th higher than the previous chords root. The voice leading is easy but the harmonic effect can be a bit confusing. It is important not to use the diminished chord in this sequence. Generally it moves from I to iii in major keys (Figure 5.9a) or from III to V in minor keys (Figure 5.9b). Inversions are not very common in this sequence.

Figure 5.9

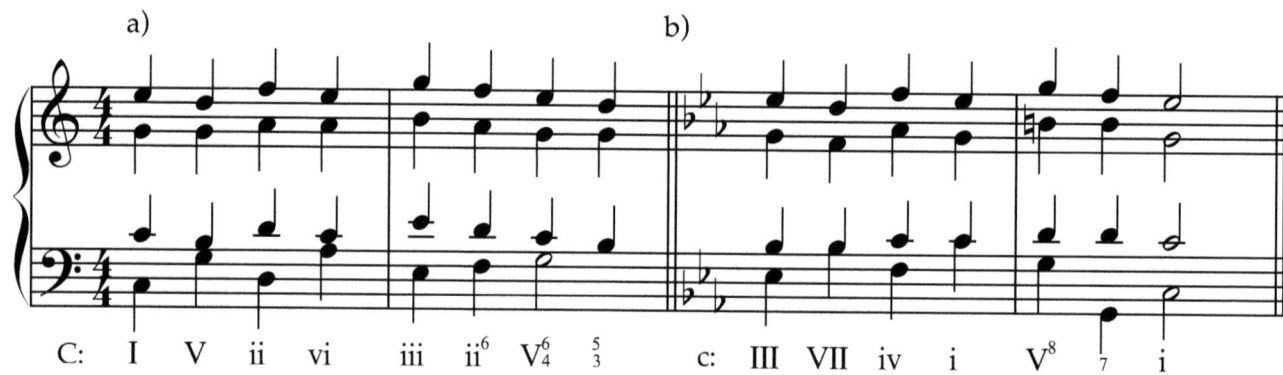

6. Provide a harmonic analysis using a functional chord symbols for the following musical excerpts.

Johann Sebastian Bach
Little Prelude BWV 924

Using Sequences

Harmonically, a sequence is a device that fills in a progresssion from one chord to another. For example, chord I can go directly to ii^6, but this progression can also be expanded with a sequence.

Ascending 5- 6: **I** (vi^6 - ii - vii^{o6} - iii - I^6 - IV) **ii^6**

Descending circle of 5ths: **I** (IV^6 - vii^o - iii^6 - vi) **ii^6**

The following chart shows typical starting and ending chords for the sequences we have studied.

Sequence	Starting Chord	Ending Chord
Descending Circle of 5ths	Tonic or mediant	any chord that creates a good progression like I, V or ii
Descending 5-6	Usually tonic	IV, I or ii
Ascending 5-6	Any stable chord	Any chord that creates a good progression
Ascending Circle of 5ths	Major keys: tonic Minor keys: mediant	Major: I leads to iii Minor: III leads to V

7. Name the key and complete each example for four voices. Add functional and root/quality chord symbols. Find and name the sequence in each example.

key: _____
sequence: _____

key: _____
sequence: _____

key: _____
sequence: _____

Chapter 5: Harmonic Sequences

Using 7th Chords in a Sequence

When 7th chords are used in a descending circle of 5ths sequence, there are several voice leading rules to take into consideration.

If all the 7th chords in the sequence are in root position, complete chords alternate with incomplete chords, in which the root is doubled and the fifth is omitted. In this progression in major keys, the leading tone, which is the root of vii^{ø7}, is doubled. This doubling is correct in this progression since the sequential pattern takes precedence over the doubling preferences of individual notes or chords.

Notice that both VII^7 and III^7 use the subtonic rather than the raised leading tone found in vii^{o7} and III^{+7}. In Figure 5.10, the sevenths of each chord are prepared as common tones and they resolve downward by step.

Figure 5.10

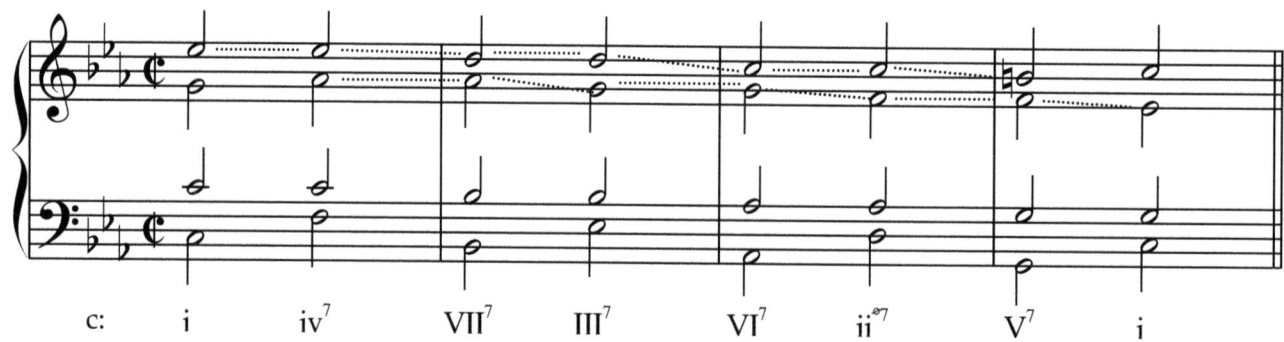

If the 7th chords in a circle of 5ths sequence are inverted, $^6_5$ chords alternate with $^4_2$ chords.

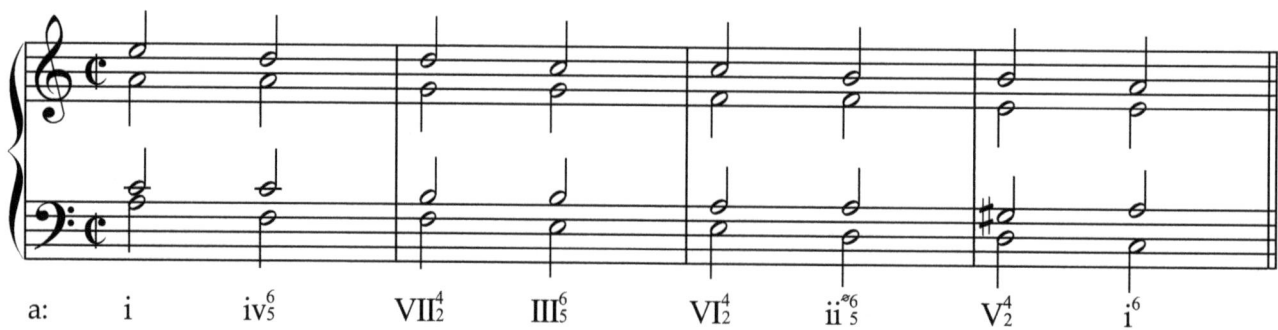

Similarly, $^4_3$ chords alternate with root position chords.

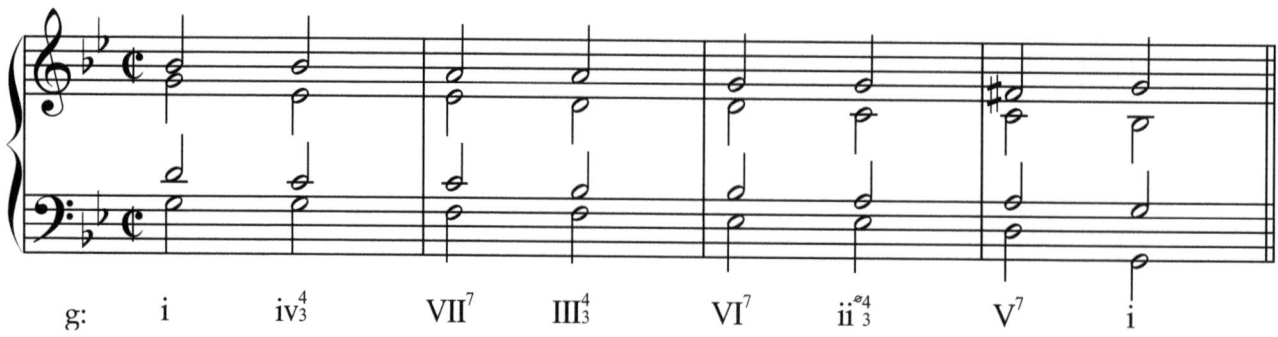

8. Provide a harmonic analysis of the following excerpts.

Mimi's aria: "Sono andate?"
from La Boheme, Act 4

Giacomo Puccini
(1858-1924)

Sonatina
op. 88, no. 3 (3rd mvt)

Friedrich Kuhlau
(1786-1832)

9. Complete the following in four parts for SATB.

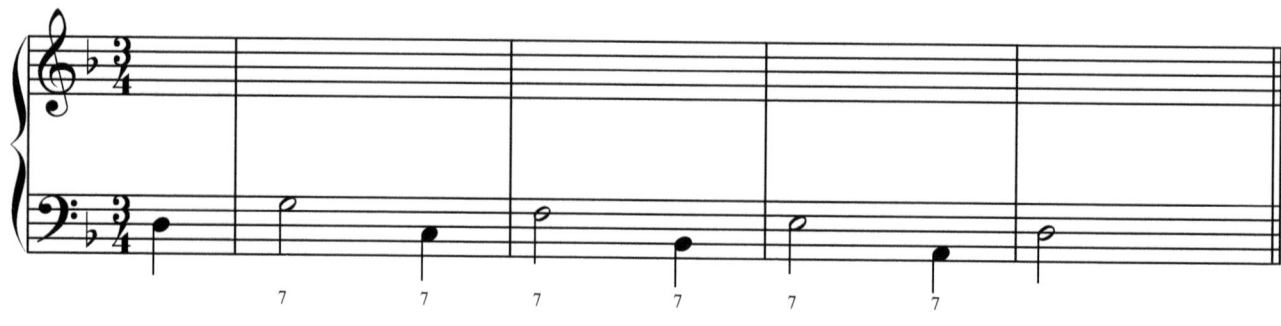

Johann Sebastian Bach
Chorale no. 105: Herzliebster Jesu, was hast du verbrochen

Chapter 5: Harmonic Sequences

6
Tonicization and Secondary Dominants

A movement of music from one key to another is called a **modulation** or a **tonicization**. Modulation implies a relatively long passage in the new key, whereas tonicization refers to a relatively shorter shift.

Tonicization means treating a chord other than the I chord like a tonic by approaching it with its dominant. In diatonic harmony, the V chord (the dominant) resolves to the I chord (the tonic). A **secondary** or **applied dominant** is a major triad or dominant seventh chord that resolves to (or tonicizes) a chord other than the I chord.

Dominant function chords covered so far include V, V^6, and vii^6, as well as V^7, vii^{o7}, and $vii^{ø7}$ and their inversions. Because all dominant function chords contain the leading tone, they have a strong tendency to resolve to tonic function chords.

This means that any chord that is preceded by a secondary dominant assumes the role of a tonic for a short period of time. Any major or minor chord can become the goal of a secondary dominant, but diminished or augmented chords cannot be tonicized because they never function as tonic chords. On the other hand, V^7 maybe proceeded by the dominant of V, even though V^7 cannot be a tonic chord.

In Figure 6.1, we hear the whole phrase in C major, but A minor appears momentarily. The chord on the last beat of m.3 (E G♯ B D) does not exist in C major: It is the second inversion of the dominant 7th of A minor (vi), and it resolves to an A minor chord. This short progression is a tonicization of A minor. For a brief instant, A minor assumes a tonic role, but this shift does not last long enough to be recognized as a real key change. The A minor chord is heard and labelled as vi. The preceding chord is labelled V^4_3 of vi (symbolized V^4_3/vi). The secondary dominant tonicizes the A minor chord, giving it special emphasis, but no change of tonic occurs.

Figure 6.1

Piano Sonata in G major
op. 14, no. 2 (2nd mvt)

Ludwig van Beethoven
(1770-1827)

I V^4_3 I^6 V^6 I ii^6 V I^6 V^4_3 I V^4_3/vi vi IV V I

Secondary Dominants in Major Keys

As stated earlier, the goal of a secondary dominant must be a major or minor chord. In major keys, ii, iii, IV, V, and vi may be tonicized. Chord I is already the tonic, and so cannot be further tonicized; vii is a diminished chord, and so cannot assume a tonic function.

Figure 6.2

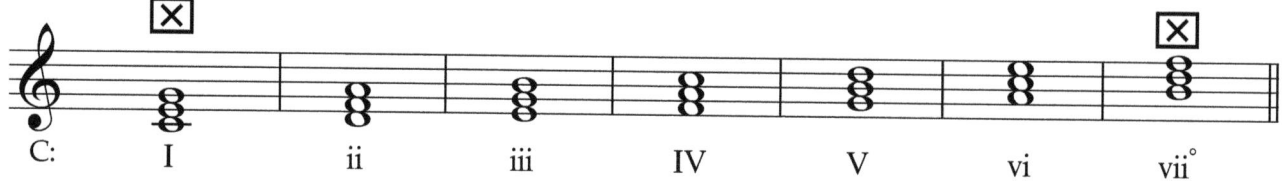

Here are five possibilities for applied dominants in C major. Notice the system for labelling these chords.

Figure 6.3

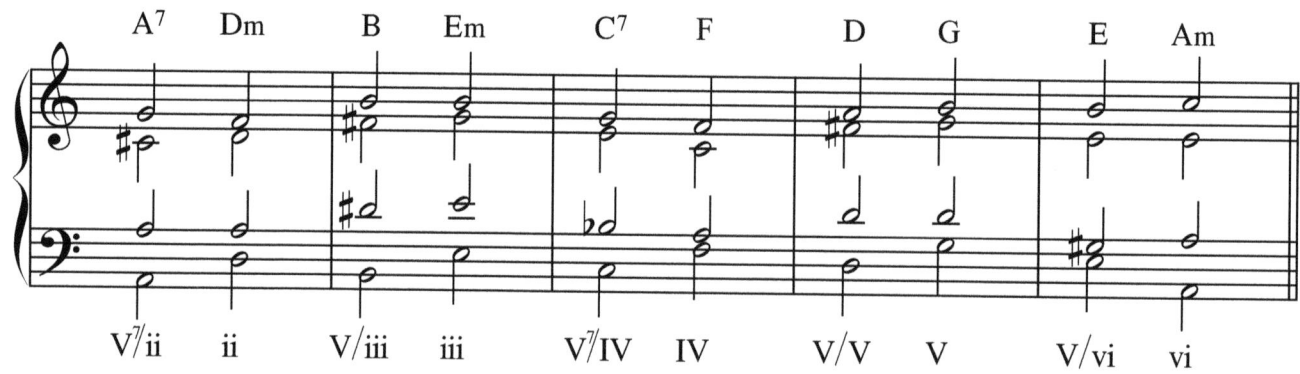

Secondary dominants are usually chromatic chords that contain accidentals. One accidental is usually the leading tone of the temporary key, but other accidentals may also occur.

In Figure 6.4 (a) in E flat major, ii is an F minor chord. In this example, the secondary dominant V/ii requires an E natural for the raised leading tone of F minor.

In Figure 6.4 (b) in A flat major, iii is a C minor chord. In this example, the secondary dominant V/iii requires two accidentals: B natural (as the raised leading tone in C minor) and D natural (because the key signature of C minor does not contain D flat).

Figure 6.4

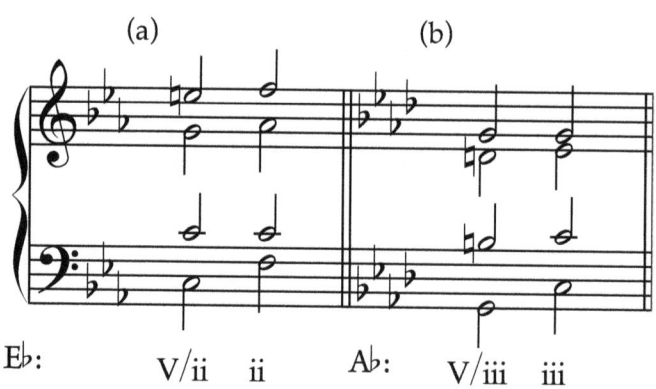

Chapter 6: Tonicization

In Figure 6.5 (a) in B major, vi is a G sharp minor chord. In this example, the secondary dominant V/vi requires an F double sharp for the raised leading tone of G sharp minor.

In Figure 6.5 (b), since V of IV does not contain any accidentals, it may not suggest a new key. For this reason, composers often use the dominant seventh (V^7/IV) instead. For example, in C major V of IV is a C major chord (C E G), but this chord is also I of C major. The dominant 7th, on the other hand, introduces B-flat, a note which is foreign to C major and which suggests the new key of F major

Figure 6.5

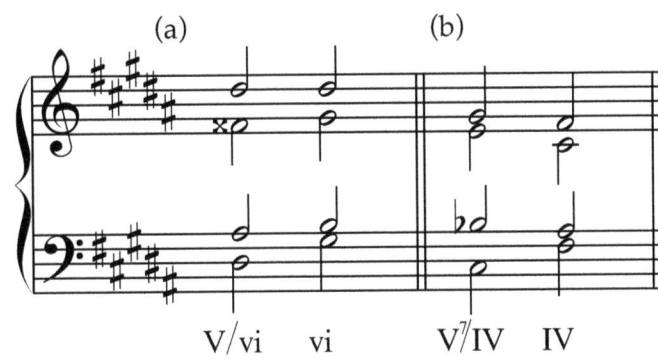

1. Provide both functional and root/quality chord symbols for the following secondary dominants.

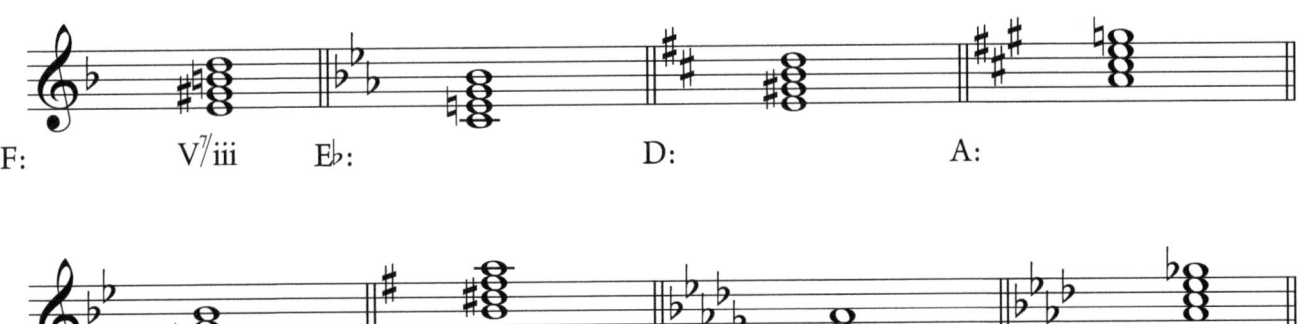

2. Write the following secondary dominants in the indicated keys. Provide root/quality chord symbols symbols.

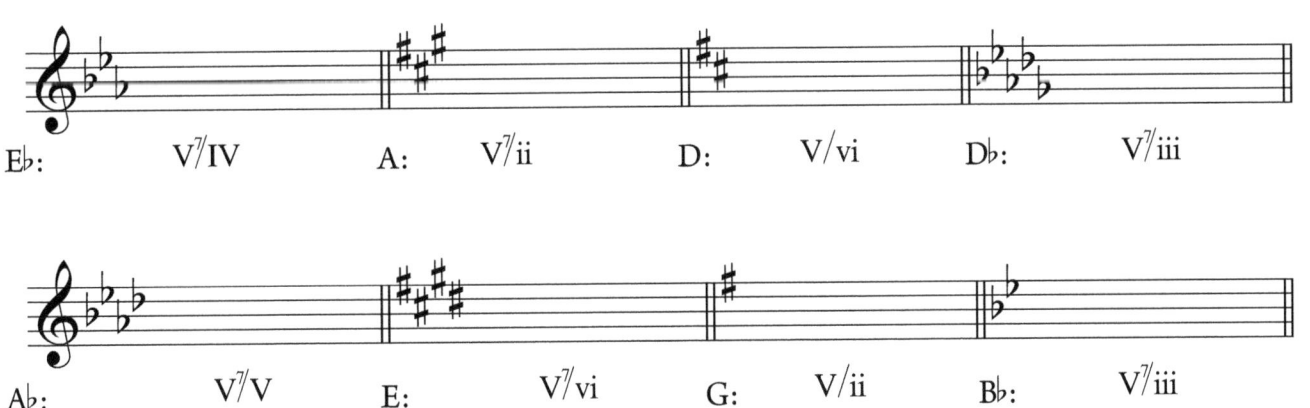

Chapter 6: Tonicization

***Note that secondary dominants follow the same rules for resolution as primary dominants.
Do not double the temporary leading tone in the secondary dominant.***

3. Complete the following progressions in four parts.

Secondary dominant 7ths maybe used in inversion, and follow the normal rules for resolution. Note that V_2^4 resolves to a first inversion chord because the seventh is in the bass in must resolve downward by step.

Figure 6.6

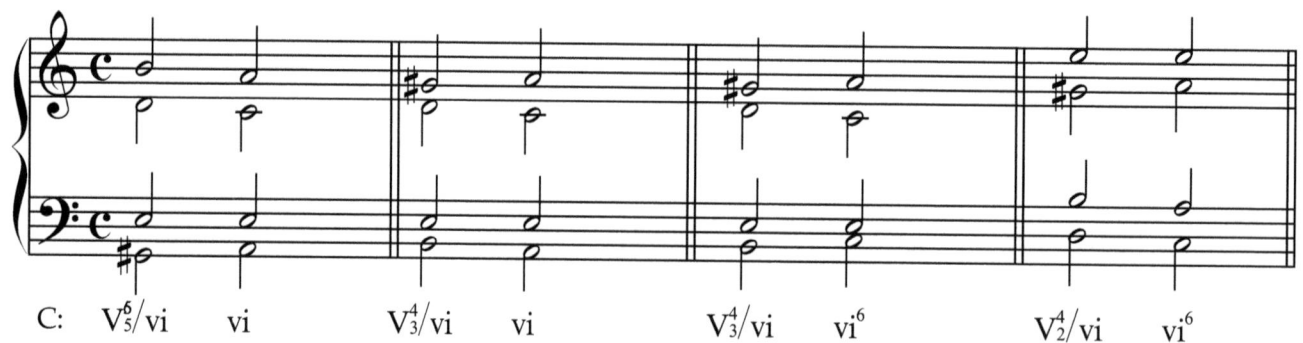

Chapter 6: Tonicization

Tonicizations of the dominant are common in both major and minor keys, and are often found at cadences. When V/V occurs at a cadential point, it acts as a prolongation of the dominant as shown in Figure 6.7.

Figure 6.7

Johann Sebastian Bach
Chorale no. 217 Ach Gott, wie manches Herzelied

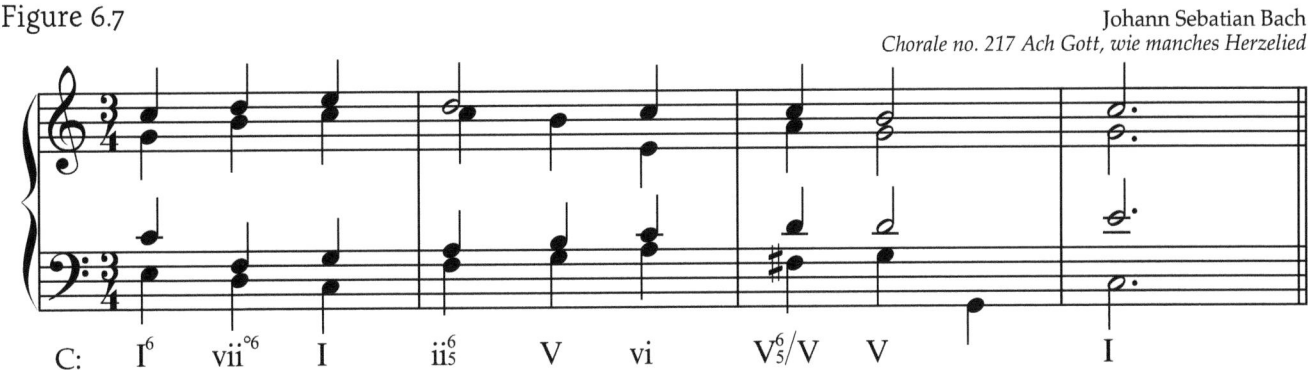

Because secondary dominants are dominant function chords, they naturally progress to tonic function chords. Since vi can function as a substitute for I in a deceptive cadence, secondary dominants may move to vi of the temporary key. Such deceptive resolutions are found most often in the progression V^7/vi - IV (or iv) as shown in Figure 6.8 (a).

Secondary dominants may be decorated with a cadential six-four in the same way as primary dominants. The cadential six-four resolves in the usual manner (Figure 6.8 (b)).

Figure 6.8

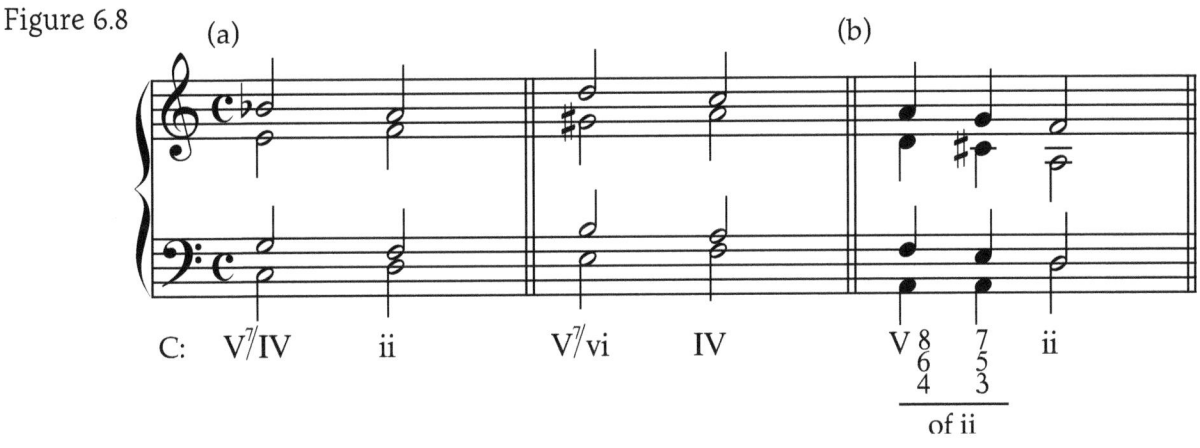

In Figure 6.9, V7/vi resolves to IV rather than vi. However this progression is the equivalent of V7/vi - VI/vi, and is a deceptive cadence.

Ludwig van Beethoven
Piano Sonata op. 53 (1st mvt)

Figure 6.9

Chapter 6: Tonicization

4. Write secondary dominants in the following keys.

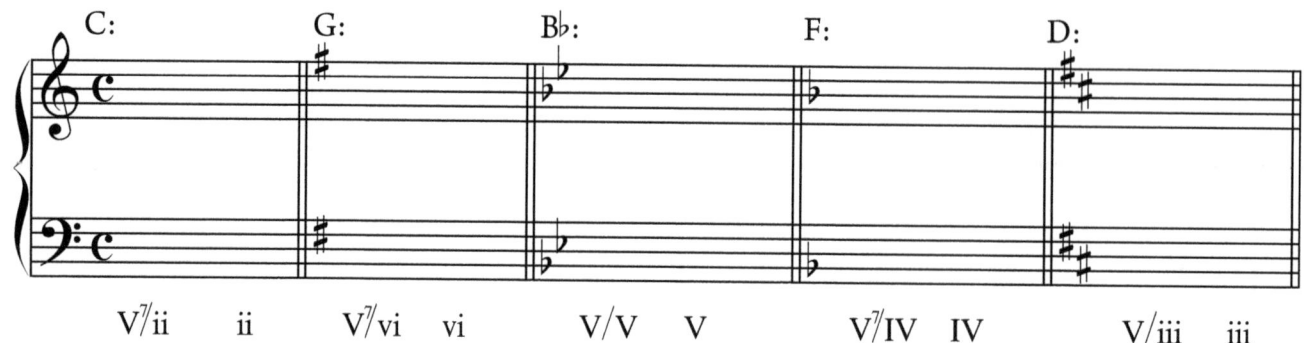

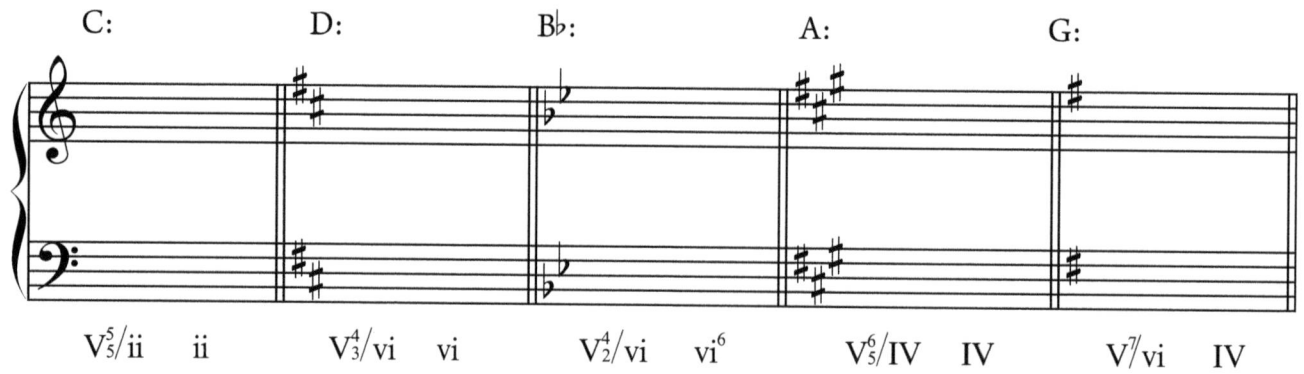

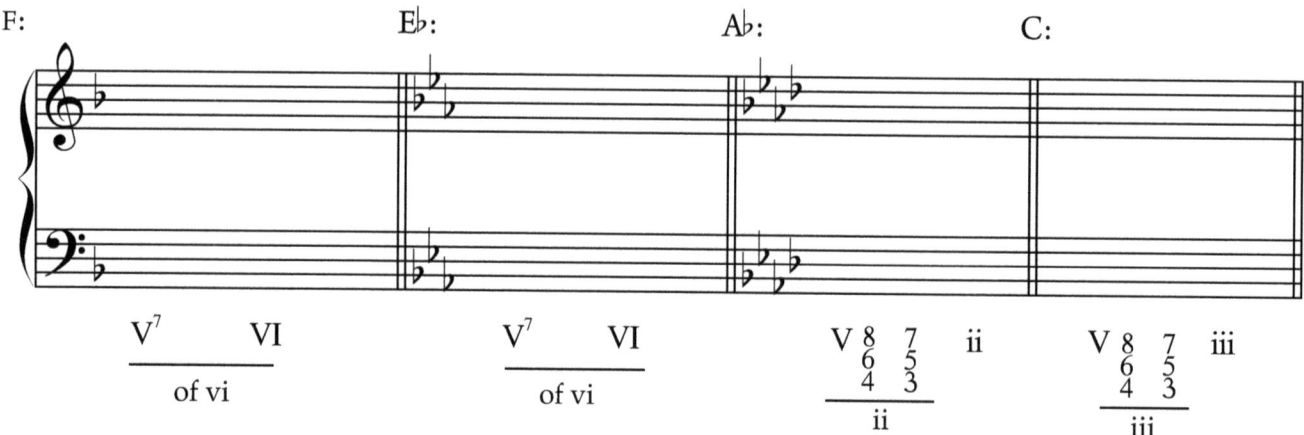

The secondary dominant in Figure 6.10 does not resolve the the usual manner. The repeated C in the bass is a tonic pedal. The secondary dominant in m.2 (V^7/V) resolves not to V or V^7 but to an altered leading tone 7th chord. This leading tone 7th, however, does have a dominant function. Thus, the basic harmonic function of the phrase is similar to the secondary dominant progressions seen earlier in the chapter. Chopin has chosen these chords in order to produce a specific musical effect.

Figure 6.10

5. Provide a harmonic analysis of the following excerpts. Circle and identify all non-chord tones.

The Creation

Franz Joseph Haydn
(1732-1809)

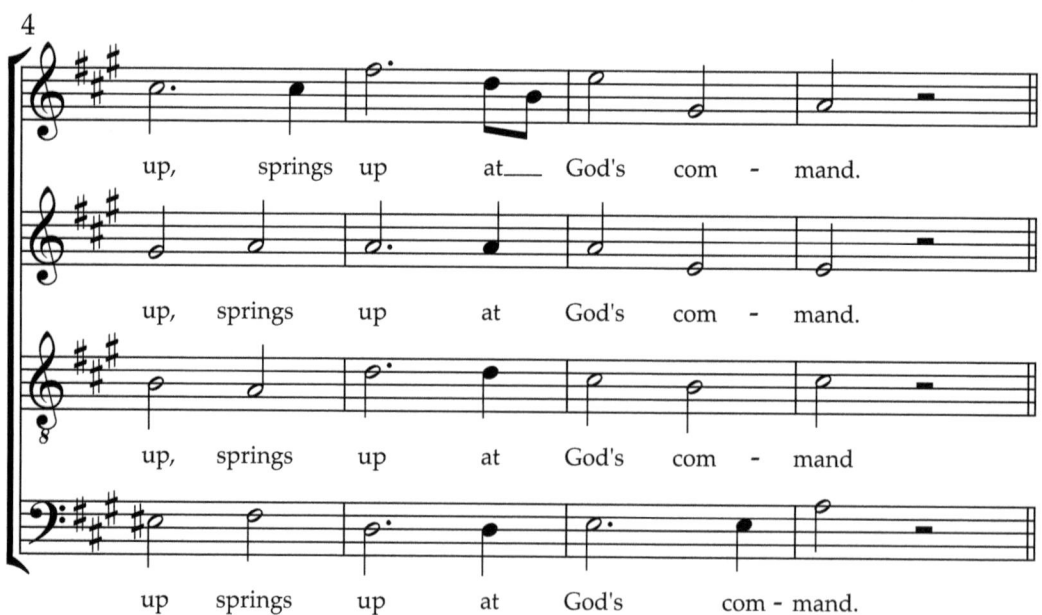

Chapter 6: Tonicization

Symphony no. 8 ("Unfinished")
D759 (2nd mvt.)

Franz Schubert
(1797-1828)

Secondary Dominants in Minor Keys

Not all of the diatonic triads produced by the three forms of the minor scale can function as goals of secondary dominants. The chords in Figure 6.11 are the most common choices for tonicizations in minor keys.

Figure 6.11

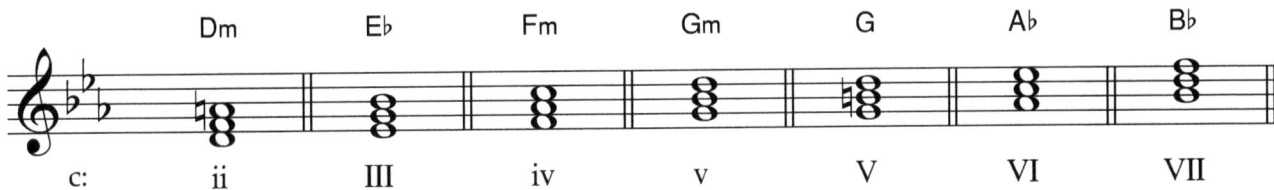

In minor keys, ii can only be tonicized when it is written using the melodic form of the minor scale (with raised $\hat{6}$). Thus V of ii has three accidentals (Figure 6.12 (a)). In a harmonic minor scale, ii is a diminished chord, and therefore cannot be tonicized.

In minor keys, III is a popular choice for tonicization because it is the relative major. It is written as a major chord (that is, without a raised leading tone). Note also that no accidentals are needed, since the minor and it's relative major have the same key signature (Figure 6.12 (b)).

Figure 6.12

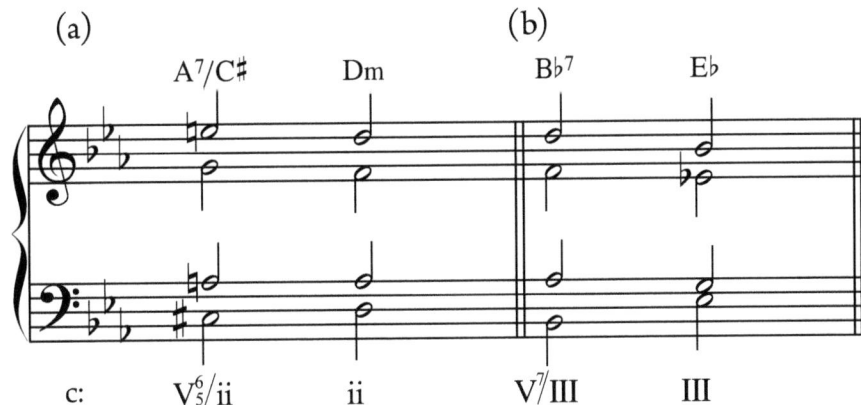

Chapter 6: Tonicization

Figure 6.13 illustrates the remaining secondary dominants used in minor keys. The secondary dominant can be either V or V^7. When tonicizing VI, it is best to use V^7; in some instances, V/VI could be analyzed as III in a minor key.

Figure 6.13

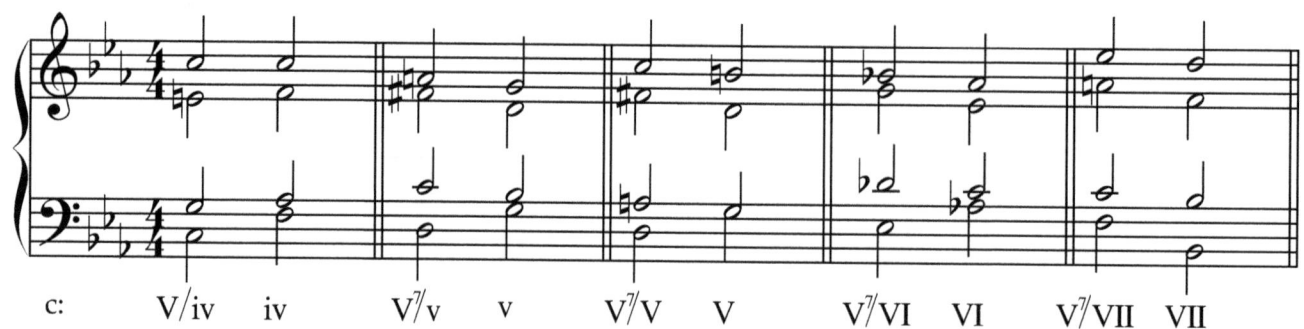

c: V/iv   iv   V^7/v   v   V^7/V   V   V^7/VI   VI   V^7/VII   VII

6. Provide functional chord symbols for the following a secondary dominants.

7. Write the following secondary dominants in the indicated keys. Add root/quality chord symbols.

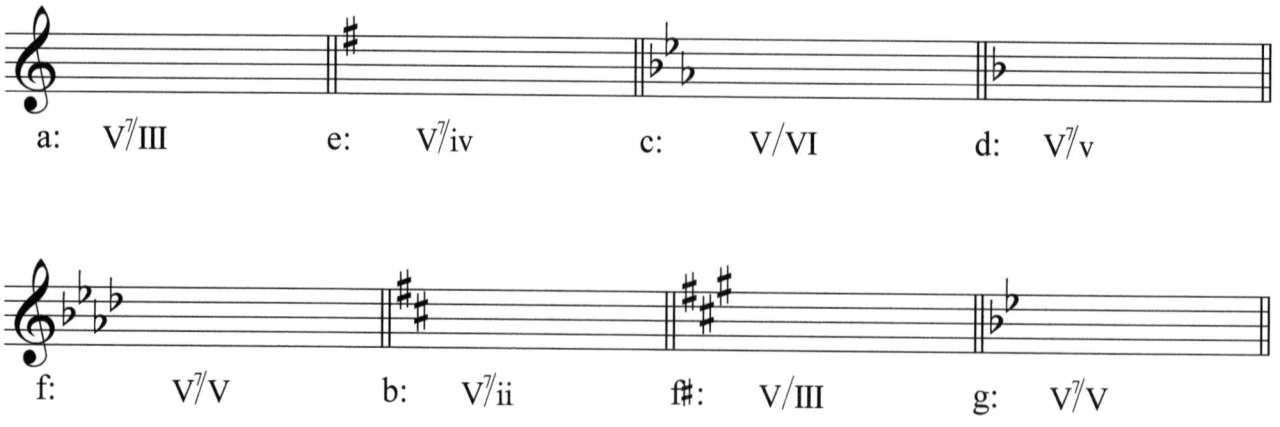

8. Name the following minor keys and write secondary dominants as indicated.

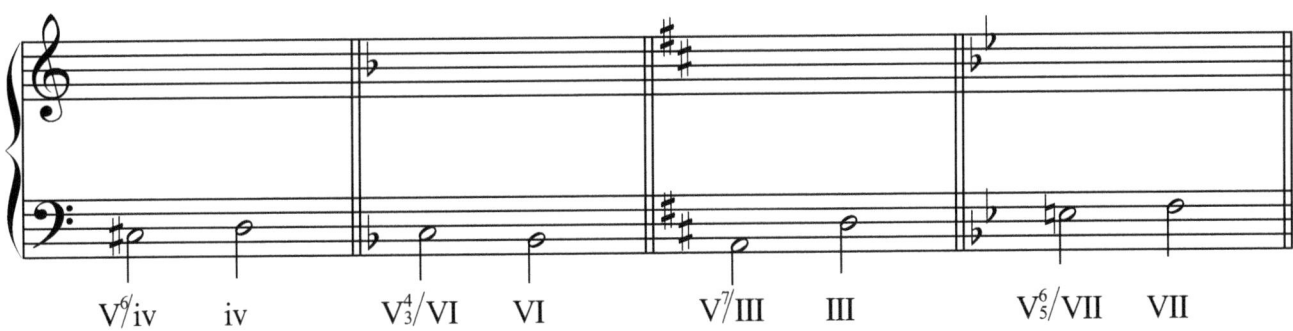

A major or minor triad that is tonacized may itself be altered to become a secondary dominant of yet another chord. Figure 6.14 illustrates two progressions where V⁷ of ii moves to V⁷ of V. Notice that the chromatic half steps are kept in the same voice.

Figure 6.14

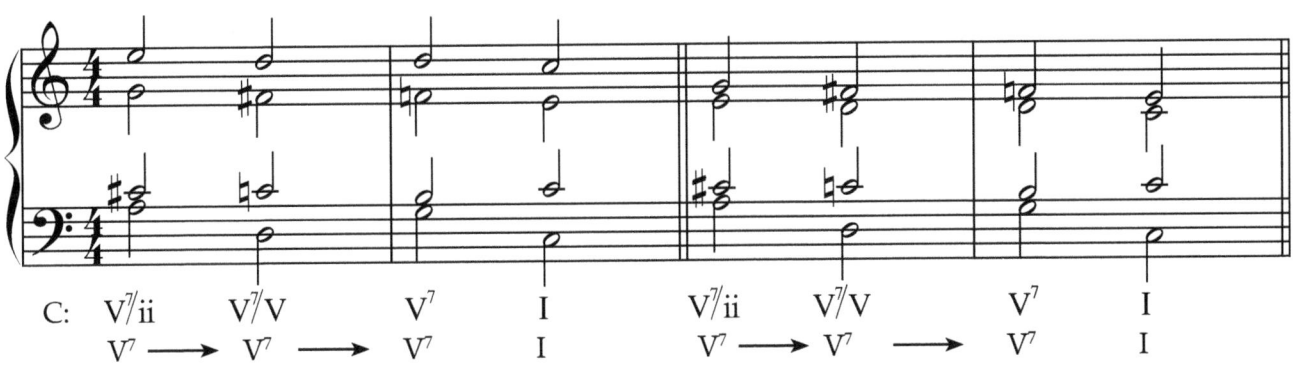

9. Harmonize the following for SATB according to the chord symbols.

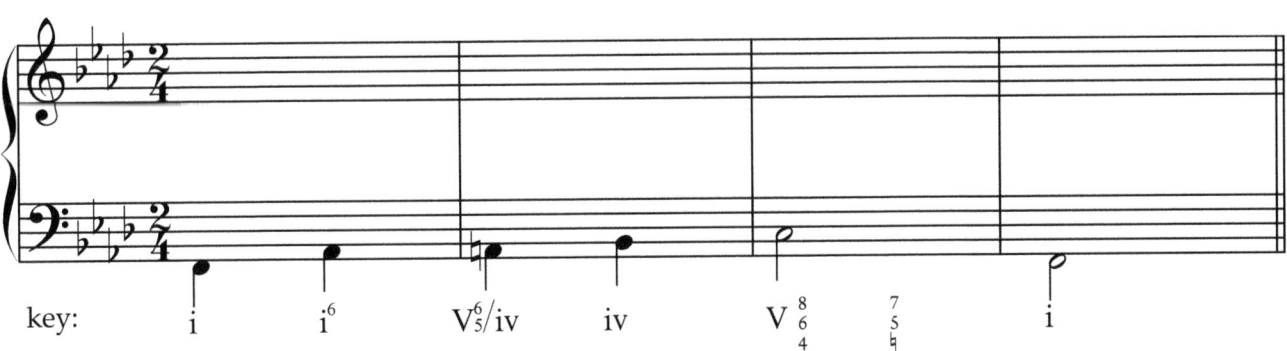

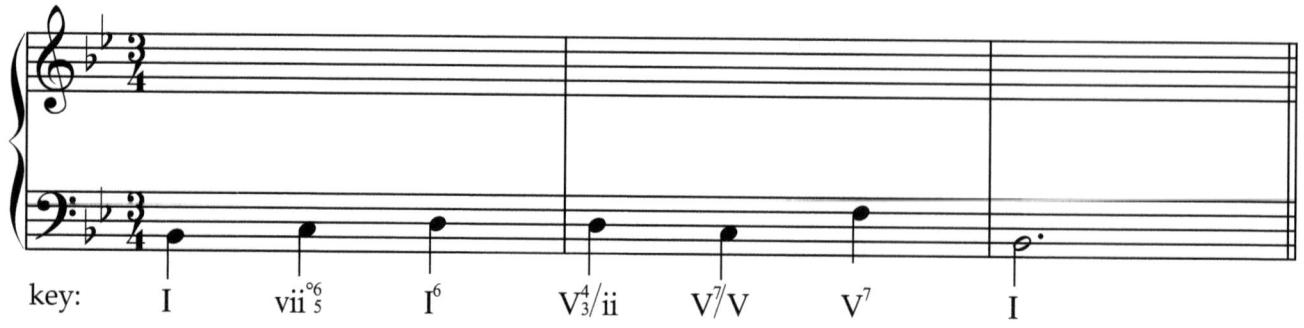

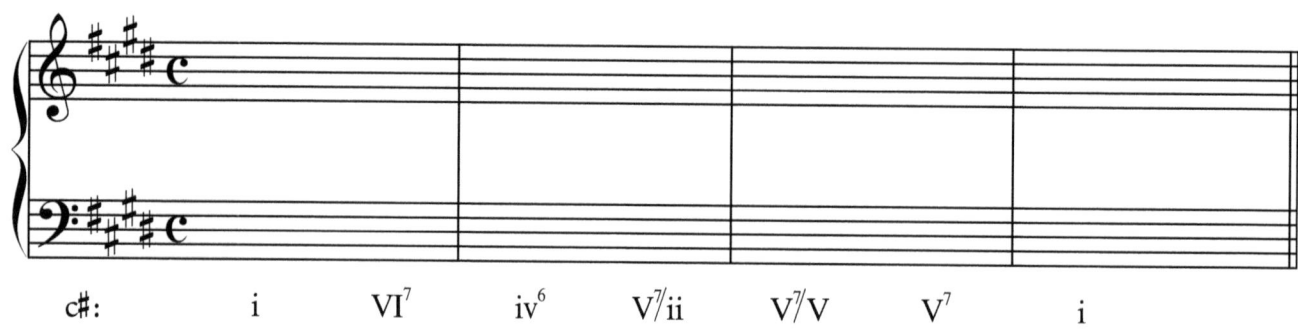

10. Provide a harmonic analysis of the following excerpts. Circle and identify any non-chord tones.

Piano Quartet no.1
op.15

Gabriel Faure
(1845-1924)

Aria: "Ah, fors'e lui"
from La Traviata, Act 1

Giuseppe Verdi
(1813-1901)

key:

Secondary Leading Tone Chords

Secondary dominants (for example V of V) have a dominant relationship with the chord that follows. However, chords that have a leading tone relationship with the following chord may also be used as secondary dominants; although their roots are different, they have the same harmonic function. Most chords that can be tonicized by V or V^7 can also be tonicized by vii, vii^{o7} or $vii^{ø7}$. As a general rule, minor chords are tonicized by vii^{o7}, and major chords by vii^{o7} or, (less often) $vii^{ø7}$.

Figure 6.15 illustrates some of the chords available for use in leading tone tonicizations. Secondary leading tone chords function in the same way as primary leading tone chords. They can be used in the same inversions and they resolve in the same way.

Figure 6.15

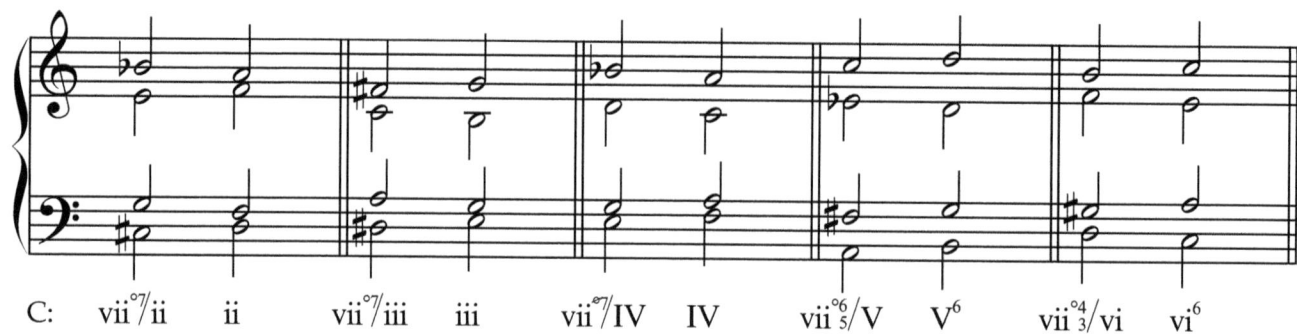

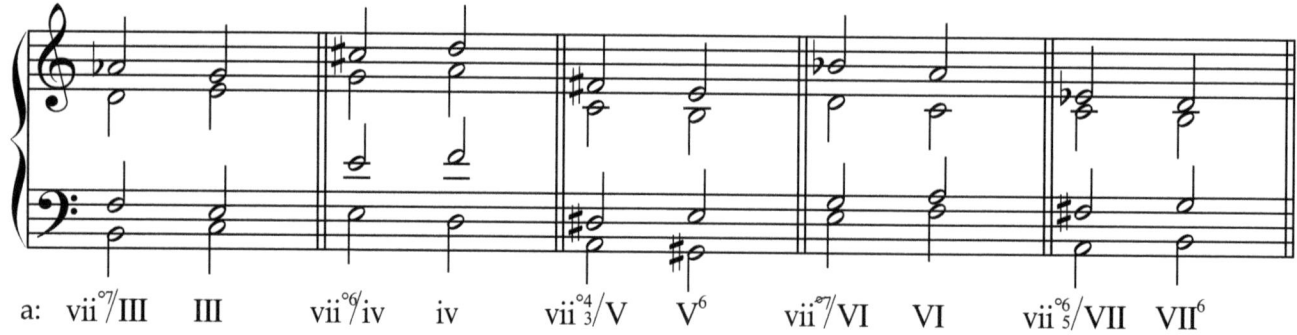

The leading tone chords of ii, IV, iv, V and vi are most commonly used; however, $vii^{ø7}$ of V is not used in minor keys.

Resolving vii°⁷/V and viiø⁷/V

The most commonly used secondary leading tone chords are vii°⁷/V and viiø⁷/V. There are several voice leading problems that are unique to these two chords. Examine the five resolutions shown in Figure 6.16.

Figure 6.16

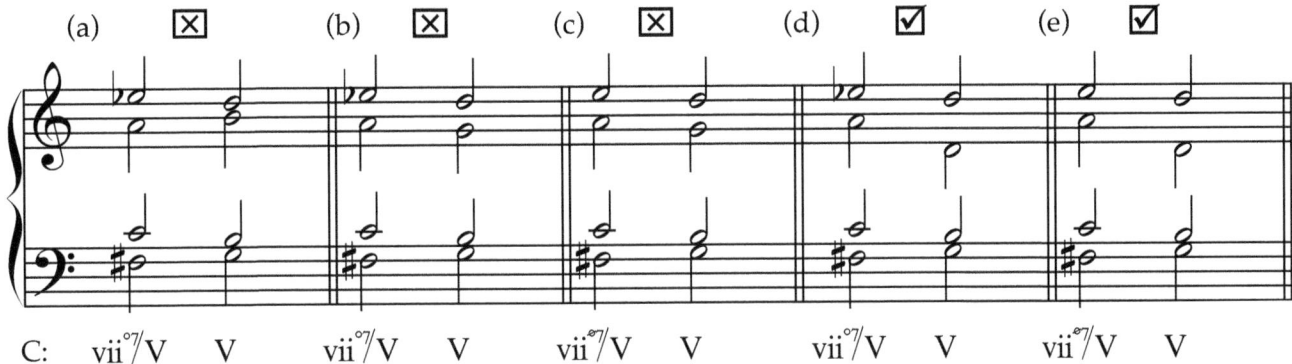

In 6.16 (a), the two tritones (F♯ - C and A - E♭) resolve regularly, but this results in a dominant chord with a doubled third (B, the leading tone), which is not acceptable. In 6.16 (b), the tritone above the bass (F♯ - C) resolves regularly, but the other diminished 5th moves to a perfect (G - D), which should also be avoided. In 6.16 (c), the voice leading from the half diminished 7th is also not acceptable, since parallel 5ths occur.

Figure 6.16 (d) and (e) are correct. Here the third of the leading tone 7th chord leaps in an inner voice, and the other notes resolve regularly. Chord V has a doubled 5th.

Often, a leap in an inner voice is followed by a melodic compensation...that is, a movement in the opposite direction. Notice the alto in Figure 6.17. The examples shown here work in both major and minor keys. The half diminished 7th is not used in minor keys.

Figure 6.17

In Figure 6.18, the upper voices of the leading tone 7th chords are arranged so that the interval between the third and the seventh is a 4th rather than a 5th. This arrangement allows for a stepwise resolution.

Figure 6.18

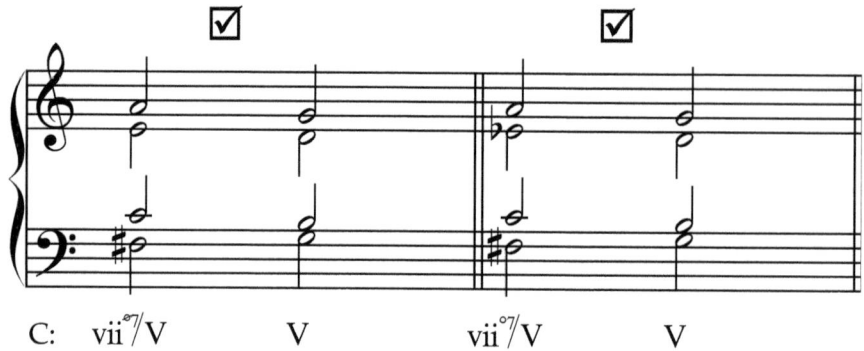

11. Name the keys and complete the following progressions in four parts.

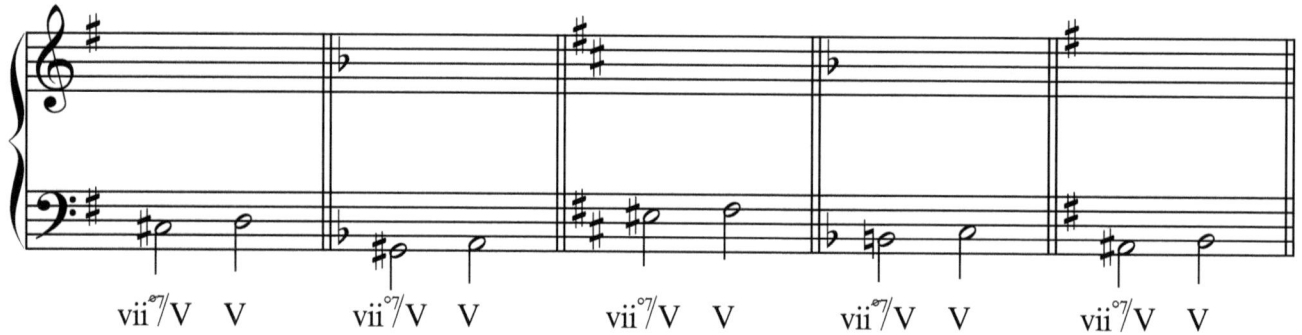

When the resolution of vii°7/V is decorated with the cadential six-four chord, the problem of parallel fifths does not arise. The resolution of the fifth and seventh of the half diminished 7th chord is delayed by the six-four chord, but occurs in the same voices when the six-four resolves (Figure 6.19(a)).

The problem of a diminished 5th moving to a perfect 5th does not arise when the resolution of vii°7/V includes a six-four chord because, once again, the resolution of the fifth and seventh are delayed (6.19 (b)).

When vii°7/V is used in a major key, the diminished 7th chord makes a detour up a half step to the cadential six-four before it resolves downward (6.19(c)).

Figure 6.19

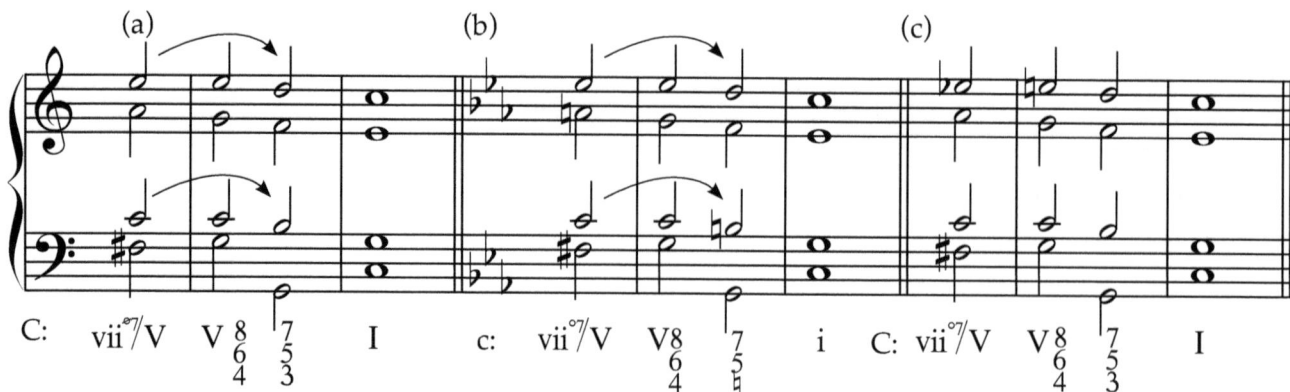

Chapter 6: Tonicization

Some composers, however, prefer not to resolve chromatically lowered note upward. In order to avoid raising the seventh, they respell the diminished 7th chord so that the top note is the sixth of the chord (in Figure 6.20, D sharp instead of E flat). A chromatically raised note moving upward makes more melodic sense. Note that the chord still functions as vii°7/V (rather than vii°$^6_5$/iii).

Figure 6.20

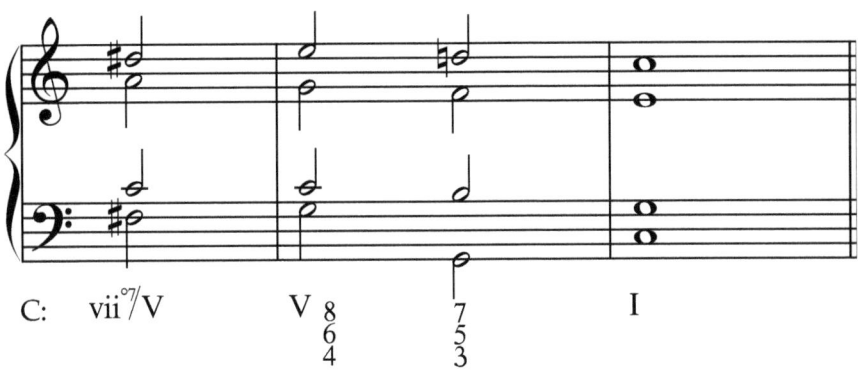

12. Name the keys and complete the following progressions in four parts.

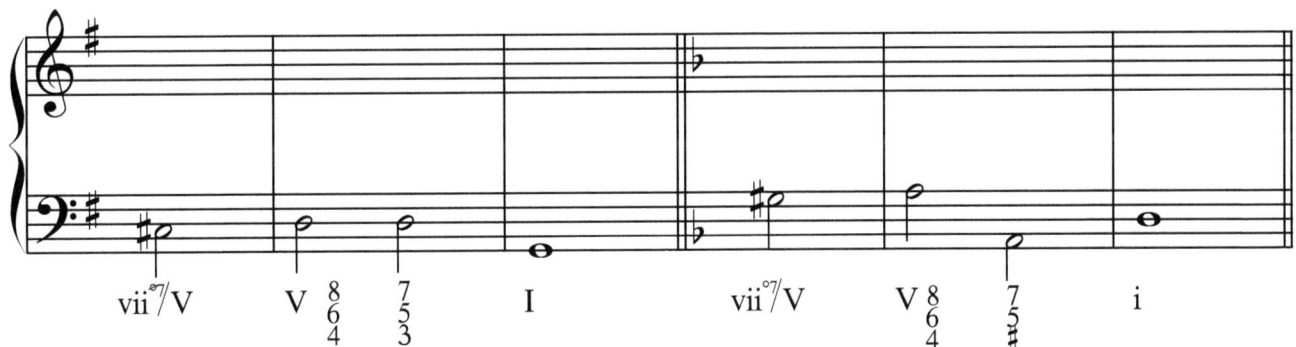

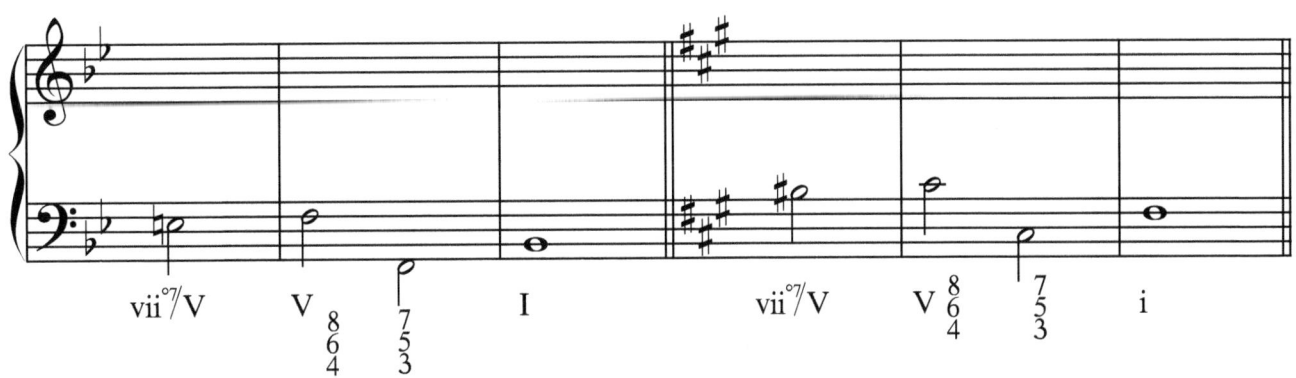

13. Write the following progressions in four parts.

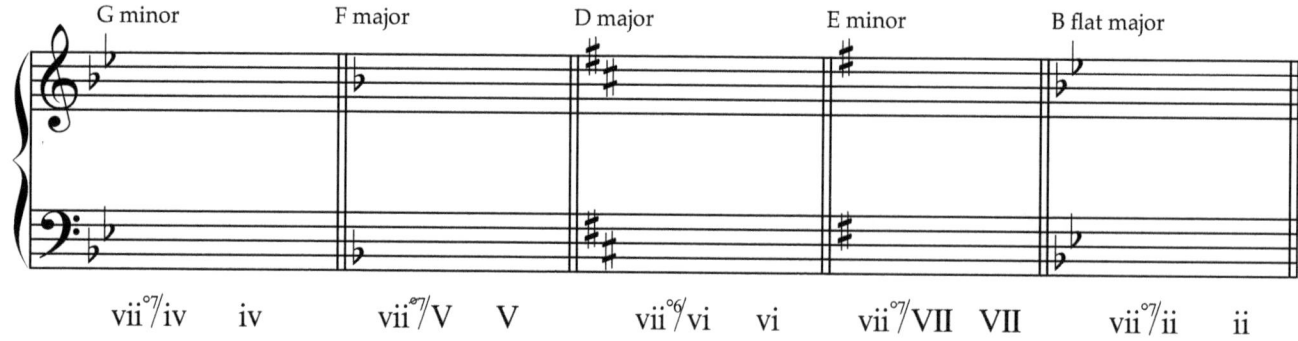

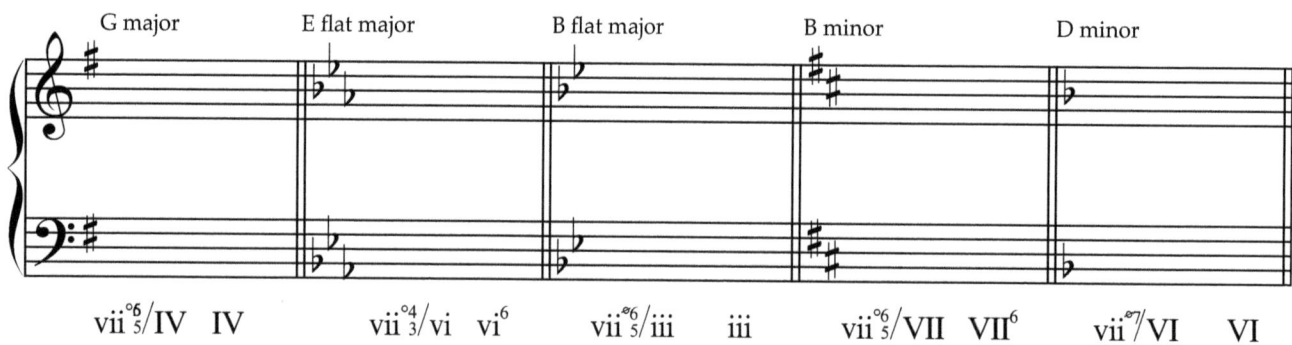

14. Harmonize the following bass lines for SATB.

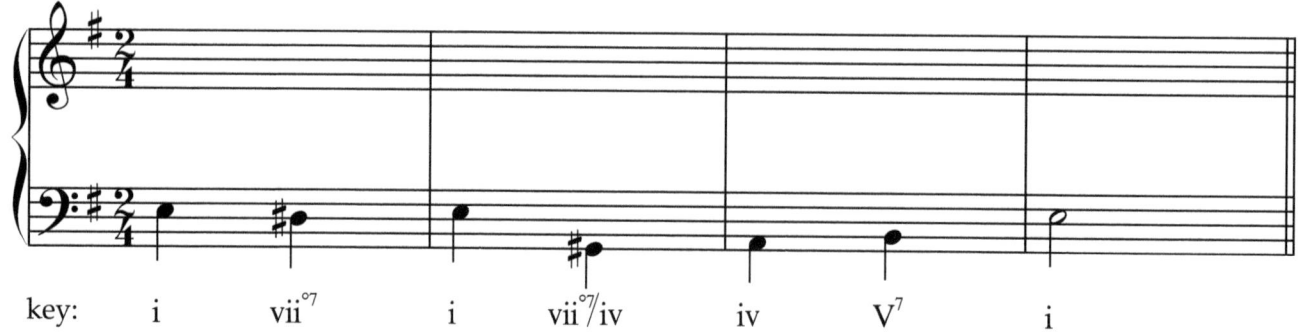

15. Provide a harmonic analysis of the following excerpt. Circle and identify any non-chord tones.

Secondary Dominants in Harmonic Sequences

Secondary dominants are often used in harmonic sequences. The most common progression is a descending circle of 5ths sequence in which secondary dominants are substituted for diatonic chords. Often, the whole progression is altered chromatically so that each chord becomes the dominant of the next. In Figure 6.21, every second chord is incomplete to allow for the preparation and resolution of the sevenths.

Figure 6.21

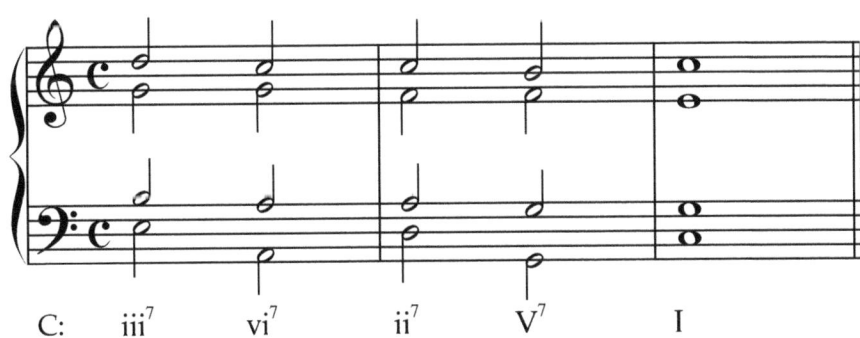

In Figure 6.22, the first three chords are chromatically altered so that each one functions as the dominant 7th of the next chord. Each leading tone moves downward to become the seventh of the next dominant 7th chord. Thus, complete chords alternate with incomplete chords.

Figure 6.22

Similarly, in the Chopin example in Figure 6.23, the 7th chord on E in m.1 is the dominant 7th of the 7th chord on A in m.2, which in turn is the dominant 7th of the 7th chord D in m.3, which is the dominant 7th of the 7th chord on G in m.4.

Figure 6.23

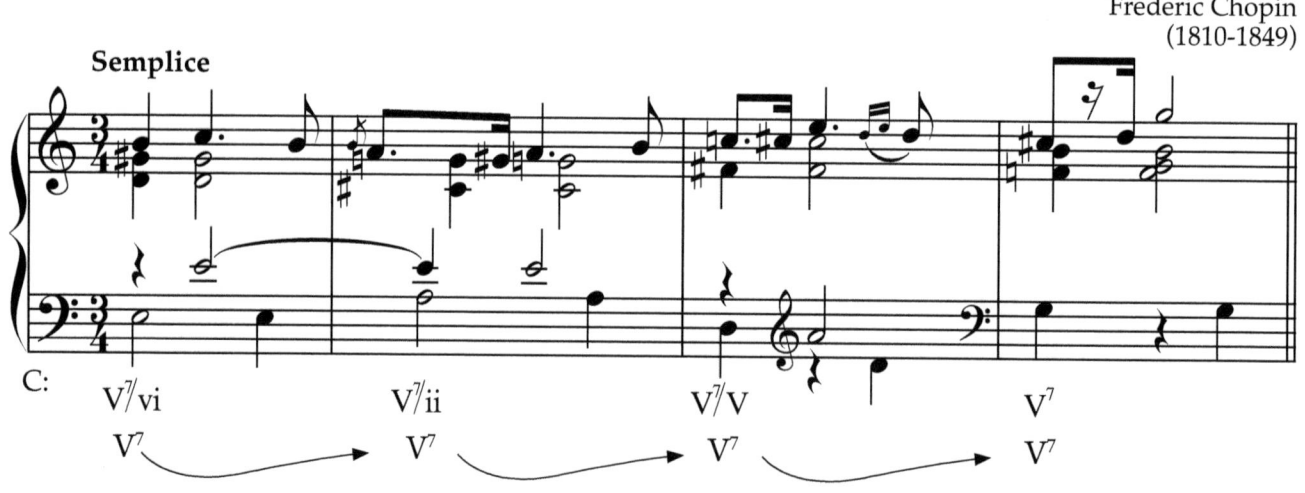

Chapter 6: Tonicization

16. Provide a harmonic analysis of the following excerpt. Circle and identify any non-chord tones.

Song Without Words
op. 102. no. 3 (Tarantella)

Felix Mendelssohn
(1809-1847)

key:

17. Harmonize the following baseline for SATB.

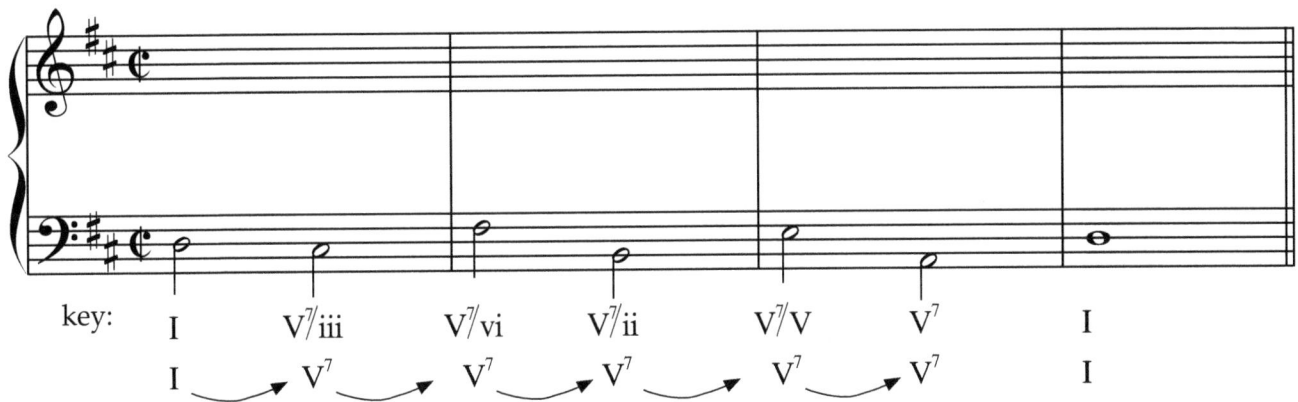

18. Provide a harmonic analysis of the following excerpt. Circle and identify any non-chord tones.

Piano Concerto no. 4
op. 58 (2nd mvt.)

Ludwig van Beethoven
(1770-1827)

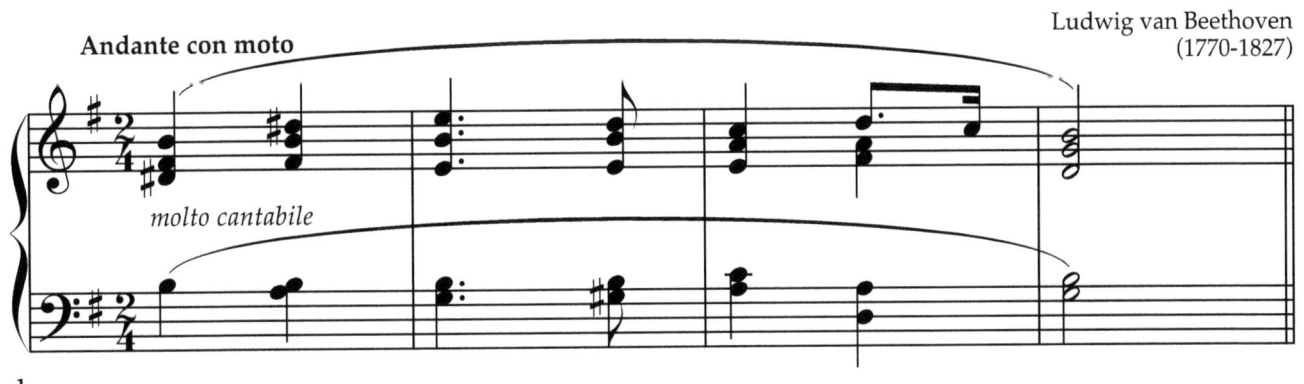

key:

19. Harmonize the following bass line using secondary dominants on the notes marked with asterisks. Provide functional chord symbols.

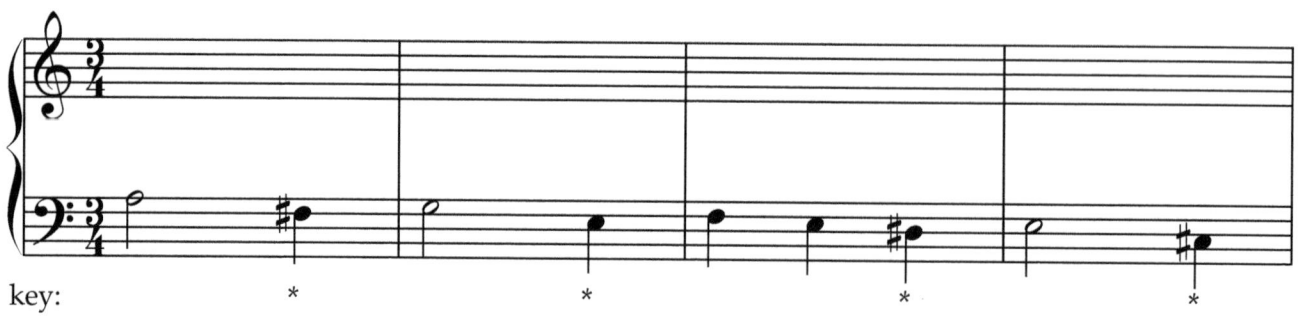

key:

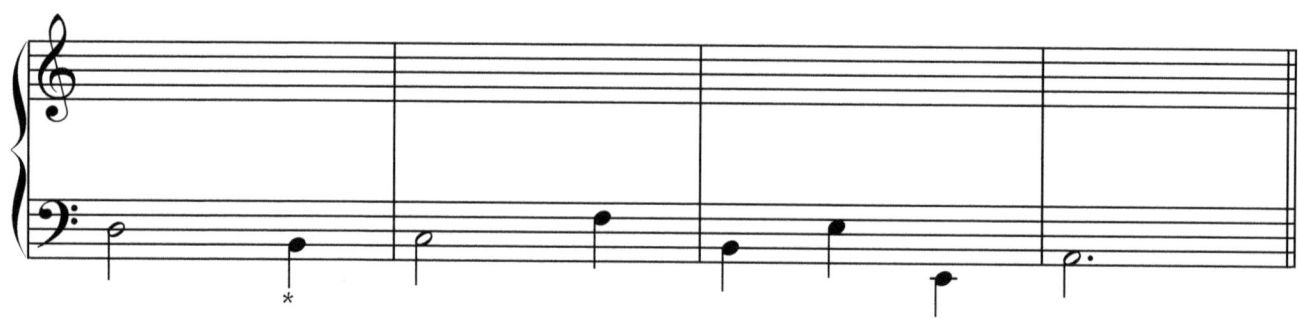

20. Harmonize the following melody using secondary dominants on the notes marked with asterisks. Provide functional chord symbols.

21. Provide a harmonic analysis of the following excerpts. Circle and identify any non-chord tones.

Kuriose Gesellschaft
from Nachstucke, op. 23, no. 2

F:

Waltz
from 36 Originaltanze (erste Walzer), D365, no. 16

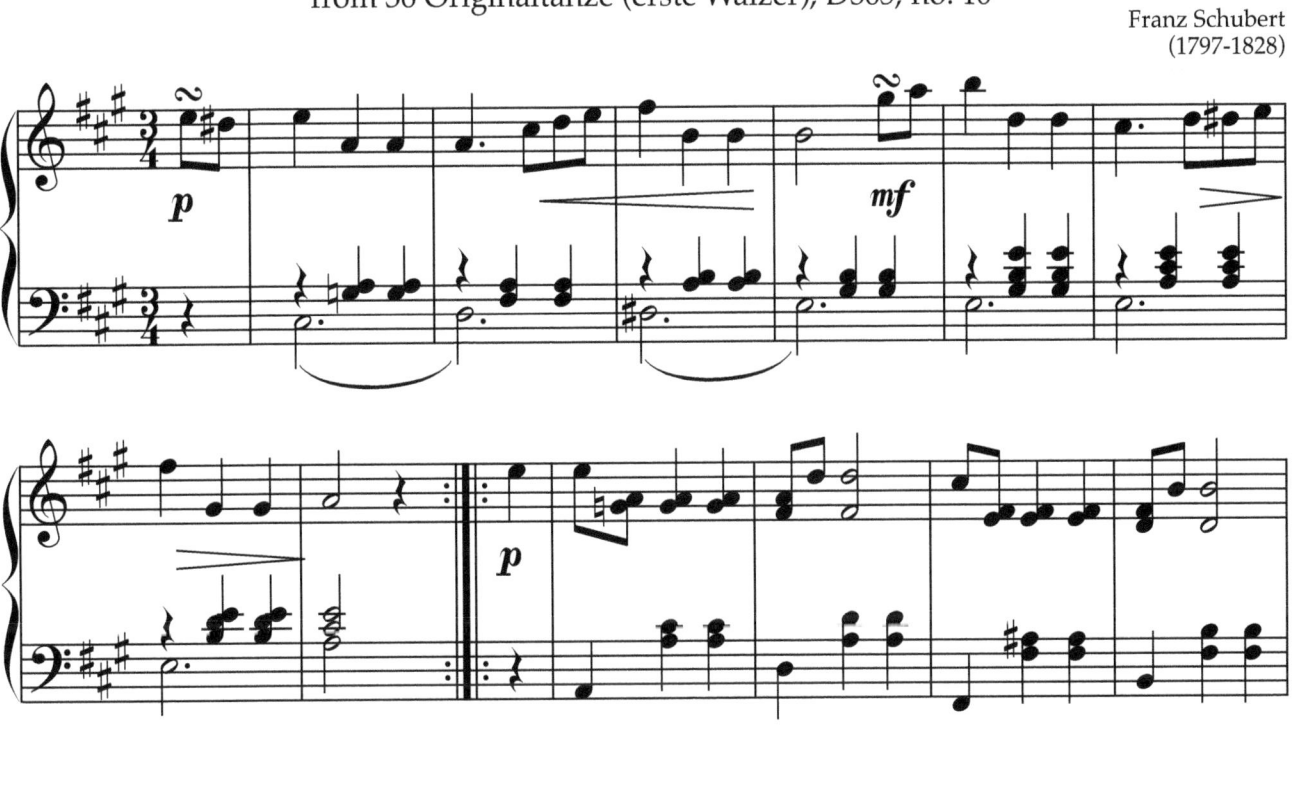

Chapter 6: Tonicization

22. Complete the following sequence in four parts.

23. Realize the following sequence in keyboard style. Add root/quality chord symbols.

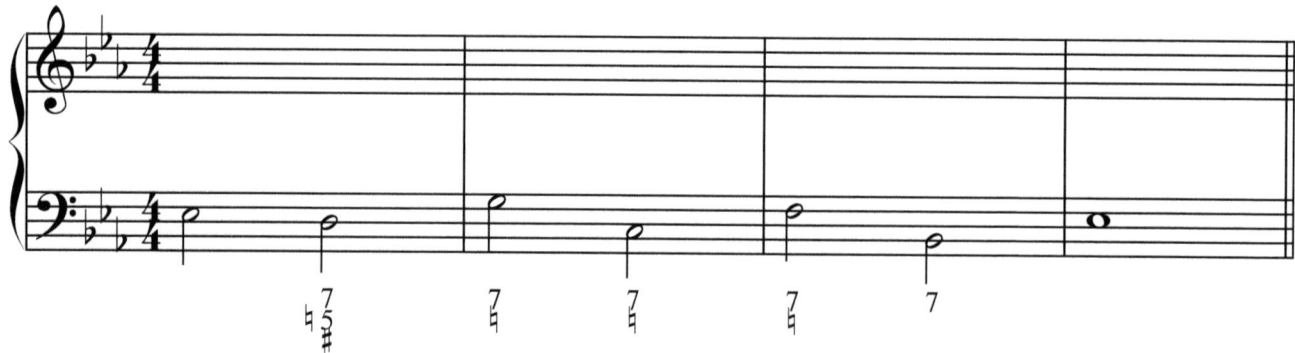

Summary

1. A chord that functions as the dominant of another key is called a secondary or applied dominant.
2. For a short period of time, the chord that follows a secondary dominant assumes a tonic role. This relatively short shift of key is called a tonicization.
3. Tonicizations of the dominant (V of V) are quite common and are found in both major and minor keys.
4. Secondary dominants may be used in inversion. They resolve in the same way as primary dominants.
5. The third of a secondary dominant chord (the temporary) leading tone must not be doubled.
6. Because secondary dominants are dominant function chords, they normally progress to tonic function chords in the temporary key. Since vi can function as a substitute for I in a deceptive cadence, a secondary dominant may progress to vi. This deceptive resolution occurs most often in the progression V^7/vi - IV (also notated V^7/vi - VI/ vi).
7. Most chords that can be tonicized by V or V^7 can also be tonicized by vii°, vii°7, or vii⌀7 and their inversions, since these chords also have a dominant function.
8. Secondary dominants are often used in harmonic sequences. The most common progression is a descending circle of 5ths sequence.

7
Modulation

Tonal compositions generally begin and end in the same key, but during the composition other tonalities may be suggested, or perhaps firmly established. A change of key, that is, a shift of tonal center, is called a **modulation**. Modulation allows for greater tonal variety within the music, and may also contribute to the form of a composition.

When a composition modulates, one tonal centre is replaced with another. The new key will almost always contain tones that are foreign to the original key. The one exception to this is a modulation from a major key to its relative minor, or vice versa, if the natural minor scale is used. Often the shift of tonal center is to a **closely related key**. Two keys are described as closely related if their key signatures are the same, or if the two key signatures differ by only one sharp or flat. For example, A major and E major are closely related because there is a difference of only one sharp between the two key signatures. Similarly, C major is closely related to F major because there is a difference of only one flat. Here are a few more examples.

F major has a key signature of *one* flat. The keys that are closely related to F Major are:

- D minor (the relative minor, which has the same key signature)
- B flat major (which has a key signature of *two* flats)
- G minor (the relative minor of B-flat major)
- C major (which has a key signature of no flats)
- A minor (the relative minor of C major)

C-sharp minor has a key signature of *four* sharps. The keys that are closely related to C-sharp minor are:

- E major (the relative major, which has the same key signature)
- G sharp minor (which has the key signature of *five* sharps)
- B major (the relative major of G sharp minor)
- F sharp minor (which has the key signature of *three* sharps)
- A major (the relative major of F sharp minor)

Modulation too closely related keys is a common feature of 18th century music. The most common modulation for a major key is to its dominant. For a minor key, the most common modulation is to its relative major. These are considered **traditional** or **standard goal keys**.

1. List all the closely related keys for the following keys. Mark the traditional goal keys with an *.

B flat major: _____ _____ _____ _____ _____

E minor: _____ _____ _____ _____ _____

A major: _____ _____ _____ _____ _____

G minor: _____ _____ _____ _____ _____

B flat minor: _____ _____ _____ _____ _____

Sectional Modulation

There are a number of different ways to change key. **Sectional modulation** is an immediate change of key at the beginning of a new section of a composition. In this type of key change, the music may include the new key signature. In Figure 7.1, the first section ends with a cadence in F major. The next section opens in the new key of C major, and the music includes the new key signature (a natural that cancels the B-flat of the previous key signature).

Figure 7.1

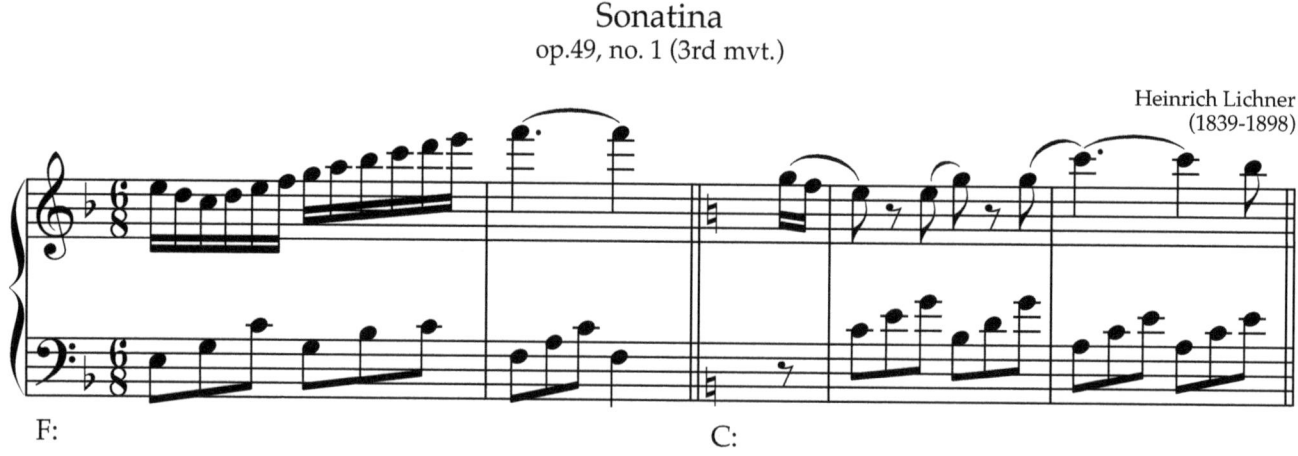

Phrase Modulation

A key change often occurs after the cadence that ends a phrase. In Figure 7.2 the first phrase ends with a cadence in A minor, and the next phrase begins with a modulation to the new key of C major.

Figure 7.2

Modulation in Mid-phrase: Pivot Chords

When two keys are closely related, they have certain chords in common. For example, G Major and D major both contain a G major triad. This triad could be analyzed as I in G major or IV in D Major. Thus, the chord of G major could serve as a **pivot chord**, which is a chord that is found in both the original and the new key, to which the music is modulating. Similarly, the D minor triad is common to both C major and A minor, And thus could be analyzed as either ii of C-major or iv of A minor.

Figure 7.3

G major: I
D major: IV

C major: ii
A minor: iv

Because pivot chords must be exactly the same in both keys, they are relatively easy to identify. For example, C major has no sharps or flats but G major has one sharp: F sharp. Since C major and G major each contain one note that is not present in the other (F in C major, and F sharp in G major), any chord that contains F or F sharp cannot function as a pivot chord between the two keys. By the process of elimination, you can determine that:

I	of C major is	IV	of G major	
iii	of C major is	vi	of G major	
V	of C major is	I	of G major	
vi	of C major is	ii	of G major	

C major: I   iii   V   vi
G major: IV vi   I   ii

Figure 7.4

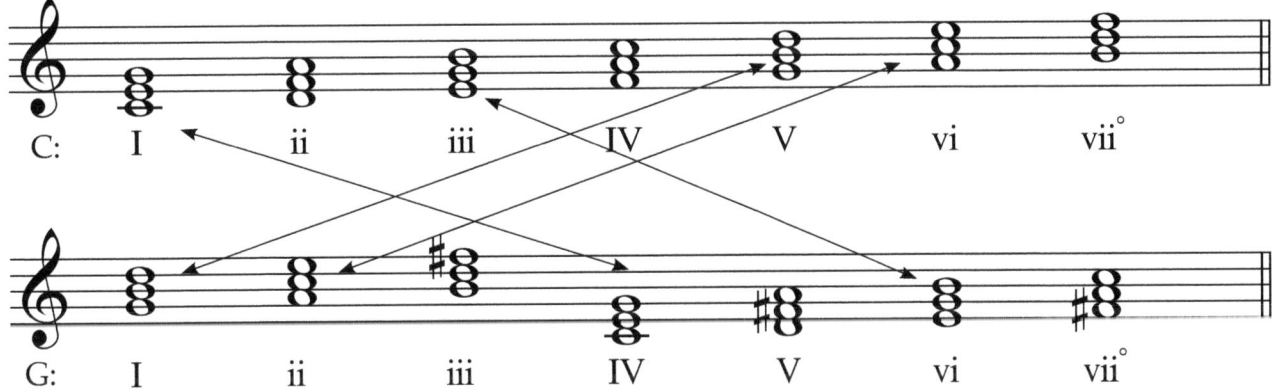

C: I ii iii IV V vi vii°
G: I ii iii IV V vi vii°

Although there are a number of chords that can function as pivots between two keys, the choice for a pivot is often either the tonic or a predominant chord of the new key, since these chords will lead to a new dominant and an authentic cadence in that key.

Tonic and predominant chords include I, I⁶, ii, ii⁶, IV, IV⁶, and vi. Notice that in the example above, all the common chords between C major and G major are pre-dominant chords in G major (IV, vi, I, and ii). Thus, any of these chords would be effective as pivots from C Major to G major. In addition, seventh chords that have a tonic or predominant function (such as ii^7, IV^7, or vi^7) can be effective choices for pivot chords.

Here is another example. There are four chords that are common to both A major and D major.

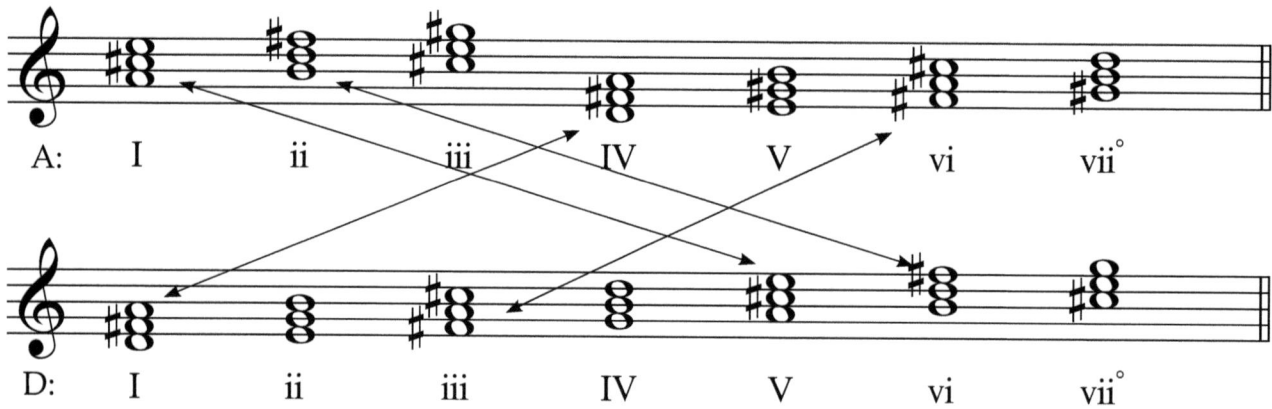

Figure 7.5

Of these four chords, the best choices for a pivot chord are I and vi of D major (IV and ii of A major). Although chords ii and V of D major (vi and I of A major) could function as pivot chords, they are not as effective as the other two choices.

The choice of tonic or predominant chords as pivots also holds true for modulations to a relative major or minor. For example, in a modulation from A minor to C major, the strongest choices for a pivot chord are vi, ii, or iv of C major (i, iv, and VI of A minor).

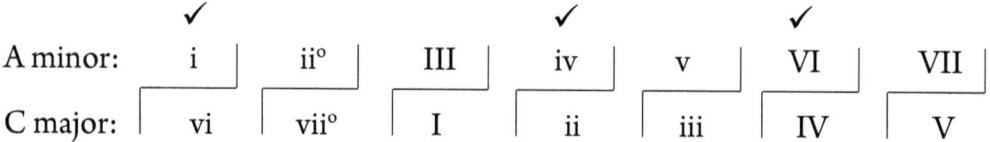

Figure 7.6

Chapter 7: Modulation

There are two steps to choosing a pivot chord.
1. Determine whether the chord is common to both the original key and the new key.
2. Determine the harmonic function of the chord in the new key.

Remember that, although the choice of pivots is not limited to tonic or predominant chords, these chords will be the most effective because they lead to the dominant and an authentic cadence in the new key.

1. Identify the following chords in the two specified keys.

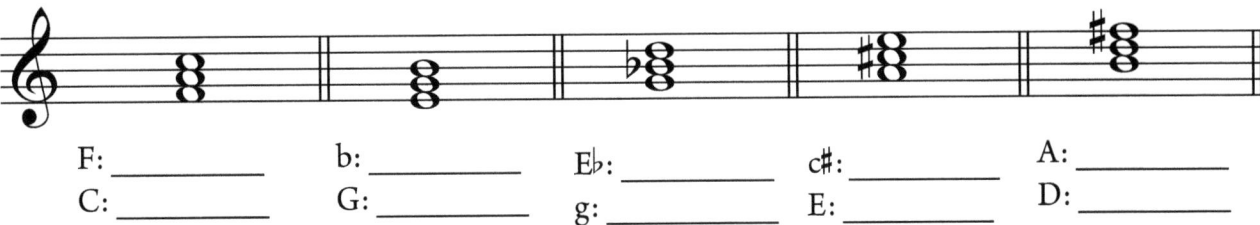

F: _____   b: _____   E♭: _____   c♯: _____   A: _____
C: _____   G: _____   g: _____   E: _____   D: _____

2. List all the available chords for the following modulations. Mark the chords that function as tonic or predominant chords in the new key with asterisks.

original key: G:
new key b:

original key: d:
new key F:

original key: a:
new key D:

There are four steps for modulating with a pivot chord.

1. Establish the original key.
2. Select a suitable pivot chord.
3. Follow this chord with the dominant of the new key.
4. Resolve the dominant chord to a tonic function chord in the new key (I, I⁶, or vi).

Figure 7.7

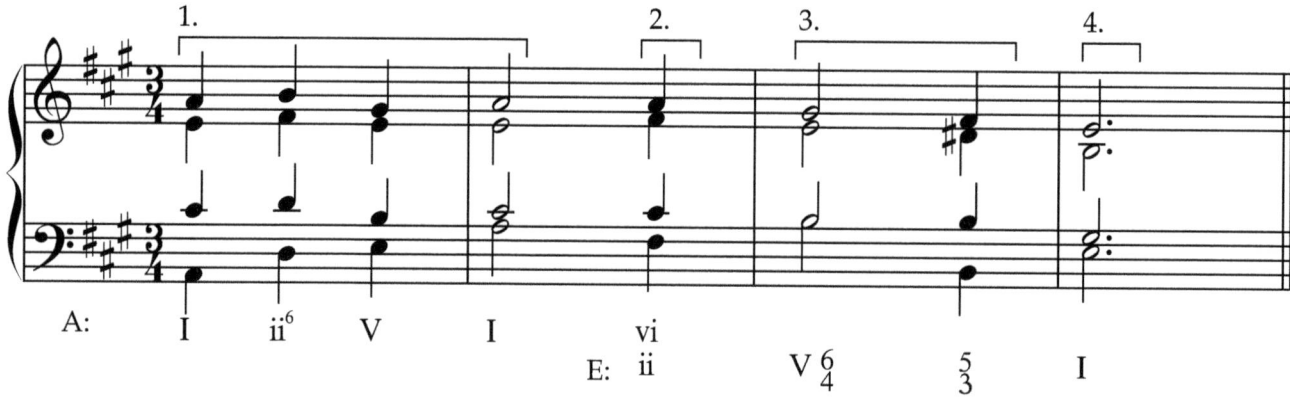

In Figure 7.7 above:

1. A major the (original key) is established through a progression that includes an authentic cadence: I - ii⁶ - V - I.
2. The pivot, an F sharp minor chord, functions as vi of A major and ii of E major.
3. The dominant area of E major (the new key) is decorated with a cadential six-four.
4. This dominant harmony resolves to the tonic, creating an authentic cadence in the new key

3. Name the key and provide a harmonic analysis of the following examples.

key: ___ ___ ___ ___   ___ ___ ___ ___

new key: ___ ___ ___ ___

Chapter 7: Modulation

key: ___ ___ ___ ___ ___

new key: ___ ___ ___ ___ ___

In Figure 7.7, the original key was firmly established with a suitable harmonic progression, and, following the pivot cord, the new key was established in the same way. If the pivot chord is the tonic in the new key, it may be followed by a progression consisting of a predominant chord followed by dominant and tonic function chords. In Figure 7.8, the pivot chord functions as the tonic of C minor (the new key). This chord is followed by pre-dominant (iv), dominant (cadential six-four), and tonic (i) harmonies, firmly establishing C minor.

Figure 7.8

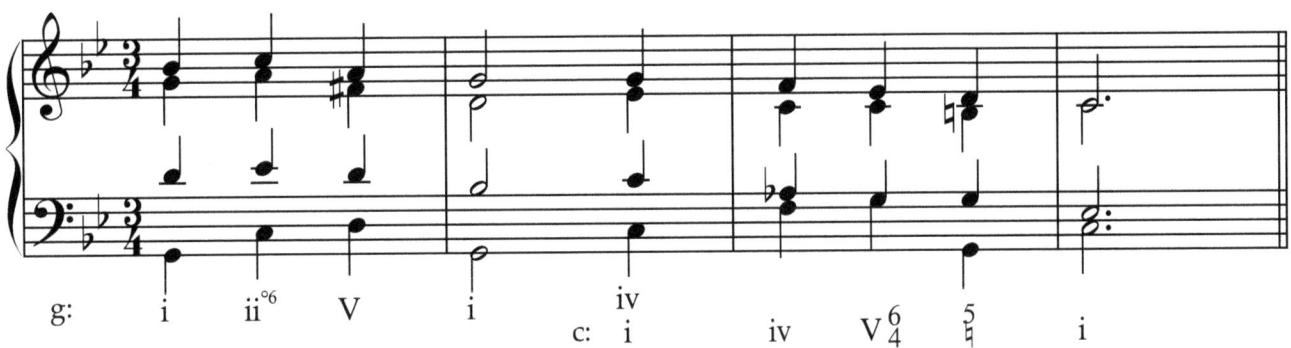

When changing keys, it is often necessary to add, remove, or change accidentals. Here, A flat (part of the key signature of C minor) and B natural (the raised leading tone) are added to m.3 to reflect the new key of C minor.

Notice also that the final melody notes, scale degrees $\hat{2}$ and $\hat{1}$ create a perfect authentic cadence in the new key. A modulation in which the melody finishes on $\hat{1}$ (the tonic) is much more emphatic than one in which the melody ends on $\hat{3}$ or $\hat{5}$.

If the pivot is a predominant chord in the new key, it may be directly followed by an authentic cadence. Alternatively, it can be followed by a half or deceptive cadence, and the new key confirmed with a V - I progression in the following phrase.

Figure 7.9

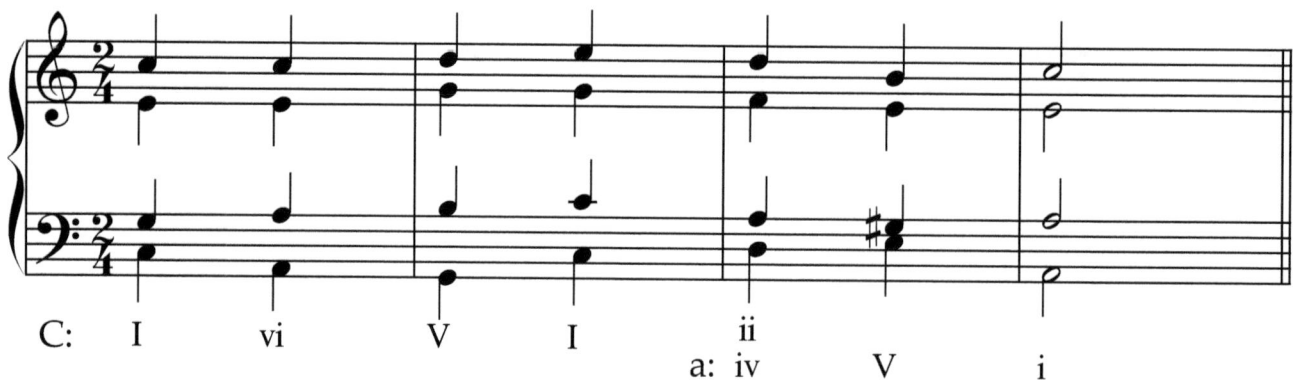

It is helpful to remember, when analyzing a modulation, that the pivot chord can be found just just before the appearance of tones that indicate the new key (that is, tones that are not found in the old key). In Figure 7.9, the D minor pivot chord comes just before the appearance of G sharp, the raised leading tone of A minor, the new key. However, the exact location of a pivot chord can be ambiguous. In a series of chords common to both keys, there may indeed be more than one valid choice as the pivot chord.

4. Harmonize the following phrases according to the given chord symbols.

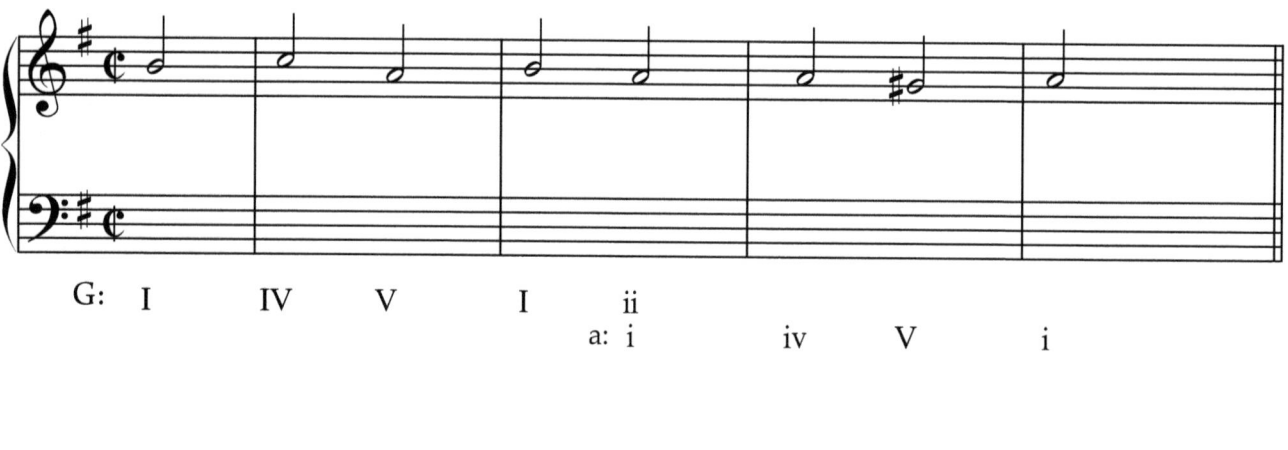

5. Harmonize the following bass lines for SATB.

Chromatic Modulation

Chromatic modulation is another method for changing keys. Here, the composer moves from one key to another by chromatically altering one or more scale degrees to reflect the new key. Chromatic modulation usually involves $\hat{4}$ - $\sharp\hat{4}$ - $\hat{5}$ in one voice, with $\sharp\hat{4}$ functioning as the leading tone in the new key.

In Figure 7.10, The F sharp in the second chord of m. 2 reflects the new key of G major. This chord is V$^6_5$ in the new key. The preceding chord (F-A-C, IV of C major) is not found in G major, and therefore does not function as a pivot chord. Instead, the chromatic bass line (F - F sharp - G, $\hat{4}$ - $\sharp\hat{4}$ - $\hat{5}$ in C major) helps to move the music into G major.

Chapter 7: Modulation

6. Provide a harmonic analysis of the following excerpts. Circle and identify all non-chord tones.

Chorus "When monarchs unite..."
From Dido and Aeneas, Act 1

Henry Purcell
(1659-1695)

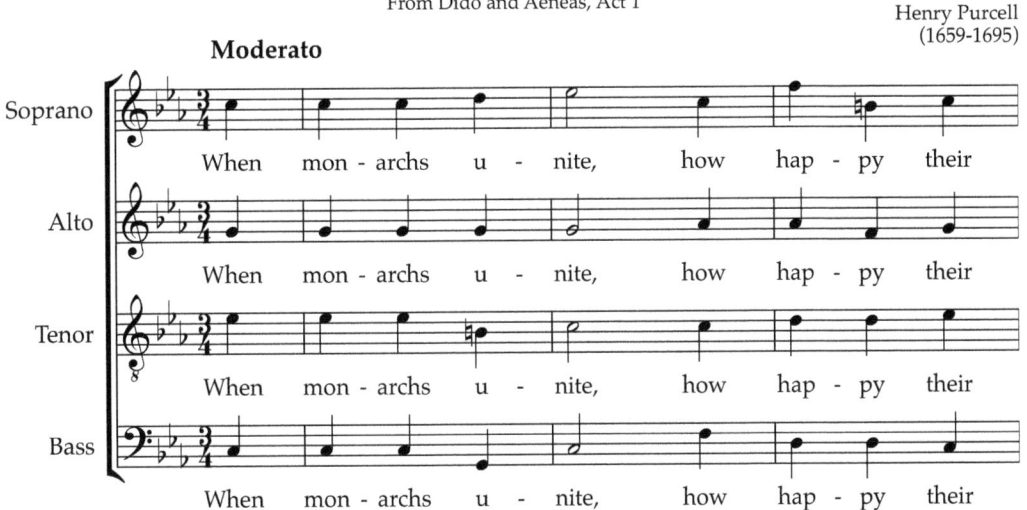

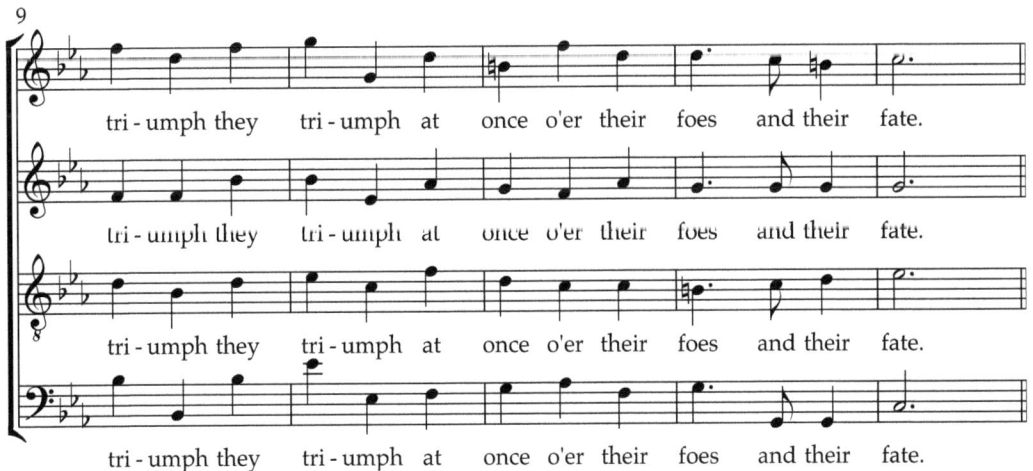

7. Harmonize the following bass lines, which contain modulations. Add functional chord symbols.

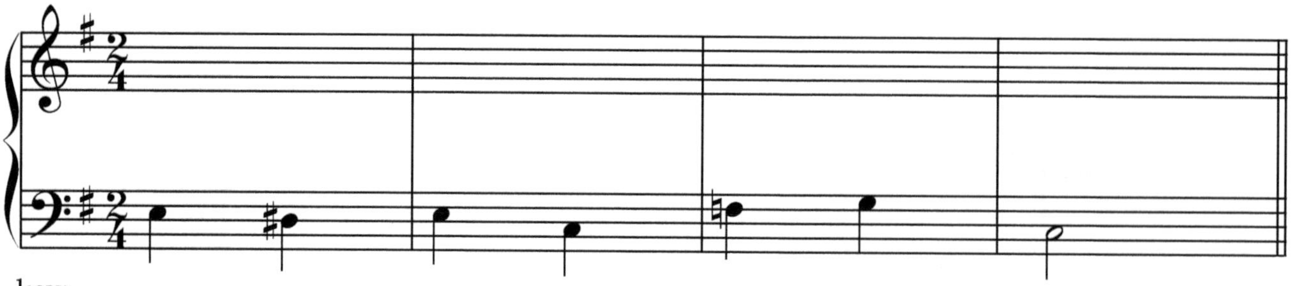

key:

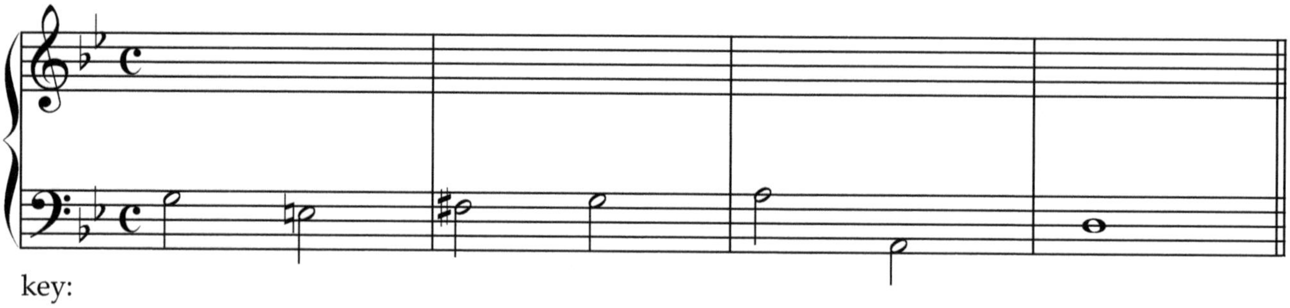

key:

key:

8. Harmonize the following melodies, which contain modulations. Add functional chord symbols.

B♭:

Chapter 7: Modulation

e:

9. Realize the following figured bass in keyboard style. Label the continuo with root/quality chord symbols

Sonata no. 1 for Flute and Continuo
BWV 1033 (Menuetto II)

Johann Sebastian Bach
(1685-1750)

126 Chapter 7: Modulation

Summary

1. A modulation is a change of key or a shift of tonal center.
2. Music often modulates to closely related keys. Two keys are said to be closely related if they have the same key signature or if their key signatures differ by only one sharp or flat.
3. A sectional modulation is an immediate change of key at the beginning of a new section.
4. A phrase modulation is an immediate change of key at the beginning of a new phrase.
5. Modulation can be achieved through a pivot chord, that is, a chord that is common to both the original key and the new key.
6. Chords that are the tonic or a predominant of the new key make affective choices for pivots since they lead to V and an authentic cadence in that key. Other choices are, however, possible.
7. In a chromatic modulation, one or more scale degrees of the old key is chromatically altered in order to initiate the change of key (for example $\hat{4}$ - $\sharp\hat{4}$ - $\hat{5}$).

8
Dominant 9th and 13th Chords

Dominant 9th and 13th chords are not often found in music of the Baroque, Classical, or early Romantic periods. By the late 19th century, however, these extended chords had become an important ingredient in the composers palette of harmonic colours; they are a particularly common feature in Impressionistic music. Although 9th and 13th chords can occur on any scale degree, they are most commonly found on the dominant.

The Dominant 9th (V^9)

The dominant 9th chord consists of a V^7 chord plus a 9th above the bass note. When this chord is written in four parts, the fifth is omitted: The incomplete chord contains the root, third, seventh, and ninth. The two forms of V^9 - major and minor - are classified according to the quality of the 9th between the bass and the top note. For example, in C Major, V^9 is a major 9th chord because the interval between G and A is a major ninth. In C Minor, V^9 is a minor ninth chord, because G to A flat is a minor 9th. The root/quality chord symbol for a major V^9 consists of the root of the chord followed by the number 9. For example, V^9 in C major would be G^9. The root/quality chord symbol for a minor V^9 consists of the root of the chord followed by $7(\flat 9)$. In C minor, V^9 would be $G^{7(\flat 9)}$.

The dominant 9th chord contains two dissonant notes: the seventh and the ninth above the root. As with most dissonances, these two notes resolve downward by step. The ninth is usually in the soprano, and should always be above the third of the chord. When resolving V^9:

- the root (scale degree $\hat{5}$) moves to the tonic
- the third (the leading tone) rises to the tonic
- the seventh falls a step
- the ninth falls a step

This resolution applies in both major and minor keys, as shown in Figure 8.1.

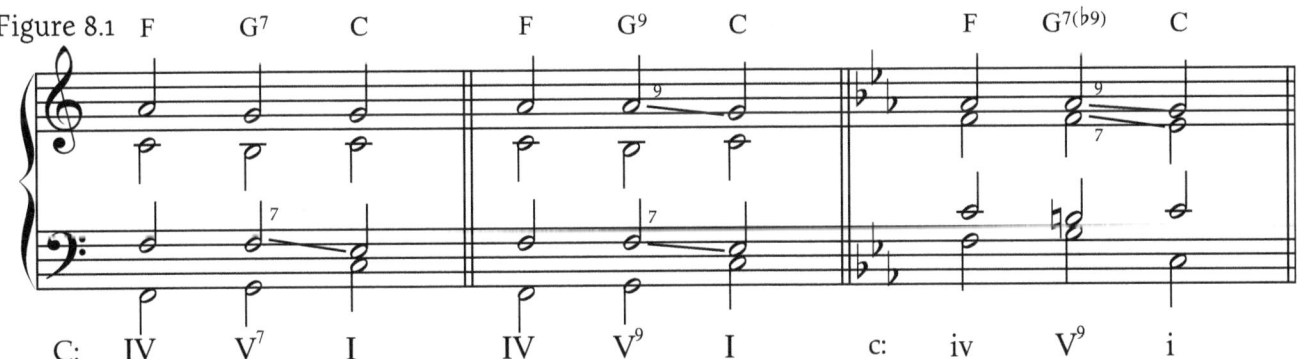

When V^9 resolves to I, the ninth (the soprano melody note) falls to scale degree $\hat{5}$. The resulting semi-closed cadence does not give as strong and final sound as a closed cadence (with the soprano on scale degree $\hat{1}$). For this reason, the progression V^9 - I is not usually used as a final cadence at the end of a composition.

The major dominant 9th can only be used in major keys, but the minor dominant 9th may be used in both major and minor keys. In Figure 8.2 a, the A flat of the minor dominant 9th is not found in C major. This note is said to be borrowed from C minor, the tonic minor. (This situation is much like that of the leading tone 7th chords: vii°⁷ can only be used in major keys; vii°⁷ occurs diatonically in minor keys, but can also be used in major keys by borrowing the diminished 7th chord from the tonic minor key).

A dominant 9th chord can be used as a neighbour chord between two statements of I, in order to prolong tonic harmony. In this progression, shown in Figure 8.2 b, the ninth is approached as a neighbour note.

A dominant 9th may also be preceded by a pre-dominant chord. In Figure 8.2 c, the ninth (A) is prepared as a common tone in the soprano. All chords that have a predominant function (ii, ii⁶, IV, IV⁶, vi, vi⁶) are good approach chords for V⁹, because they allow for a common tone preparation of the ninth. When harmonizing a passage containing a dominant 9th chord, it may be helpful to start by writing the ninth in the soprano, and then work backwards to sketch in the approach.

Figure 8.2

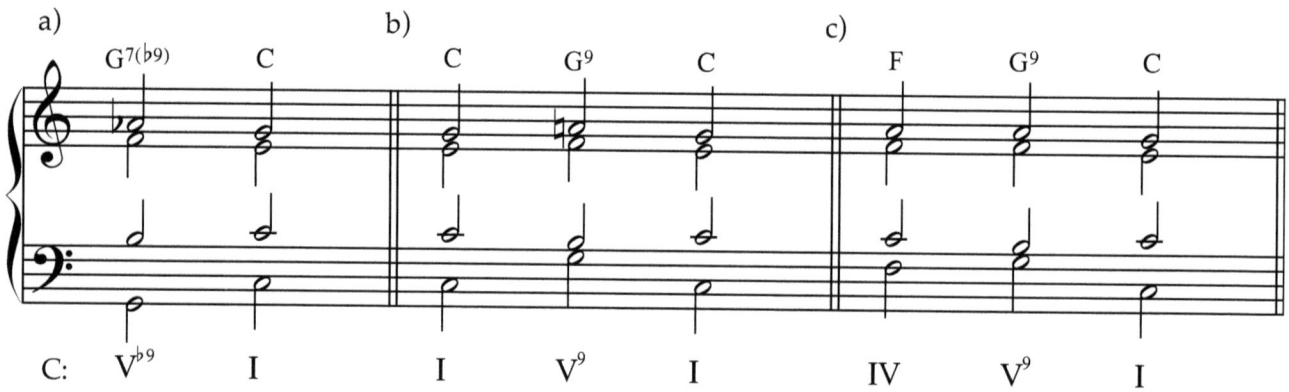

In Figure 8.3, the ninth of V⁹ falls a step to its root (scale degree $\hat{5}$) and the chord becomes a dominant 7th. This progression can be analyzed in three ways, all of which are correct.

Figure 8.3

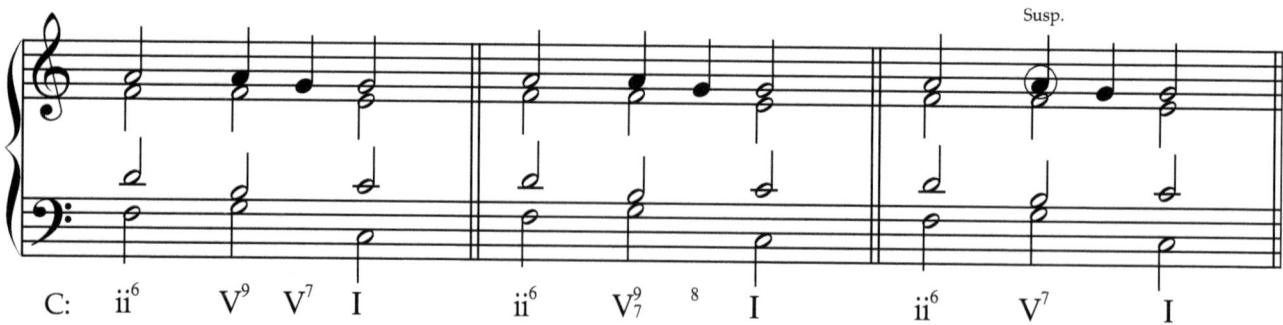

In Figure 8.4, the ninth of V⁹ moves to the seventh of the chord, either with a leap (8.4a) or with a passing tone (8.4b).

Figure 8.4

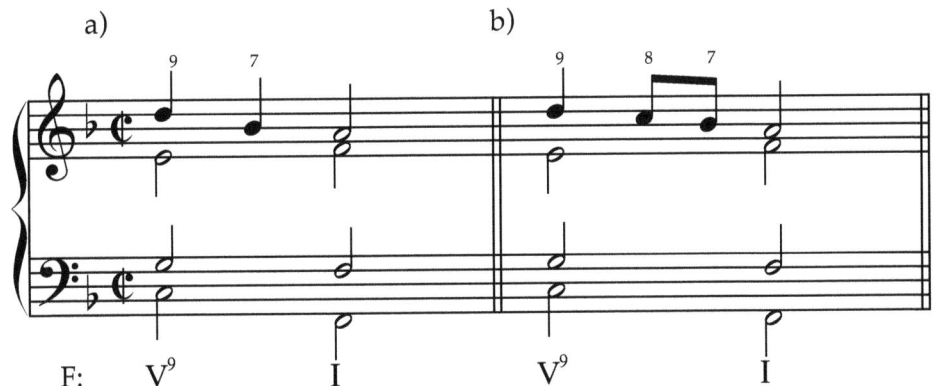

As we have seen, the ninth of V⁹ usually resolves downward by step to scale degree $\hat{5}$. However, occasionally, when the ninth occurs with the seventh and the seventh resolves normally, the ninth does not resolve. In Figure 8.5, Beethoven resolves the seventh downward by step to E flat in m. 2, but the ninth (the high A flat in m. 1) does not resolve.

Figure 8.5

This style of writing is characteristic of free instrumental textures. In vocal writing, which is the primary focus of this textbook, the constraints of voice leading are generally observed with more care.

Dominant 9th Chords as Secondary Dominants

Dominant 9th chords may also function as secondary dominants. In Figure 8.6, V⁹ functions as a secondary dominant of V. The ninth is in the upper voice and resolves by step.

Figure 8.6

1. Complete the following progressions according to the chord symbols.

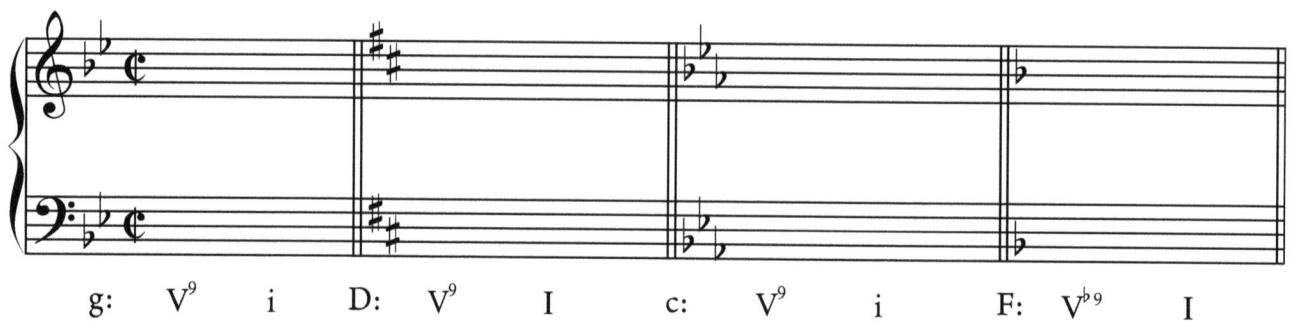

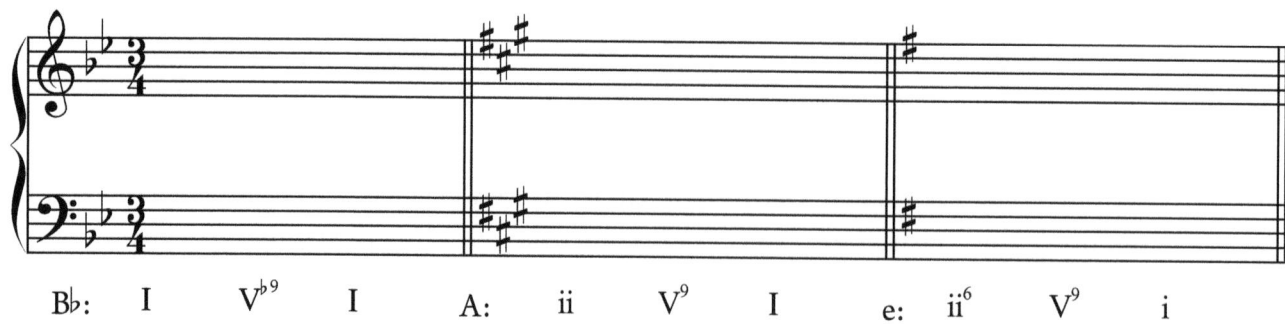

2. Realize the following figured basses in keyboard style.

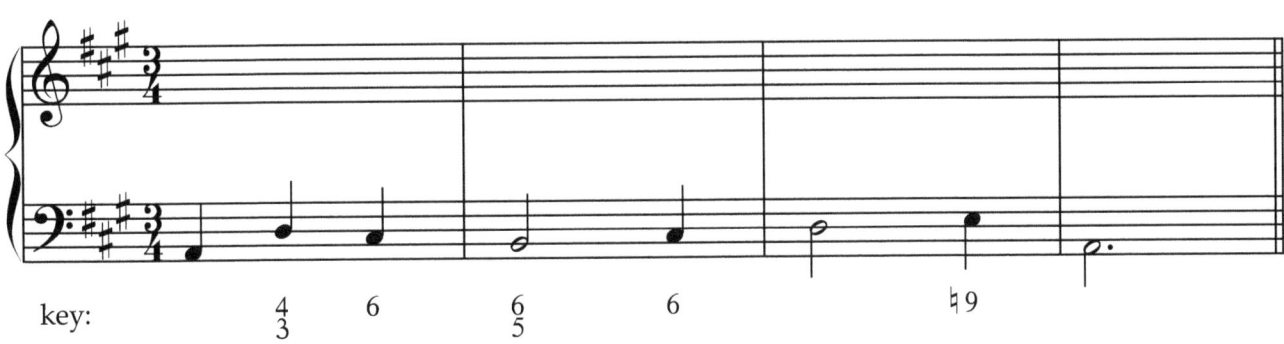

3. Provide a harmonic analysis of the following excerpts. Circle and identify any non-chord tones.

Waltz
from 36 Originaltänze (Erste Walzer), D 365, no. 3

Franz Schubert
(1797-1828)

Allegretto

key: ___

The Dominant 13th Chord

The dominant 13th chord (V^{13}) consists of a dominant 7th chord with a thirteenth added above the bass. Writing this chord in four parts, the fifth is usually omitted, so that the chord contains the root, third, seventh, and thirteenth. The thirteenth should be in the soprano. The root/quality chord symbol for a major V^{13} consists of the root of the chord followed by the number 13. For example, V^{13} in C major would be G^{13}. For a minor V^{13}, the symbol consists of the root followed by $7(\flat 13)$. For example, V^{13} in C minor would be $G^{7(\flat 13)}$.

The dominant 13th chord resolves to a tonic chord in both major and minor keys.

- The root (scale degree $\hat{5}$) moves to the tonic.
- The third (the leading tone) either rises by step to the tonic or falls a 3rd to the dominant.
- The seventh falls a step to scale degree $\hat{3}$.
- The 13th falls a third to the tonic.

Figure 8.7

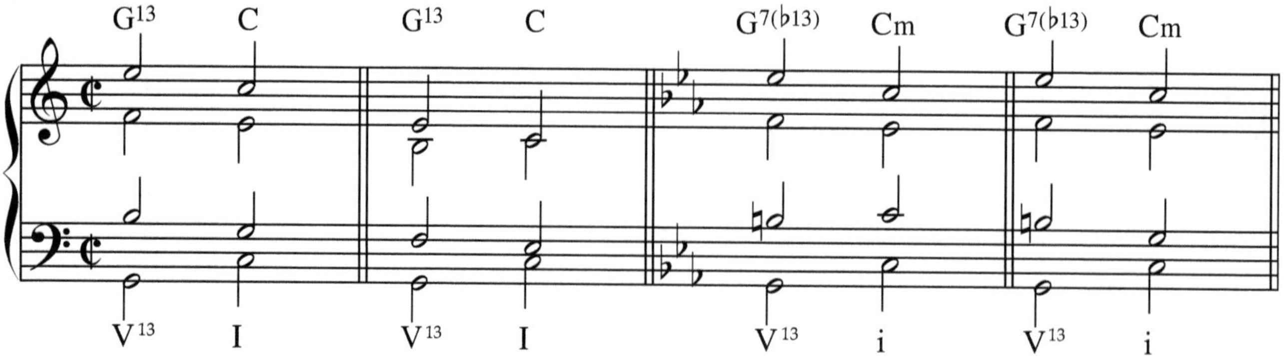

Chapter 8: Dominant 9ths and 13ths

Because the dominant 13th resolves to a tonic chord with the soprano in the tonic, this chord is effective in an authentic cadence at the end of a composition.

The dominant 13th chord is also effective in a deceptive cadence (V^{13} - vi) as shown in Figure 8.8.
- the root rises a step to scale degree $\hat{6}$
- the third (the leading tone) rises a step
- the seventh falls a step
- the 13th falls a third to the tonic

Figure 8.8

A dominant 13th chord may be approached by I, or by any chord that has a predominant function, as shown in Figure 8.9. Note that in C minor, the third of ii⁶ (scale degree $\hat{6}$) is raised in order to avoid a melodic augmented 2nd in the tenor.

Figure 8.9

A dominant 13th chord may move through a dominant 7th on its way to the tonic. In Figure 8.10, the 13th (E) moves to the 5th of V^7 (D) before resolving to I. This progression may be analyzed in two ways, both of which are correct:
- as a passing tone between the dominant 13th and the tonic chord
- as an appoggiatura that resolves into the dominant 7th

Figure 8.10

In Figure 8.11, V^{13} is decorated with a cadential six-four. Notice the chord symbols for this progression. The fourth and the doubled root of the six-four chord (C and G) each drop a step, while the sixth (E) in the soprano remains stationary to become the thirteenth of V^{13}. (Even though a lower number is used in the figuration - 6 instead of 13 - this note sounds best in the soprano).

Figure 8.11

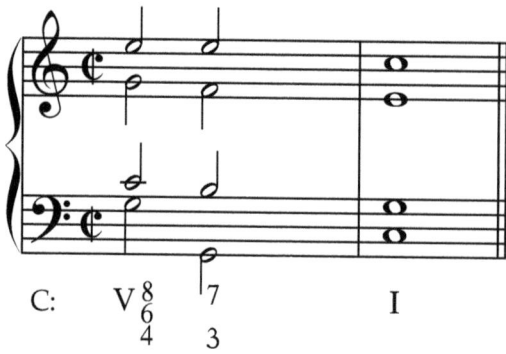

1. Name the keys. Provide root/quality chord symbols and resolve the following chords.

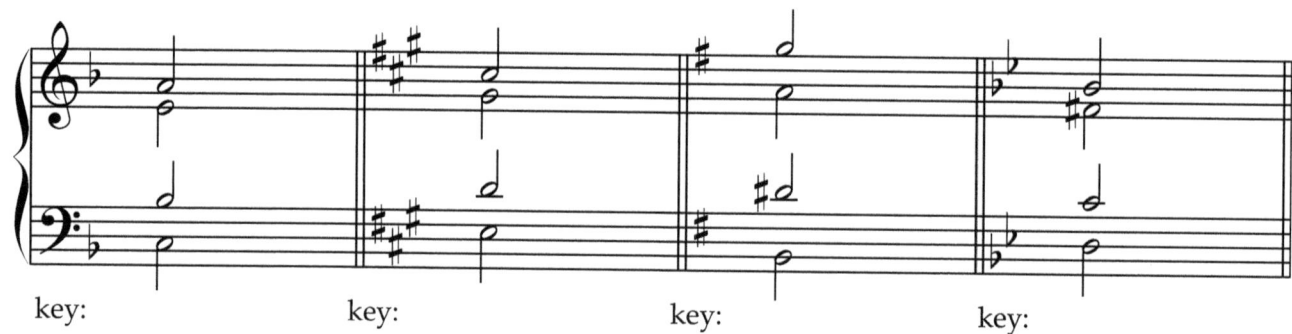

2. Complete the following progressions in four parts.

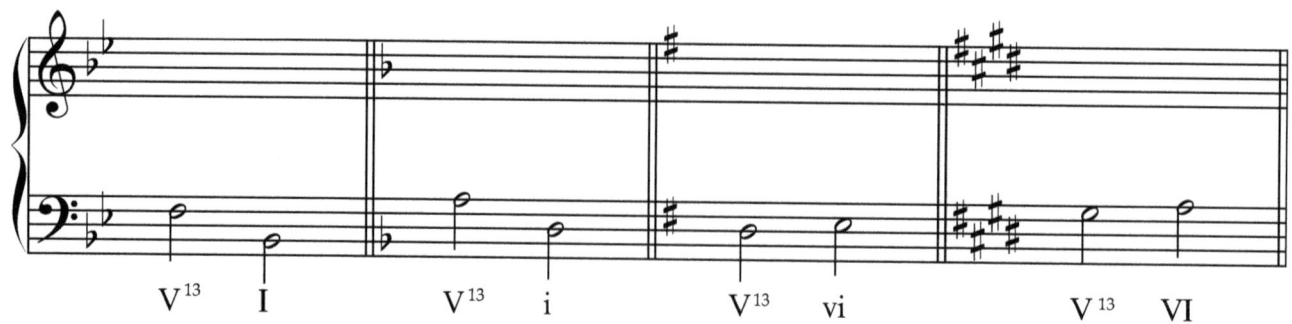

3. Write the following progressions in four parts.

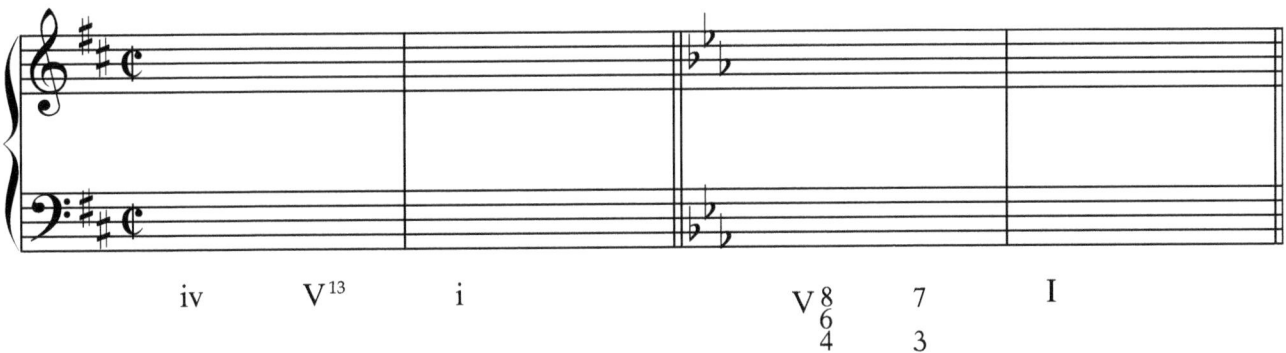

iv   V^{13} i   V$^{8\,7}_{6\,-}$ I
$\phantom{iv \ V^{13} \ i \ \ \ \ V}{}^{6\,-}_{4\,3}$

4. Complete the following progressions for SATB.

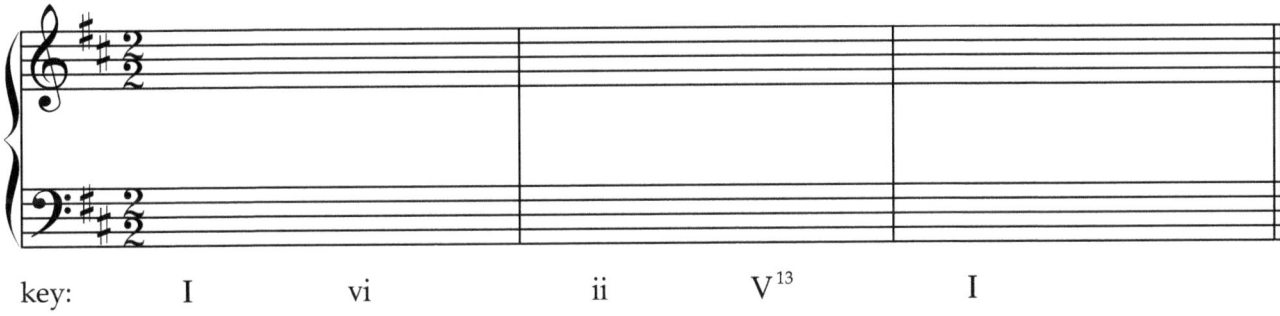

key: I   vi   ii   V^{13} I

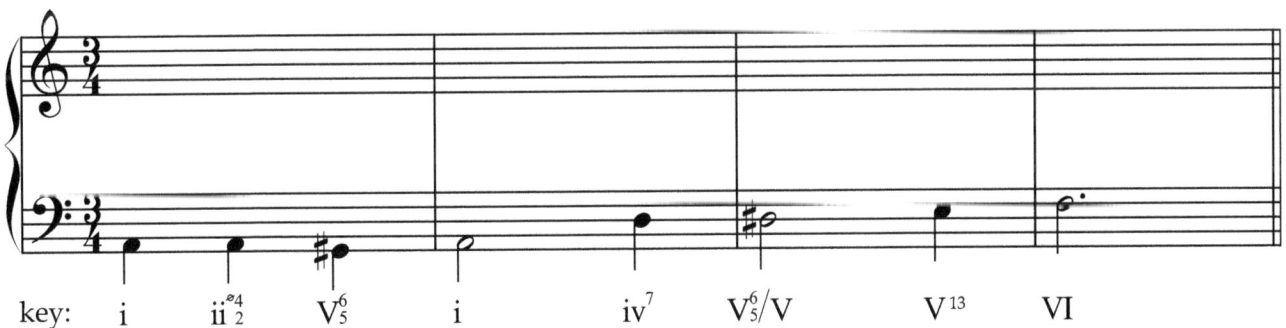

key: i   ii$^{ø 4}_{2}$ V$^6_5$ i   iv^7 V$^6_5$/V   V^{13} VI

Chord Type	Interval Structure	Symbol	Example
Major triad	root, maj 3, per 5	letter only	C
Minor triad	root, min 3, per 5	m	Cm
Diminished triad	root, min 3, dim 5	dim or °	Cdim (or C°)
Augmented triad	root, maj 3, aug 5	aug or +	Caug (or C+)
Dominant 7th chord	root, maj 3, per 5, min 7	7	C7
Diminshed 7th chord	root, min 3, dim 5, dim 7	dim7 or °7	Cdim7 (or C°7)
Half diminished 7th chord	root, min 3, dim 5, min 7	ø7	Cø7
Minor 7th chord	root, min 3, per 5, min 7	m7	Cm7
Major 7th chord	root, maj 3, per 5 , maj 7	maj7	Cmaj7
Dominant 9th chord	root, maj 3, (per 5), min 7, maj 9*	9	G9
Dominant minor 9th chord	root, maj 3, (per 5), min 7, min 9*	7(♭9) (or m9)	G7(♭9) (or Gm9)
Dominant 13th chord	root, maj 3, (per 5), min 7, (maj 9), maj 13*	13	G13
Dominant minor 13th chord	root, maj 3, (per 5), min 7, (maj 9), min 13*	7(♭13) (or m13)	G7(♭13) or Gm13

* notes in parenthesis are usually omitted

5. Provide harmonic analysis of the following excerpt. Use both functional and root/quality chord symbols. Circle and identify all non-chord tones.

Summary

1. Although the 9th and 13th chords can occur on any scale degree, they are most commonly found on the dominant.

2. A dominant 9th in four parts usually consists of the root, third, seventh, and ninth. The fifth is omitted. The ninth should be placed above the third, and is usually found in the soprano.

3. A dominant 13th in four parts usually consists of the root, third, seventh, and 13th. The fifth is omitted. The 13th is in the soprano and resolves down a 3rd to the tonic. This chord is effective in a final authentic cadence at the end of a composition.

9
The Bach Chorales

The early hymn tunes of the German protestant church are known as chorales. Many of these chorales had their origins in Latin hymns, plainsong chants, or folk melodies, but some were original compositions. A number of composers wrote four part harmonizations of chorale tunes, and some of the finest examples are by Johann Sebastian Bach (1685- 1750).

Characteristics of Bach's Chorale Harmonizations

Bach's Chorale settings have a number of common features.

1. Most are in 4/4 time, but a few are in 3/4 time.
2. The melodies are simple. The range is small and the notes move mostly by step.
3. Each phrase ends with the fermata at the cadence.
4. The harmonizations are written for four voices (SATB) and each voice has an individual melodic shape.
5. The texts are set up in a syllabic style with one or perhaps two notes per syllable. Each voice sings the same word or syllable at the same time.
6. There is a fairly regular flow of eighth notes in the three lower voices. Common non-chord tones include passing tones, neighbour notes, appoggiaturas, suspensions, and anticipations. Échappées and incomplete neighbor notes are used less frequently.

Figures 9.1 and 9.2 illustrate these features and some others.

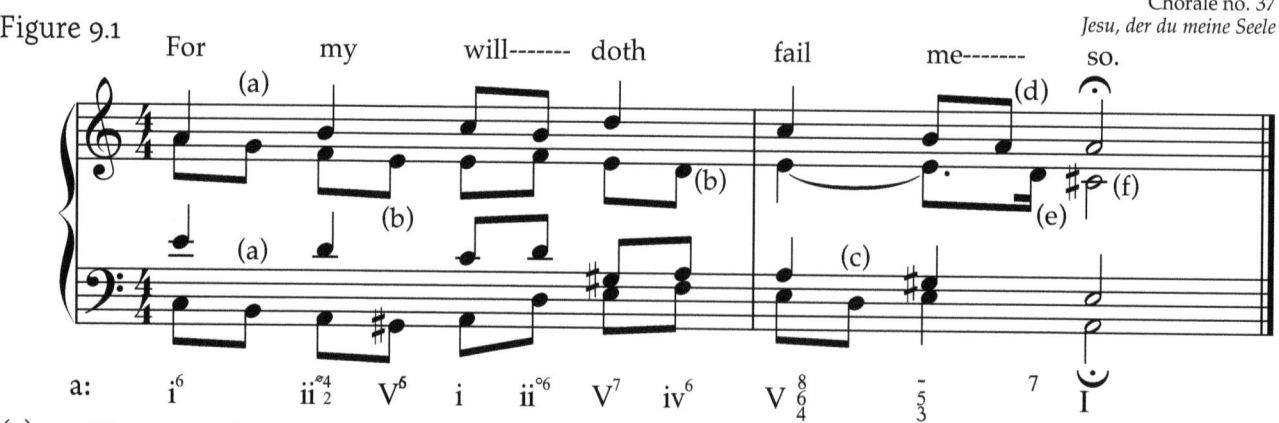

Figure 9.1

Chorale no. 37
Jesu, der du meine Seele

(a) Unaccented passing tones occur frequently, often in two voices at the same time.
(b) Changes of harmony on the eighth note beats provide harmonic movement or variety.
(c) Neighbour notes occur frequently, often in two voices at the same time.
(d) Anticipations are found most often in the soprano, especially at cadences.
(d) The seventh of the dominant 7th chord is introduced as a passing tone that resolves downward by step.
(e) In minor keys, the final chord sometimes includes a Picardy third (*tierce de picardie*, a raised third).

Figure 9.2

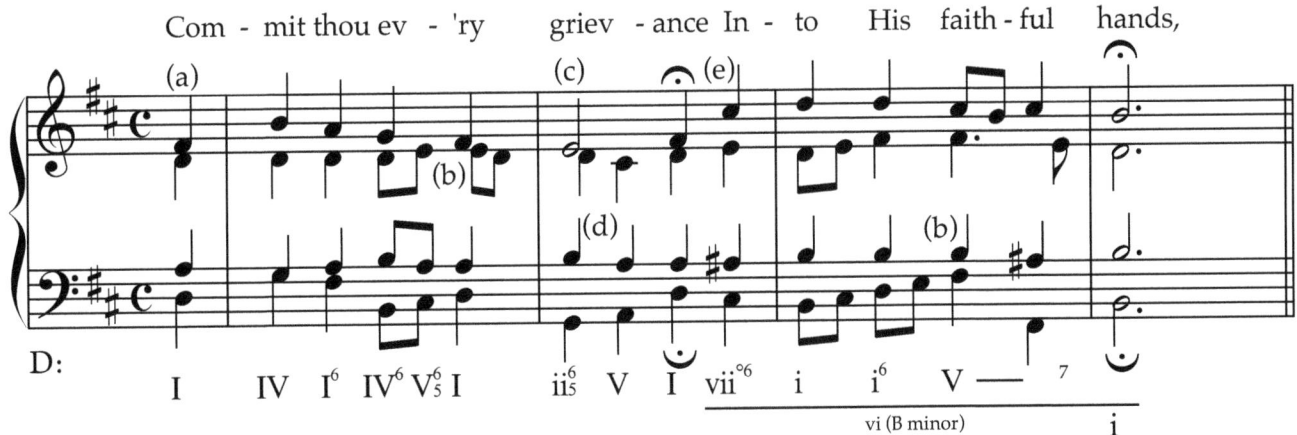

(a) An upbeat (anacrusis) is usually harmonized with I, V, V⁶, or V⁷ and its inversions.
(b) Suspensions are not always tied.
(c) A half note in the melody is often harmonized either with two chords or with one chord that is highly decorated with non-chord tones.
(d) Secondary 7th chords especially ii⁷, vi⁷, and IV⁷ occur frequently as predominant chords.
(e) Bach often uses phrase modulation. The listeners ear accepts the immediate change of key at the beginning of a phrase because of the pause at the preceding cadence.

Decoration of an Authentic Cadence

The authentic cadence is the most common cadence in Bach's chorale harmonizations, but half cadences also occur regularly. Plagal and deceptive cadences are seen less often. Figures 9.3 to 9.5 illustrate Bach's sometimes elaborate decorations of the dominant chord at authentic cadences.

In an authentic cadence, Bach usually states the V chord first, and then introduces the seventh on a weaker beat or a weaker part of the beat

Figure 9.3

Bach usually uses a complete tonic chord (doubled root, third, and fifth) in an authentic cadence. The incomplete tonic chord (tripled root and third) appears less often. In Figure 9.4, notice the Picardy third.

Figure 9.4

When the leading tone occurs in an inner voice (in Figure 9.5, G sharp), Bach often drops it down a third to the fifth of chord I.

Figure 9.5

Often there may be more than one way to analyze a musical excerpt. The following example shows two different but equally correct analyses of the same passage. If both functional and root/quality chord symbols are used, they must be consistent. If as in Figure 9.6 a, you choose to label the second chord Dm7/F, it must also be labeled as ii$^6_5$. If you choose to label it as Fmaj7 as in Figure 9.6 b, the functional chord symbol must be IV^7. The non-chord tones must also reflect the analyzed harmony. Study these examples and notice how the function of the non-chord tones change with the choice of harmony.

Figure 9.6

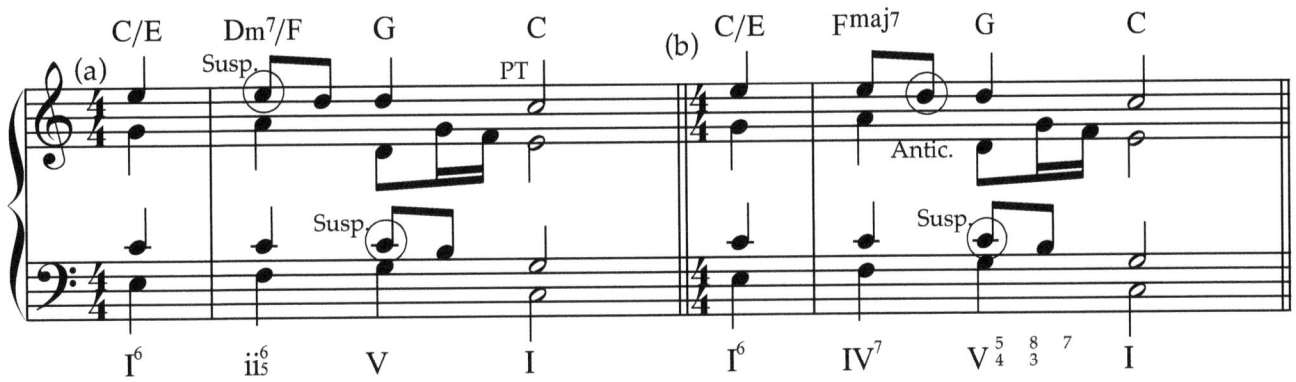

1. Provide a harmonic analysis of the following chorales. Circle and identify any non-chord tones.

Chorale no. 277
Herzlich lieb hab'ich dich, o Herr

142   Chapter 9: The Bach Chorales

Chorale no. 153
Alle Menschen mussen sterben

key:

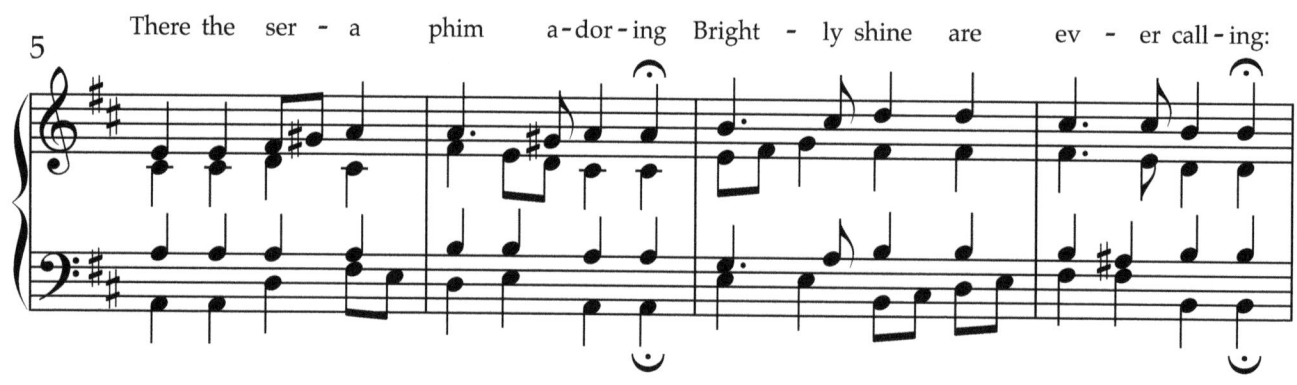

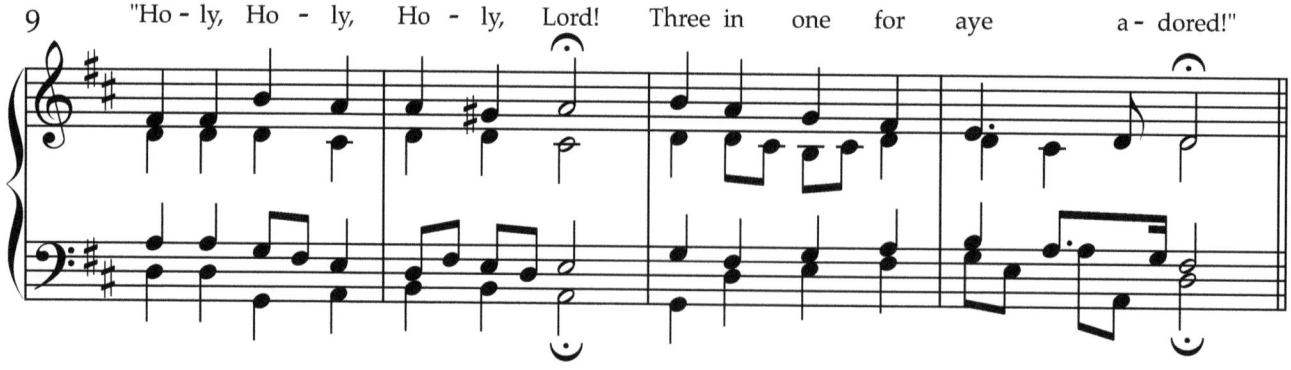

2. Complete the following chorales for four voices (SATB). Show all functional chord symbols.

Chorale no. 98
O Haupt voll Blut und Wunden

Chorale no. 303
Herr Christ, der ein'ge Gott'ssohn

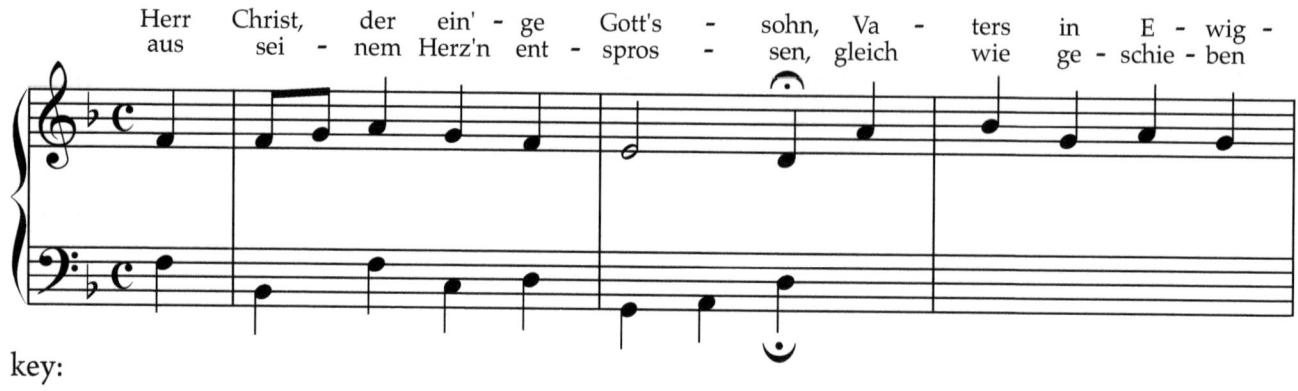

key:

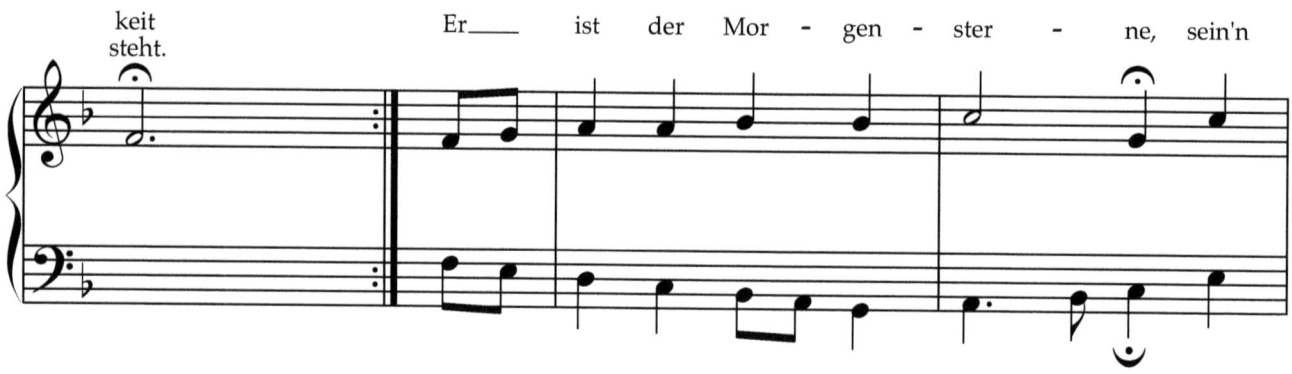

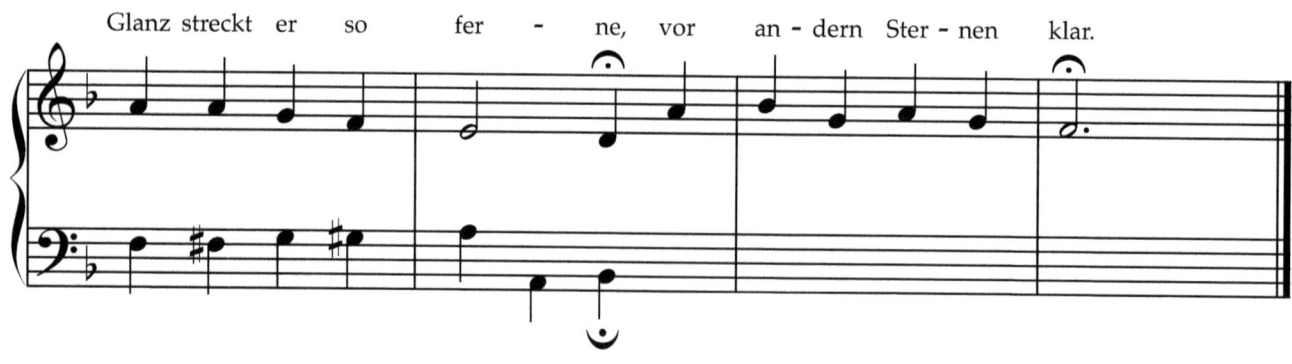

Chapter 9: The Bach Chorales

Chorale no. 245
Christe, der du bist Tag und Licht

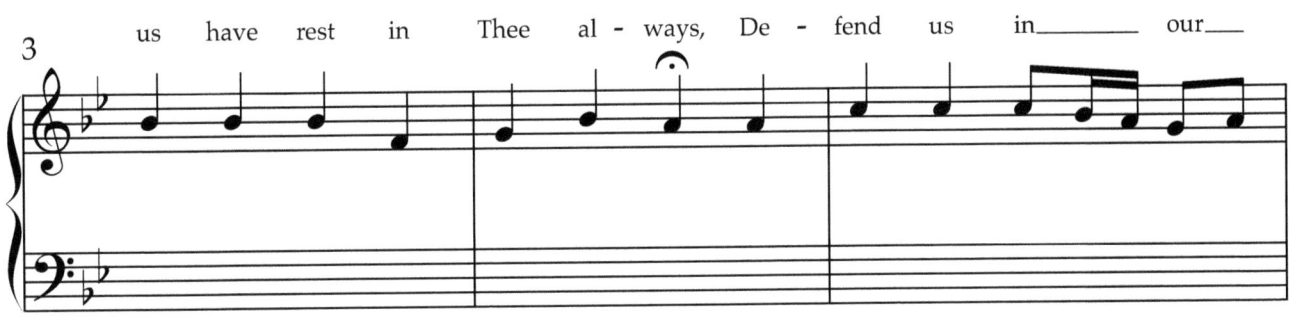

Chapter 9: The Bach Chorales

3. Provide a harmonic analysis of the following chorales. Use both functional and root/quality chord symbols. Circle and identify any non-chord tones.

Chorale no. 147
Wenn ich in Angst und Not

key:

Chapter 9: The Bach Chorales

Chorale no. 40
Ach Gott und Herr wie gross und schwer

key:

Chapter 9: The Bach Chorales

10
Form and Analysis

Music has been defined as a collection of sounds arranged in a specific order according to a number of principles. **Form** is the organization and structure of a musical composition. Form involves several aspects. What is the arrangement of the music, including compositional techniques such as repetition, contrasting themes, motives, dynamics, phrasing, and rhythm? A second aspect is the **harmonic structure** of the composition. Harmonic structure involves the overall tonal plan of a movement of a larger musical work.

Binary Form

Binary form has two parts or sections. Often (but not always) each section is repeated. The first section is labeled **A**, and the second section is labeled **B**.

$$\|: A :\| \quad \|: B :\|$$

The A and B sections are usually contrasting in character. Often, especially in simpler compositions, both sections consist of two or more four measure phrases, but composers also use irregular phrase lengths. Binary form may fall into different categories.

Simple Binary: In this form material from the first section does not reappear in the second section. If the two sections are relatively different, the form may be represented as AB (or $\|: A :\| \|: B :\|$ to indicate the repeats).

Balanced Binary: In this form the cadential formula from the first section returns at the end of the second section (usually just a measure or two, but sometimes as much as a phrase).

Rounded Binary: In this form, material from the beginning of the first section returns after a digression in the second section, resulting in an $A^1\ BA^2$ form (with repeats, $\|: A^1 :\| \|: BA^2 :\|$).

The analysis of Johann Pachelbel's Bourée in B flat major in Figure 10.1 illustrates a typical tonal plan for a piece in binary form.

Section A: start in the tonic (B♭) and ends with an authentic cadence in the dominant (F).

Section B: begins in the key where Section A ended (F major), and modulates to C minor (ii) at the end of its first phrase. The final phrase modulates back to the tonic (B♭) and ends with an authentic cadence in the tonic.

Figure 10.1

Study Figure 10.2 which illustrates a typical piece in rounded binary form.

151 Chapter 10: Form and Analysis

Ternary Form

Ternary form consists of three parts or sections. Two sections are the same. The A section is repeated fter the B section. The A and B sections are often contrasting in character. The three sections may (or may not) be separated by double bar lines, and the may (or may not) be repeated.

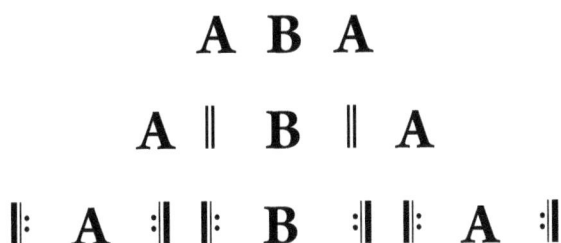

In some cases, the return of the A section is indicated with the marking *"Da capo al Fine."* Note that when this is done, the end of the A section will be marked *"Fine."*

Study Figure 10.3 which is in Ternary form.

Figure 10.3

Bourree in A minor

Form: Ternary

Johann Krieger
(1652-1735)

Sonata Form

Sonata form is often found in individual movements of larger multi-movement works such as sonatas, string quartets, symphonies, and concertos. This form reached its height in the classical period with the works of Haydn, Mozart, and Beethoven. A sonata form consists of three major sections: an **exposition**, a **development**, and a **recapitulation**.

The Exposition

In the exposition, the composer introduces several musical ideas that are called **themes**. The **first theme** is presented in the tonic key, and is followed by a short section that is called a **bridge**. The function of the bridge is to modulate from the tonic key to the key of the second theme. If the composition is in a major key, this new key is usually the dominant. If the composition is in a minor key, the new key may be either the relative major or the dominant minor. However, other closely related keys are sometimes used.

The second theme usually has a contrasting musical character to the first theme, but this is not always the case. The primary difference between the first and second themes is one of the key rather than of character. Following the presentation of the second theme, composers often add a short ending section called a *codetta*. The codetta is in the same key as the second theme, and functions as a closing or cadential section. The entire exposition section is often (but not always) repeated.

The Development

There is no established plan for development sections. As the name implies, the composer uses the development section to develop, expand, fragment, or sequence the material presented in the exposition. Occasionally, new material is also introduced. The most significant characteristic of the development is found in the modulations or key changes. Themes and motives from the exposition are presented in new keys. Often, the new keys are closely related to the tonic key of the movement. In major keys, the tonic minor is commonly used.

The development section often ends with a strong emphasis on the dominant where chord V is prolonged, often with a dominant pedal. This **dominant preparation** leads to the return of the tonic key in the recapitulation.

The Recapitulation

The musical events that took place in the exposition normally recur in the same order in the recapitulation section, with one important difference: both themes are presented in the tonic key. The bridge is present, but since there is no modulation, the second theme is stated in the tonic key, either as an exact repetition or with slight variations. Although the entire recapitulation is based on the tonic key, there may be brief excursions to other keys.

The movement ends with a codetta, which is often lengthened. Sometimes the composer chooses to end the movement with a coda in which new material is presented. The coda either follows or replaces the codetta at the end of the recapitulation.

In sonata form movements from the early classical period, the development and recapitulation sections are often repeated together, much like the B and A^2 sections of rounded binary form. It's also important to note that, in sonata form, composers did not limit themselves to regular four measure phrases. Irregular phrase lengths can be found, especially in larger, more complex works.

How to Analyze a Movement in Sonata Form

1. Name the key of the movement or piece.
2. Find and label the exposition, development, and the recapitulation sections.
3. Make a complete analysis of the exposition. Find and label the following elements:

    - two essential keys
    - any excursions into unexpected keys
    - first theme
    - bridge
    - second theme
    - codetta

    Often Composers will present more than one distinct melodic idea in a key area. This is especially likely to occur in the second key area. Use letters to differentiate the melodic ideas presented in each key area (for example, theme 2a, theme 2b, etc.).

4. Name the cadences at the end of each part of the exposition section, and identify the chords with functional chord symbols.
5. Make a complete analysis of the development section. Determine and label the main key (or keys) and the dominant preparation (if present). Identify the main materials according to their labels in the exposition (for example, "derived from theme 2, mm. 9-10").
6. Make a complete analysis of the recapitulation section. Find and label the following elements:

    - main key and (any brief modulations, if present)
    - first theme
    - bridge
    - second theme
    - codetta(if present)

7. Name the cadences At the end of each part of the recapitulation section, and identify the chords with functional chord symbols.
8. Determine whether or not there is a coda. If a coda is present, name the cadences and identify the chords with functional chord symbols.

Finally, it is important to keep in mind that sonata form is not carved in stone. Not all movements in sonata form are the same. The outline provided above is intended as a general guide that will help you explore the many possible variations of sonata form. You may encounter unexpected modulations in the exposition, or new material in the development or recapitulation sections. Point out any such unusual or unique features you encounter in your analysis. It is these variations and innovations that make the study of music in this form fascinating both for beginning students and for advanced scholars.

The analysis of the first movement of Friedrich Kuhlau's Sonatina in C major will serve as a basic example of sonata form.

Sonatina in C major
op. 20, no. 1 (1st mvt)

Form: Sonata
Exposition

Friedrich Kuhlau
(1786-1832)

1. The following movement is in sonata form.

   (a) Indicate the following elements directly on the score:

         exposition
         principal key
         theme 1
         bridge
         theme 2
         key of theme 2
         development
         recapitulation
         recapitultion of theme 1
         key of the recapitulation of theme 1
         recapitulation of the bridge
         recapitulation of theme 2
         key of the recapitulation of theme 2

   (b) Indicate the following elements directly on the score:

         the source of the material of the bridge
         the source of the material of the development
         one key in the development

   (c) Briefly discuss the changes made to the following elements in the recapitulation:

       (i) the bridge _____

       _____

       (ii) theme 1 _____

       _____

   (d) For mm. 16 to 23 inclusive, symbolize the chords using root/quality chord symbols, and identify and label any non-chord tones.

Sonatina
op. 36, no. 1 (1st mvt)

Muzio Clementi
(1752-1832)

Chapter 10: Form and Analysis

Rondo Form

The main feature of rondo form is the recurrence of the initial theme, **section A**, which is often called the **refrain**. This refrain opens the piece and returns at least two more times. Between the statements of the A section, there are a number of contrasting sections that are called **episodes**. These episodes are in different keys and may introduce new themes. Usually there is only one episode between two statements of the refrain. The episodes are labelled alphabetically: **section B**, **section C**, and so on. Thus, a basic rondo form looks like this:

A B A C A

Section A may be written in one of the smaller forms, such as binary or rounded binary, and the episodes may also be in one of these forms. Three types of rondos were common in the classical period: A **five-part rondo**, a **seven-part rondo**, and a **sonata rondo**. For now, we will limit our discussion to the five and seven part varieties.

Five-Part Rondo Form

A five-part rondo contains three statements of section A (the refrain). The movement or piece falls into one of two patterns:

$A^1 \; B^1 \; A^2 \; B^2 \; A^3$

$A^1 \; B \; A^2 \; C \; A^3$

Section A^1 is in the tonic key, and can be any length. **Section B^1** is often in a new key (with or without a change of key signature), and usually presents a new theme. **Section A^2** is in the tonic key and is an exact or slightly varied repetition of section A^1. So far, the two five-part rondo patterns are alike.

Section B^2 (if present) is often a transposed version of section B^1, with or without a change of key signature. If the composer is following the pattern with two different episodes, **section C** presents new material and is usually in a new key. **Section A^3** is another repetition of the A^1 material in the tonic key. Some rondos end with a *coda* based on existing or new thematic material.

Seven-Part Rondo Form

Seven-part rondo form contains four statements of section A (the refrain).

$A^1 \; B^1 \; A^2 \; C \; A^3 \; B^2 \; A^4$

The four A sections are all in the tonic key, and are either exact or slightly varied repetitions. The two B sections present new thematic material. The B^1 section is often in a new key, with or without a change of key signature. The B^2 section is often a transposed version of the B^1 section, and may be either in the tonic key or in the tonic major or minor. The C section, like the B sections, presents new material, usually in a different key, with or without a change of key signature. The rondo may conclude with a *coda* based on new or existing thematic material.

A rondo often contains modulations between the end of one section and the beginning of the next. If the music moves from the tonic to a new key, this short modulatory passage is called a **transition**. If the music moves from a foreign key back to the tonic. The passage is called a **re-transition**. A re-transition passage often ends with, or consists entirely of, a dominant preparation.

How to Analyze Rondo Form

1. Name the key of the movement or piece.
2. Find the main theme (the refrain) and label it with uppercase letters (A^1, A^2, A^3, etc.). Comment briefly on any differences between the various a sections (for example, length, variation of a motive, ornamentation). Name the key of each section Identify the cadence at the end of each section and label the chords with functional chord symbols.
3. Find the episodes and label them with the appropriate uppercase letters (B^1, B^2, C). Name the key of each section. Identify the cadence at the end of each section and label the chords with functional chord symbols.
4. Find and label the coda (if present), and identify the source of existing materials used there.
5. Determine whether any of the sections are in one of the smaller forms (binary, rounded binary, or ternary). Identify the forms, and label the subsections with lowercase letters.
6. Find and label any transition or re-transition passages. Label any significant dominant pedals or dominant preparation's.

The analysis of the rondo movement from Mozart's *Piano Sonata* K 570, illustrates five part rondo form.

1. Analyze the following movement in rondo form by answering the questions below.

(a) Label the following sections directly on the score. Use capital letters for A, B, and C.

    A section (A^1)

    B section

    A section (A^2)

    C section

    A section (A^3)

(b) Name the main key of each of the sections listed in part (a) above. Label the keys directly on the score at the beginning of each section.

(c) Label a transition or re-transition passage directly on the score.

(d) Name the internal form of each of the following sections:

    The first A section:_____

    The B section: _____

    The C section:_____

(e) Verify the form of each section listed in question (d) with small (lowercase) letters placed directly on the score.

(f) For mm. 81 to 93 inclusive, symbolize the chords using both functional and root/quality chord symbols, and label and identify any non-chord tones.

(g) Compare A^2 and A^3 with A^1. Comment on any differences.

Piano Sonata
Hob XVI: 37 (3rd mvt)

Franz Joseph Haydn
(1732-1809)

key:

Compound Ternary Form

Composers of the Classical period often used **minuet and trio form** for the middle movement of a three movement sonata, string quartet, or symphony, or for the third movement of a four movement work. The complete movement consisted of a minuet, a trio, and then the complete minuet again. This type of large scale **ABA** form is called **compound ternary**. Each of these three sections is a closed, independent piece, and each of the sections is often in one of the binary forms. This form may also appear as a **scherzo and trio** or a **march and trio**, replacing the minuet with another type of piece.

Thus, we have three smaller formal structures within a single larger one.

Section A^1, often, but not always a minuet, usually ends with an authentic cadence in the tonic key. Minuets are generally constructed in four measure phrases, but irregular phrase lenghths are sometimes found.

Section B, often, but not always a trio, has a contrasting character. It may be in a new but closely related key, like the subdominant, or perhaps the tonic minor or major. Trios usually end with either an authentic cadence in the new key, or a half cadence in the tonic key. Again, four measure phrases are found most often, but irregular phrase lengths do occur.

Section A^2 is an exact or slightly varied repetition of A^1. Sometimes the repetition is written out, but often it is indicated by the markings *Da capo al Fine* or *Menuetto da capo* at the end of the B section.

Some minuet and trio movements also include a short *coda*.

Transition passages (modulating from the tonic to a new key) and **retransition** passages (modulating from a foreign key back to the tonic) are also common in compound ternary form. A retransition passage often ends with, or consists entirely of a dominant preparation.

Common Key Structures in Compound Ternary Form

These are some of the most common, but not the only, key schemes found in compound ternary form.

- A^1, B, and A^2 are all in the same key
- I - i - I or i - I - i The B section is in the tonic minor or tonic major
- I - IV - I The B section is the the subdominant

How to Analyze Compound Ternary Form

1. Determine the key of the composition.
2. Find and label the sections A^1, B, A^2.
3. Determine the form of each section (binary, rounded binary, etc.) and indicate these forms by labelling the individual parts with the appropriate lowercase letters.
4. Mark the phrases, name the cadences, and identify the chords with functional chord symbols.

The following analysis of the minuet and trio from Beethoven's *Piano Sonata* op. 2, no. 1, illustrates a minuet and trio in compound ternary form. Notice the irregular phrase lengths in the trio section.

Form: **Compound Ternary**
Form of Minuet (A): **Rounded binary**
Form of Trio (B): **Rounded binary**

Piano Sonata op.2 no. 1 (3rd mvt.)

Ludwig van Beethoven
(1770-1827)

Chapter 10: Form and Analysis

1. The following movement is in **compound ternary form**. Analyze the movement by answering the following questions below.

    (a) Identify and label the minuet and trio with uppercase letters written directly on the score.

    (b) Write the main key of the minuet and the main key of the trio on the score.

    (c) Name the internal forms of the minuet and trio sections.

    Minuet:_____

    Trio:_____

    (d) Verify these forms with lowercase letters written directly on the score.

    (e) Mark the phrasing directly on the score.

    (f) Provide functional chord symbols for the cadences, and name the cadences at the end of phrases. Name the key if the cadence is not in the tonic key.

    (g) For mm. 1 to 10 inclusive, symbolize the chords with root/quality chord symbols and identify any non-chord tones.

Divertimento
Hob XVI:9 (2rd mvt.)

Franz Joseph Haydn
(1732-1809)

The Fugue

The **fugue** is a contrapuntal composition consisting of three or more melodies that are played together. This form flourished in the Baroque era and one of the most famous collections of fugues can be found in *The Well-Tempered Clavier* composed by J. S. Bach.

The individual melodic lines of the fugue are called **voices**. The voices are named after the four singing ranges: soprano, alto, tenor and bass. Most fugues are written for three or four voices.

In a four voice fugue the two upper voices (soprano and alto) are usually written in the treble clef on the upper staff and the two lower voices (tenor and bass) are written in the bass clef on the lower staff. Figure 10.4 contains an excerpt from a four voice fugue.

Figure 10.4

In a three voice fugue the soprano is written in the treble clef on the upper staff, and the bass voice is written in the bass clef on the lower staff. The middle voice (the alto) uses both the upper and lower staves depending on the range of the part. Higher notes use the treble staff, and lower notes use the bass staff. Figure 10.5 shows an excerpt from a three voice fugue.

Figure 10.5

The Exposition

The first section of the fugue is called the **exposition**. In the exposition the main themes are introduced in each voice.

Elements of a Fugal Exposition

The Subject: This is the first thing you hear; it lasts until the next voice enters with the answer.

The Answer: – The answer is the imitation of the subject in the second voice, transposed into the dominant. Answers can be written in two ways:

- real answer – an exact, note-for-note transposition in the dominant.
- tonal answer – a subject transposition in which some intervals have been altered in order to pull the tonality back to the tonic key.

A fugue will normally use a tonal answer when:

- the tonic and dominant are used prominently in the subject.
- the subject modulates.
- the subject has many skips.

The Countersubject: This is what the first voice does when it has finished with the subject, and the answer has entered in another voice. Simply put, the countersubject is counterpoint against the answer. Sometimes a fugue may not have a countersubject.

The exposition ends when all voices have entered with the subject or answer and there is a cadence, (authentic or half). The cadence may be in the home key or a closely-related key.

Optional material: Things you may or may not find in a fugue exposition:

The Link: Your fugal exposition may include short sections between the answer and subject entries. We call these links. Links frequently make use of a motive from the subject, for instance with sequential repetition of a short fragment. They may appear between any or all voice entries and may be of varying lengths. These links are often modulatory in nature.

Redundant Entry: An extra occurrence of the subject in the exposition after all the voices have stated the subject (or countersubject), So, in a 3-voice fugue it will be the 4th occurrence of the subject.

Structure of a 3-voice Fugue (voices may enter in any order)					
Voice 1:	subject (I)	countersubject	optional link	new material	cadence
Voice 2:		answer (V)		countersubject	
Voice 3:				subject (I)	

Structure of a 4-voice Fugue (voices may enter in any order)						
Voice 1:	subject (I)	countersubject	optional link	new material	new material	cadence
Voice 2:		answer (V)		countersubject	new material	
Voice 3:				subject (I)	countersubject	
Voice 4:					answer (V)	

Figure 10.6 is an analysis of the exposition of a 3-voice fugue.

Figure 10.6

Johann Sebastian Bach
Fugue 2 in C minor BWV 847

Chapter 10: Form and Analysis

1. Analyze the following fugal exposition by answering the questions below.

   (a) Name the key.

   _____

   (b) Label all the appearances of the subject (S) and answer (A) directly on the score.

   (c) Name the key of the answer.

   _____

   (d) Name the type of answer (real or tonal).

   _____

   (e) Label the countersubject on the score.

   (f) Label the link on the score.

   Johann Sebastian Bach
   Fugue 20 BWV 889

2. State the form of the following movements. Identify directly on the music all the characteristics applicable to this form.

Form: _____

Sonatina
op. 168, no. 1 (1st mvt)

Anton Diabelli
(1781-1858)

Form: _____

Sonatina
op. 157, no. 4 (2nd mvt)

Fritz Spindler
(1817-1905)

Form: _____

Sonatina
op. 120, no. 1 (3rd mvt)

Friedrich Kuhlau
(1752-1832)

190 Chapter 10: Form and Analysis

Form: _____

Sonatina
op. 36, no. 2 (1st mvt)

Muzio Clementi
(1752-1832)

Chapter 10: Form and Analysis

Form: _____

Piano Sonata
K 545 (3rd mvt)

Wolfgang Amadeus Mozart
(1756-1791)

Chapter 10: Form and Analysis

Form: _____

Partita (Divertimento)
Hob XVI:1 (3rd mvt)

Franz Joseph Haydn
(1732-1809)

Form: _____

Sonatina
op.49, no. 1 (3rd mvt)

Heinrich Lichner
(1839-1898)

204   Chapter 10: Form and Analysis

Chapter 10: Form and Analysis

3. Analyze the following fugal exposition by answering the questions below.

   (a) Name the key.

   _____

   (b) Label all the appearances of the subject (S) and answer (A) directly on the score.

   (c) Name the key of the answer.

   _____

   (d) Name the type of answer (real or tonal).

   _____

Johann Sebastian Bach
Fugue in C major

4. Analyze the following fugal exposition by answering the questions below.

   (a) Name the key.

   _____

   (b) Label all the appearances of the subject (S) and answer (A) directly on the score.

   (c) Name the key of the answer.

   _____

   (d) Name the type of answer (real or tonal).

   _____

   (e) Label the link on the score.

Johann Sebastian Bach
Fugue 21 BWV 890

Chapter 10: Form and Analysis

5. Analyze the following fugal exposition by answering the questions below.

   (a) Name the key.
   _____

   (b) Label all the appearances of the subject (S) and answer (A) directly on the score.

   (c) Name the key of the answer.
   _____

   (d) Name the type of answer (real or tonal).
   _____

   (e) Label the countersubject on the score.

   (f) Label a link directly on the score.

   (g) Label any redunant entries on the score.

Johann Sebastian Bach

Chapter 10: Form and Analysis

6. Analyze this exposition of a four voice fugue.

Johann Sebastian Bach

11
Counterpoint and Melody Writing

Counterpoint Review

The term counterpoint comes from the Latin expression *punctus contra punctum* which means point against point or note against note. Generally, counterpoint involves the writing of musical lines that sound different from each other but sound harmonious when played together. Counterpoint focuses on the interaction of melodies. Secondary to this interaction are the harmonies produced by the counterpoint. Still, you cannot separate the harmony from the counterpoint. It is impossible to write two lines of music without creating harmony, and impossible to create harmony without linear activity.

Counterpoint was used extensively in the Renaissance period, especially in the music of Giovanni Palestrina (1525 - 1594), but it reached its culmination with the composers of the Baroque period. It is often referred to as *polyphony* and the two terms are almost interchangeable. Historically, music created in the Baroque period is described as *contrapuntal*, while music composed before the Baroque period is described as *polyphonic.*

The Baroque was a very active period for contrapuntal writing. Prominent composers from this period that were in Germany are Johann Sebastian Bach (1685-1750), Dietrich Buxtehude (1637-1707), Johann Pachelbel (1635-1706) and Georg Phillipp Telemann (1681-1767). In Italy and Spain composers of this genre were Arcangelo Corelli (1653-1713), Antonio Vivaldi (1678-1741) and Domenico Scarlatti (1685-1757). In France composers included François Couperin (1668-1733) and Jean-Phillipe Rameau (1683-1764); and in England George Frideric Handel (1685-1759).

Figure 11.1 is an example of two voice counterpoint from the 18th century.

Figure 11.1

George Frideric Handel
Passepied

Writing Two Part Counterpoint

This chapter focuses on writing two part counterpoint in 18th century style. An important aspect of this writing can be seen in the intervals that occur between the two voices. Figure 11.2 shows the intervals that occur between the two voices of the Handel Passepied.

Figure 11.2

George Frideric Handel
Passepied

Two part contrapuntal writing in 18th century style involves three basic types of motion between the voices.

Similar Motion
Similar motion is when two voices move in the same direction either by step or by leap. The numbers in Figure 11.3 indicate the intervallic distance between the voices. If the voices move in the same direction by the same interval (as in this example in parallel 3rds) it is considered parallel motion. Note that we are expressing compound intervals in their simple form. (e.g. 10 = 3, 12 = 5, etc.)

Figure 11.3

Figure 11.4

Contrary Motion
Contrary motion is when two voices move in the opposite direction. Figure 11.4

Figure 11.5

Oblique Motion
Oblique motion is when one voice moves and the other voice remains stationary. Figure 11.5

Intervals Between Voices

The following intervals are considered consonant and are used frequently between voices in two part counterpoint.

major 3rd, minor 3rd, major 6th, minor 6th, perfect octave, perfect 5th, perfect unison

Two dissonant intervals that are used fairly frequently since they imply dominant 7th harmony are the:

augmented 4th, diminished 5th

Other dissonant intervals that may be used are:

minor 7th, perfect 4th, major 2nd

Two dissonant intervals that are **not used** are:

minor 2nd and **major 7th**

Most Commonly Used Intervals	⟶		Least Commonly Used Intervals	
major and minor 3rds major and minor 6ths	perfect octaves		perfect 5ths perfect unisons minor 7ths major 2nds perfect 4ths	augmented 4ths diminished 5ths

We can study these vertical intervals and their uses beginning with the most commonly used.

Thirds

Vertical major and minor 3rds are used frequently. The 3rd often implies a triad in root position. You can use up to four vertical 3rds in a row. Using more than four in a row can make the counterpoint sound boring or uninteresting.

Figure 11.6

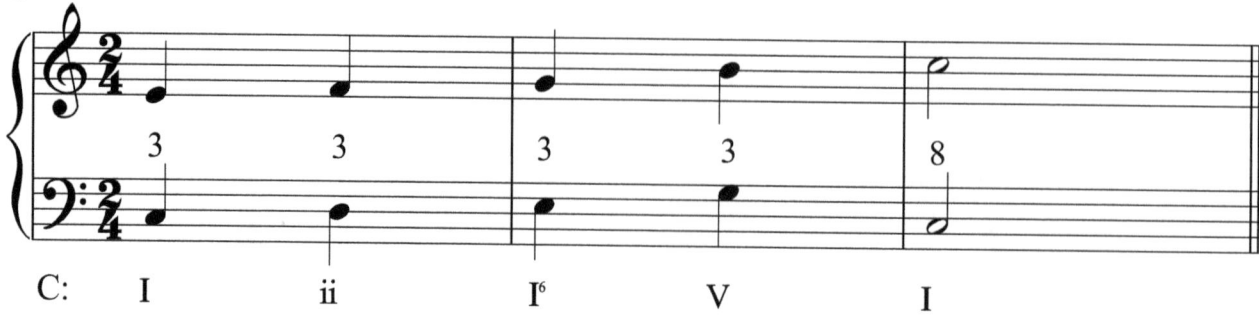

Chapter 11: Counterpoint

Sixths

Vertical major and minor 6ths are used frequently. The 6th often implies a triad in first inversion. You can use up to four vertical 6ths in a row.

Figure 11.7

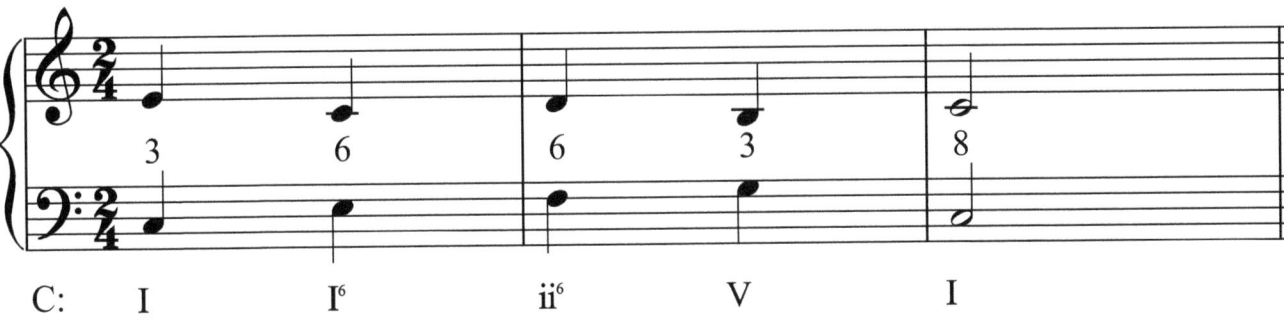

Perfect Octaves

Perfect octaves occur most commonly at the beginning and ends of phrases. They may be used elsewhere in a phrase but are usually found on a weak beat. Perfect octaves are found most frequently on the tonic and dominant notes of the key, but may occur on any note of the scale except the leading tone.
The approach to the octave is important. It is most often approached by contrary motion as in m.2 of Figure 11.8. It is correct to approach the octave in similar motion as long as the melody moves by step (mm.3-4). This is a common progression that occurs at the ends of phrases with an authentic cadence.

Figure 11.8

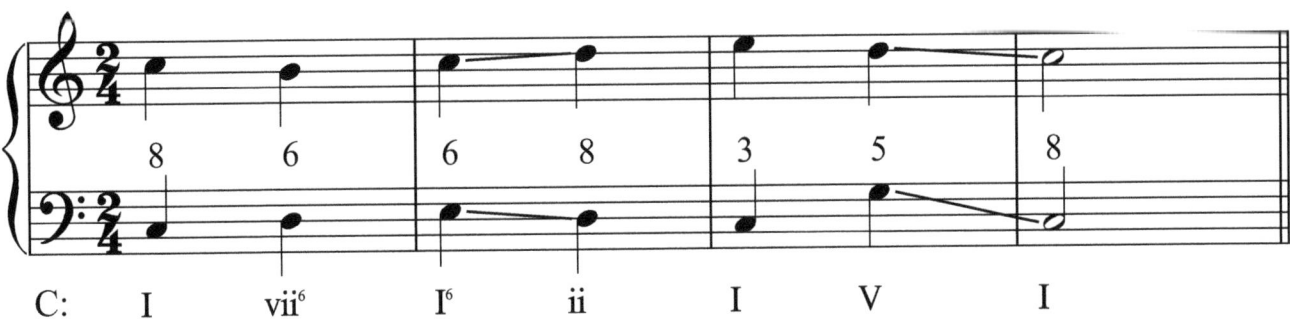

Do not use more than one octave in a row. This is the error of parallel octaves, and is considered wrong Figure 11.9. (a) The passing tone in (b) does not hide the faulty parallel octaves. When octaves are approached by a leap in similar motion, the error of hidden or direct octaves occur Figure 11.9 (c). Do not leap to an octave with similar motion.

Figure 11.9

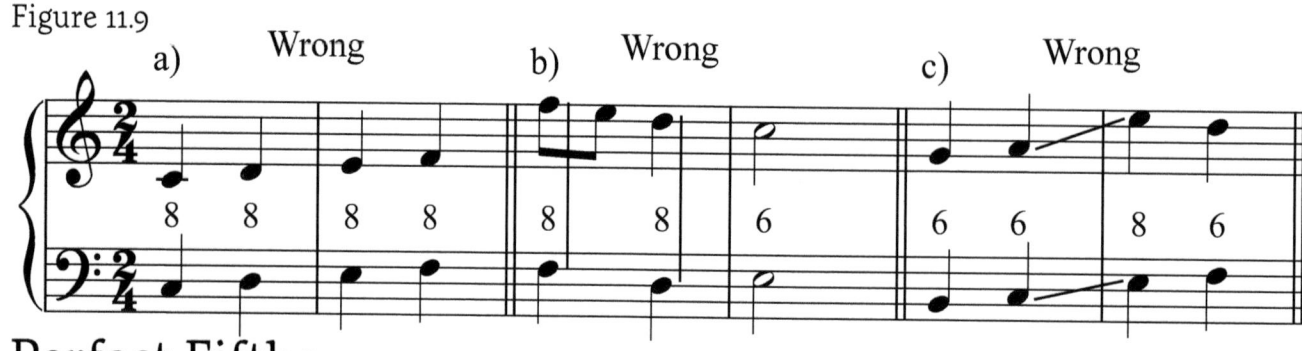

Perfect Fifths

The perfect 5th is most commonly used at the beginning and ends of phrases. It has a hollow sound and if it is used within the phrase it is usually found on a weak beat. The perfect 5th is usually approached by contrary motion Figure 11.10 (m. 2). An approach by similar motion is possible if the melody moves by step (mm.3-4).

Figure 11.10

Do not use more than one 5th in a row. This is the error of parallel 5ths and is wrong Figure 11.11 (a). The passing tone creates faulty parallel fifths in (b). When 5ths are approached by a leap in similar motion an error called hidden or direct 5ths occurs Figure 11.11 (c). Do not leap to a 5th with similar motion.

Figure 11.11

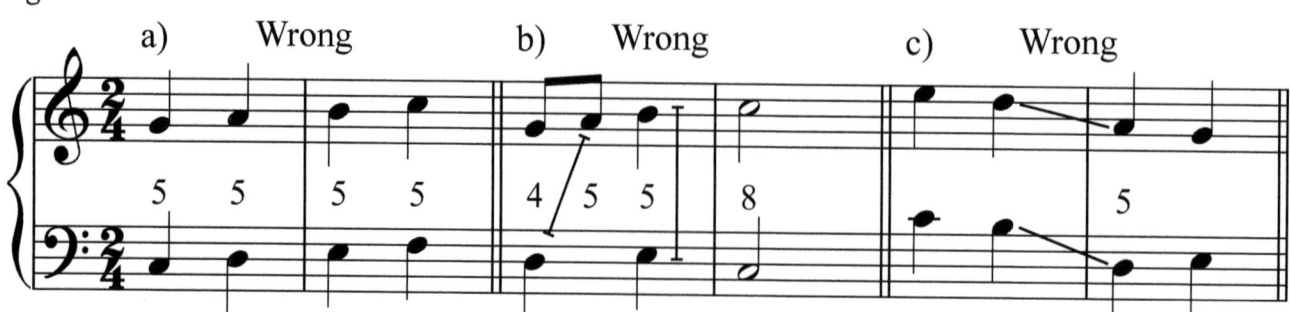

Sevenths

Major 7ths are almost never used because they are very dissonant. We do however use the minor 7th to imply V^7 or ii^7. The root of V^7 rises a 4th or falls a 5th to the root of I and the 7th falls a step to the 3rd of I Figure 11.12(a). In the progression V^7—vi, the root of V^7 rises a step to the root of vi and the 7th falls a step to the 5th of vi Figure 11.12(b).

Since ii^7 resolves to V certain rules of resolution are required. The 7th of ii^7 is prepared with common tone motion and falls a step to the 3rd of chord V. The root of ii^7 move to the root of chord V Figure 11.12(c). *Note that the leading tone must always rise to the tonic in two part writing and the implied 7ths must always resolve downward by step.*

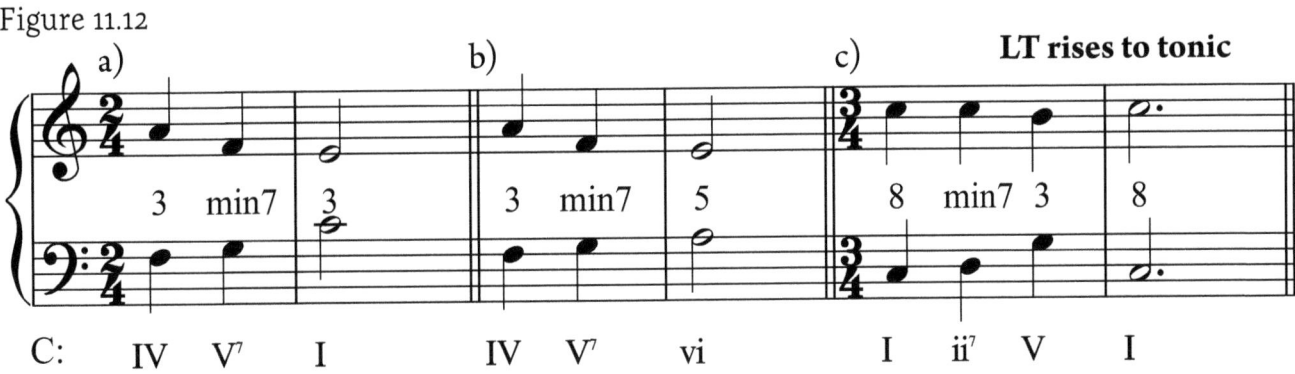

Figure 11.12

In Figure 11.13 the 7th of V^7 falls a step in its resolution to I and the 7th of ii^7 falls a step in its resolution to V.

Figure 11.13

1. Complete the following progressions in two part counterpoint according to the following chord symbols. Be sure to resolve the 7ths in each 7th chord correctly.

key: IV   V⁷   I   key: ii°⁶   V⁷   i   key: I   ii⁷   V

2. Complete the following progressions in two part counterpoint according to the following chord symbols.

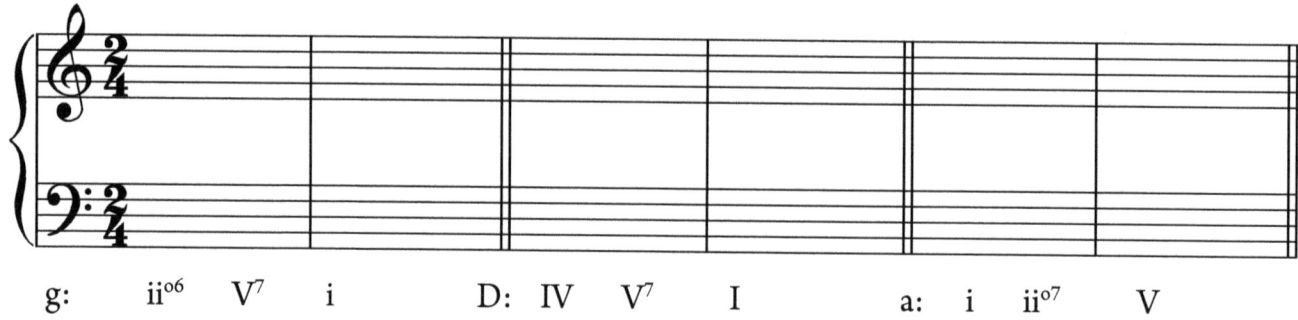

g: ii°⁶   V⁷   i   D: IV   V⁷   I   a: i   ii°⁷   V

The Perfect Unison

The perfect unison is used at the beginning and ends of phrases. It is not often used in the middle of a phrase because a unison can cause the counterpoint to sound like one voice has dropped out. It is best to approach a unison by contrary motion. Do not use more than one perfect unison in a row. Parallel perfect unisons are wrong.

Figure 11.14

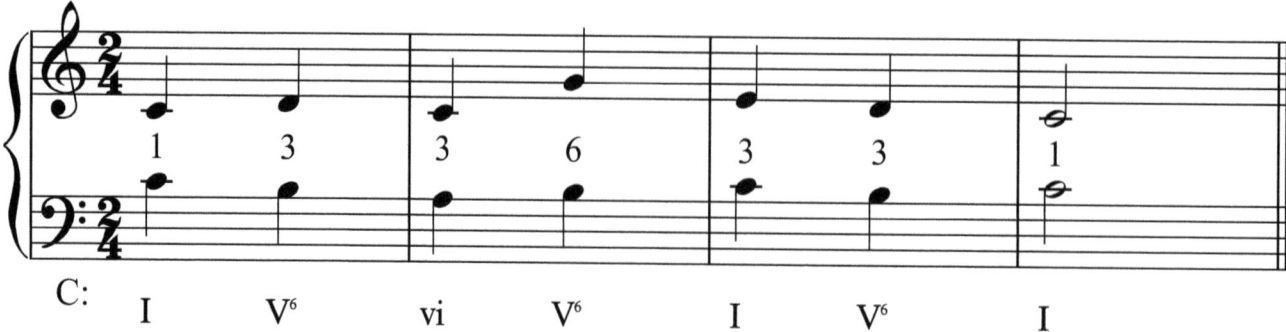

C: I   V⁶   vi   V⁶   I   V⁶   I

The Augmented Fourth and Diminished Fifth

The augmented 4th and diminished 5th are vertical intervals that require resolution. These two intervals imply inversions of the dominant 7th chord. The diminished 5th occurs between the leading tone in the bass and the subdominant in the treble. This implies the V^6_5 chord or less frequently an inversion of a diminished 7th chord.

The subdominant is the 7th of V^6_5 and must resolve down by step to the 3rd of chord I. The dim 5th resolves inwardly to the interval of a 3rd. Dim 5ths should be approached by contrary or oblique motion.

Figure 11.15

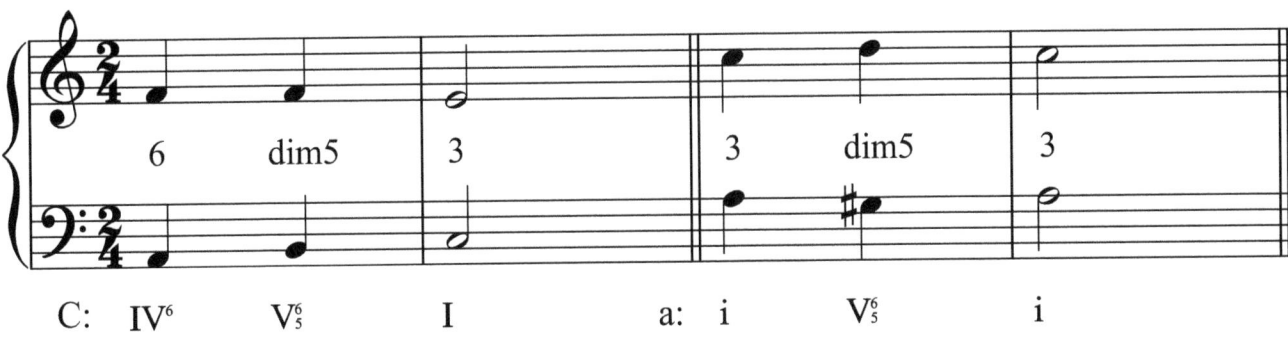

The augmented 4th implies V^4_2, or less frequently, an inversion of a diminished 7th chord. The aug 4th occurs between the subdominant in the bass and the leading tone in the treble. This interval resolves outwardly to the interval of a 6th. Augmented 4ths should be approached by contrary or oblique motion.

Figure 11.16

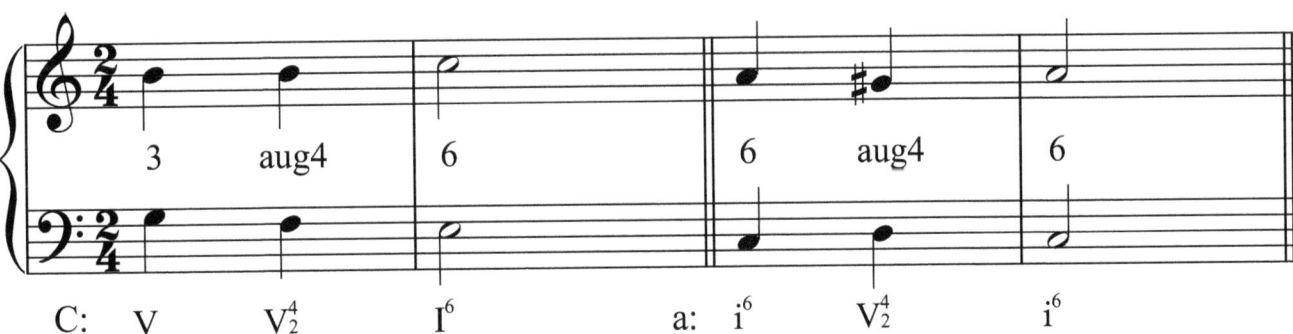

3. Complete the following progressions in two part counterpoint according to the following chord symbols.

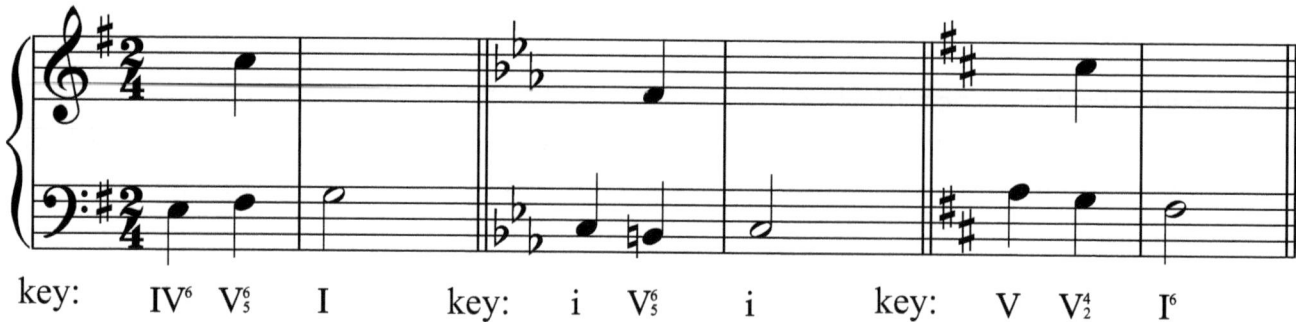

key: IV⁶   V⁶₅   I   key: i   V⁶₅   i   key: V   V⁴₂   I⁶

4. Complete the following progressions in two part counterpoint according to the following chord symbols.

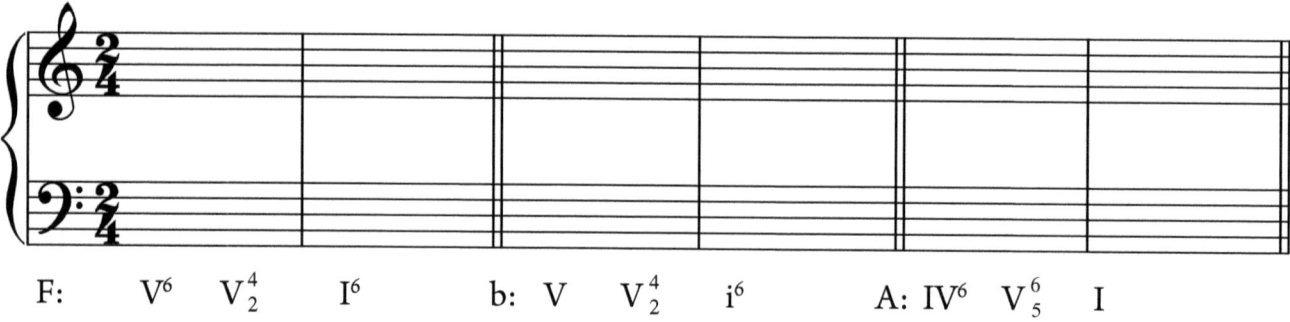

F: V⁶   V⁴₂   I⁶   b: V   V⁴₂   i⁶   A: IV⁶   V⁶₅   I

The Major Second

The major 2nd can be used as an interval between voices. The minor 2nd however is not. This interval is used occasionally to imply V^4_2 or ii^4_2. Here, the bass note is the 7th and must resolve downward by step to a first inversion chord. The upper note may repeat as a common tone as in Figure 11.17 (a), or leap up a 4th as in Figure 11.17 (b).

Figure 11.17

C: ii   V⁴₂   I⁶   c: i   ii⁴₂   V⁶   i

The Perfect Fourth

The perfect 4th used between two voices is usually found at the end of a phrase and implies a cadential six-four. Because the 4th is considered dissonant it requires resolution.

Study the following examples using the perfect 4th. In Figure 11.18 (a) the 6 resolves to 5 maintaining the dominant in the bass. Here, the bass drops an octave, but it could also repeat.
In Figure 11.18 (b) the 4 resolves to 3 over the dominant in the bass. Care should be taken when approaching the 4th. It is usually approached by common tone or by stepwise motion from above.

Figure 11.18

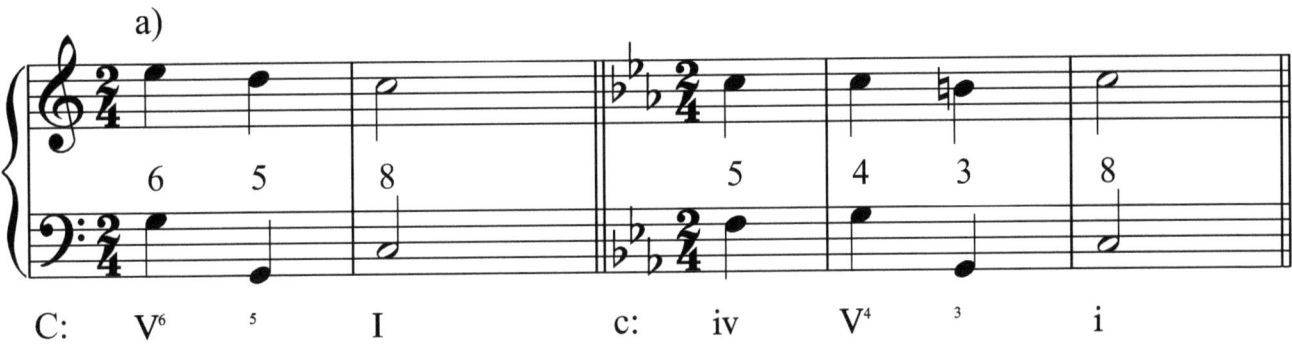

5. Complete the following progressions in two part counterpoint according to the following chord symbols.

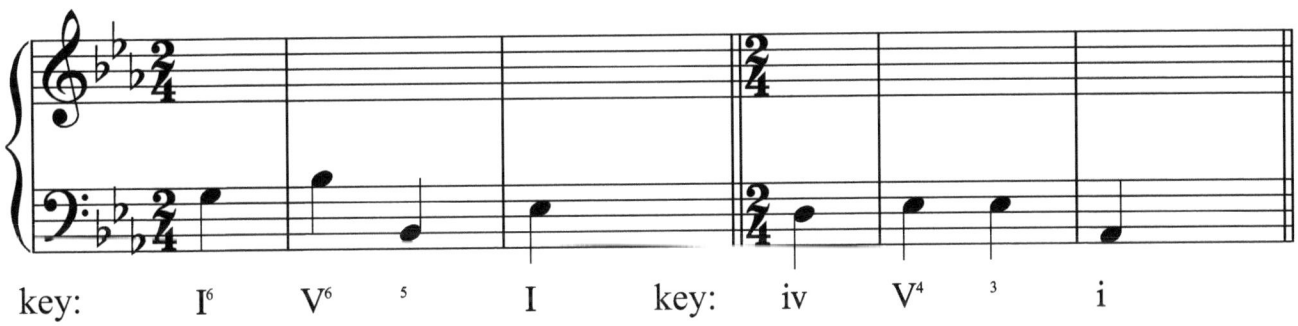

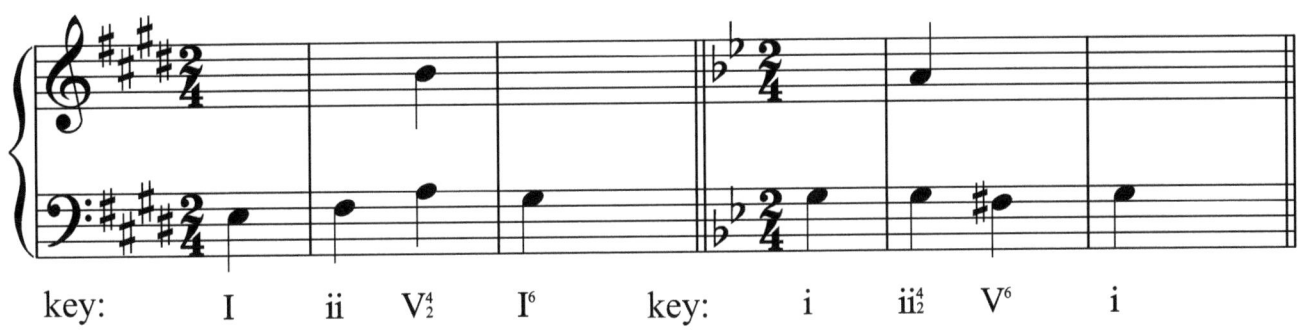

Implied Harmony

In 18th century counterpoint not only are the interval combinations considered, but also the harmonic progressions implied by the interval combinations. The music must be logical and have a sense of direction both as independent melodic lines and as a harmonic progression.

It is best to keep the progressions simple. Following the plan of: beginning tonic – predominant– dominant- ending tonic is effective most of the time. Staying within this harmonic framework in your two part writing will help to make your work harmonically sound and give it musical sense.

Figure 11.19 shows two different harmonies for the same bass line. Both examples function in the same way. Measures 1 and 2 are a prolongation of the beginning tonic. Measure 3 contains the predominant and dominant harmony followed by the ending tonic in measure 4.

Figure 11.19

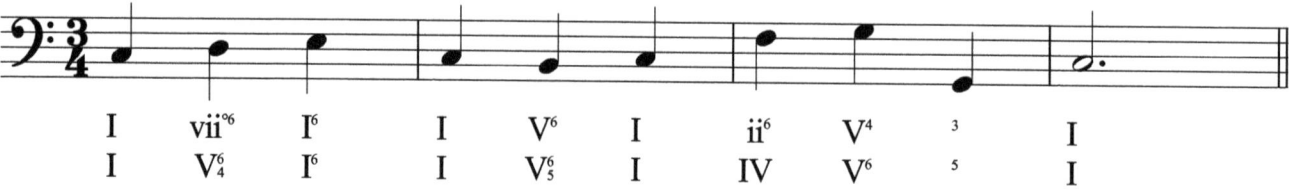

6. Study the following progression. Using Roman numerals indicate the implied harmony under the score.

key:

Strict note against note counterpoint is not used very often for an entire composition in 18th century style since it provides very little rhythmic interest when both voices use the same note values. We often see the addition of non chord tones or chordal skips to provide rhythmic interest and movement.

Study the example of strict note against note counterpoint in Figure 11.20

Figure 11.20

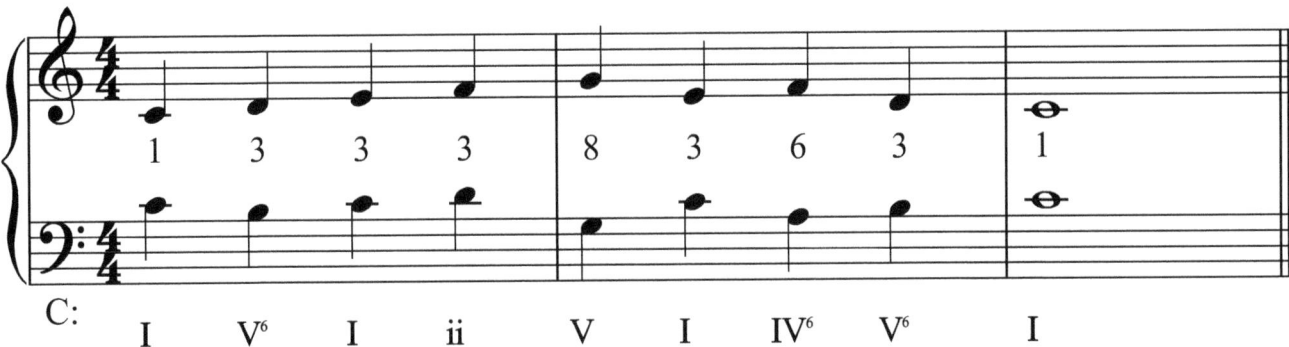

Figure 11.21 is the same example with the addition of passing motion in m.2. These notes give interest and movement to the melody. However, care must be taken when adding non chord tones. Always check your work to see if the addition of non chord tones has created faulty parallel motion.

Figure 11.21

Tips for Writing Counterpoint Above A Bass Line

Study the following steps for writing counterpoint above a given bass.

1. Study the given example and name the key.

2. Decide on a harmonic plan. Here it may be best to start at the end of the phrase, deciding on a cadence and a good pre-cadential chord. Sketch in the predominant and cadence.

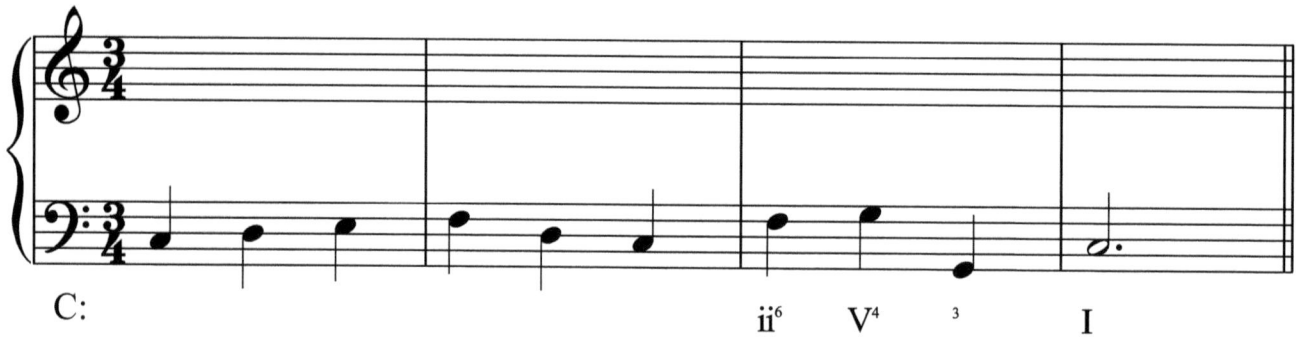

3. Start at the beginning and complete the harmonic plan for the exercise. Try to follow the basic harmonic plan of: beginning tonic—pre-dominant—dominant—ending tonic if you can. Look for common and idiomatic progressions like I-vii°6 –I6 shown below. Sketch in a basic chord progression bearing in mind that you may have to make changes when you actually add the upper voice.

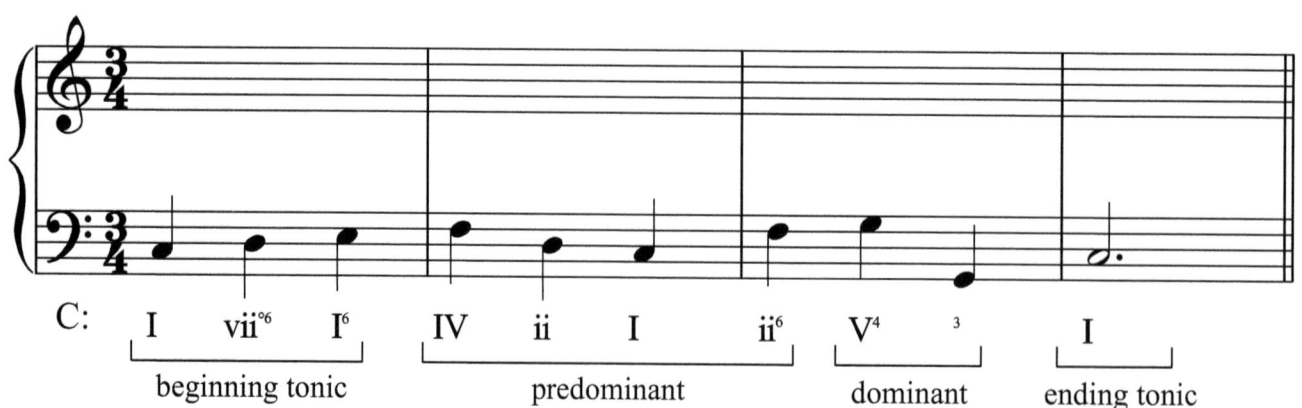

4. Write the counterpoint according to your harmonic plan. Write out the vertical intervals occurring between the voices. Check your work for the following:

- Are there any incorrect parallel perfect unisons, 5ths or octaves?
- Are there any melodic intervals that are not allowed like the aug4th and major 7th?
- Are there more than four vertical 3rds or 6ths in a row?
- Are all perfect unisons, 5ths and octaves approached correctly?
- Are 7th chords and six-four chords resolved correctly?
- Are large leaps treated correctly and left with stepwise motion in the opposite direction or an interval within the leap?
- Are there too many leaps in one direction outlining a dissonance?
- Does the phrase contain a climax?

5. Think about adding a few non chord tones or chordal skips to give the example rhythmic momentum and interest, but be careful to avoid faulty parallels. Here a paassing tone is added to m.1, a chordal skip to m.2, and an suspension to m.3. The chordal skip works here because it outlines the notes of the IV chord. When writing these skips be careful avoid a dissonant interval. The suspension is an extension of cadential six-four. 4 is held off for a half beat longer before it resolves to 3.

7. Name the key, provide chord symbols, and write a melody to accompany the following bass lines in two part counterpoint.

The 18th Century Dance and Melody Writing

This section covers writing melodies in the style of an 18th century dance. Study the melody in Figure 11.22.

Figure 11.22

Figure 11.22

This melody is based on two motives. A motive is a short melodic or rhythmic pattern that recurs throughout a composition. These two motives are contrasting in rhythm as well as interval structure.

Measures 3 and 4 are derived from the opening motives. Here, the composer uses the same rhythms but change the intervals between the notes. This provides repetition and contrast, which are both essential elements in a good melody.

The beginning of the second phrase is derived from motive A. Here the composer uses a melodic sequence, repeating the motive one step lower. Sequences are effective in melody writing, but do not usually occur more than three times in a row.

The rhythm slows at the end of the second phrase for the cadence. The dotted half note provides a place of rest for the final note of the cadence.

1. Analyze the following melody by marking the phrasing and labelling the motives, material derived from the motives, and any melodic sequences.

Harmonic Rhythm and Implied Harmony

Chorale tunes have simple melodies characterized by stepwise motion and quarter note rhythm. The harmonic rhythm is relatively fast, with a new chord or sometimes two chords on each beat. The melodic style explored in this chapter is quite different. The melodic lines are more active, with a wider range, frequent skips, and relatively intricate rhythms. One result of this increased melodic activity is that the harmonic rhythm tends to be slower, often only one or two chords per measure.

In Figure 11.23, the implied harmony is fairly obvious. The chord tones in the melody give little doubt about the implied chords.

Figure 11.23

Not all melodies suggest a harmony so clearly, the chords may well be implied, especially if a specific chord progression is understood. In Figure 11.24, the opening tonic is an obvious choice. A change to the dominant on beat 2 would not be likely if the melody has a fast tempo. The second measure is not as clear; a IV chord or a ii chord would work equally well.

Figure 11.24

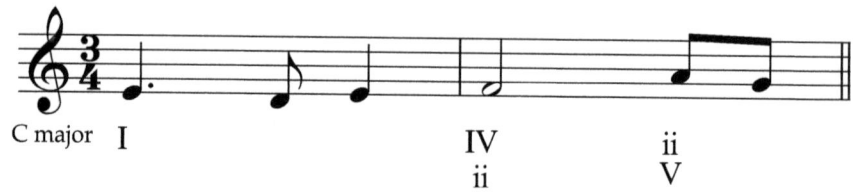

How to Write a Melody

When writing a melody, the first step is to determine a harmonic foundation. The harmony will depend on the style of the melody. It is best to keep the harmonic foundation fairly simple for your first attempts at melody writing. Later, you may want to introduce more complex harmonies, such as secondary 7ths and diminished 7ths, especially since these chords will be helpful for modulations.

In melody writing exercises, you are often asked to continue a two measure opening such as the one in Figure 11.25, to create a 16 measure composition.

Figure 11.25

The first step is to study this opening fragment and answer the following questions.

1. *What is the tempo and the time signature?* These elements will influence the type and quality of your melody.

2. *What is the key? What is the implied harmony?*

Figure 11.26

3. *Are there motives? What is the shape of the melodic fragment?* Examine the rhythm and the direction of the notes and the intervals between the notes. *What are the predominant rhythmic patterns? Do they move in steps, or leaps, or both? What are the melodic intervals? Are there broken chords?*

Figure 11.27

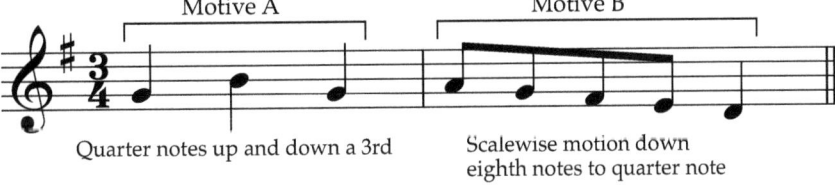

This initial investigation will provide you with the building blocks for your melody. Remember that if you base your melody on the given opening fragment, it will be easier to maintain unity. Here are some additional techniques that you can use to introduce variety and musical interest into your melodic writing.

1. Repeat a motive from the opening fragment sequentially at a higher or lower pitch.

Figure 11.28

2. Invert the entire fragment, or portion of it, that is, turn it upside down. Always be aware of the implied harmony when you do this. An exact inversion of an entire fragment may not work. It is usually better to make small adjustments so as to accommodate a cadence.

Figure 11.29

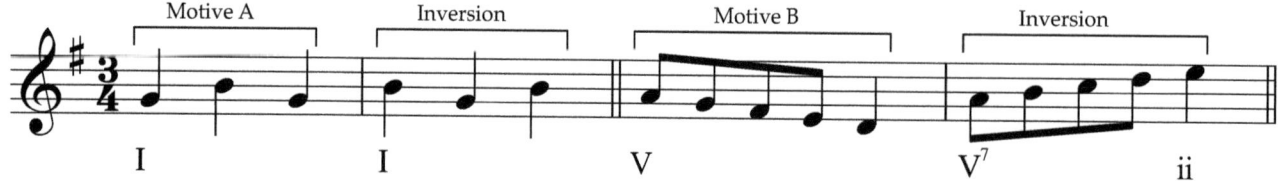

3. Alter the rhythm slightly.

Figure 11.30

4. Change the intervals between the notes.

Figure 11.31

Finally, it is important to remember that music has its roots in singing. You should be able to sing your melody. If it feels a little awkward, it may need reworking. Singers need to breathe. Make allowances for this when you plan the phrase structure. Aim for well proportioned phrases with a blend of leaps and stepwise motion. Think of a melody has a series of phrases and sentences, similar to a verse of poetry.

We will be composing melodies in 18th century style. Melodies from these dances have a number of common characteristics.

1. Melodies are usually diatonic, with an emphasis on authentic cadences and some use of secondary dominants.
2. The phrases are fairly regular and are usually four measures long.
3. Pairs of phrases often occur in a question and answer or antecedent and consequent pattern: the first phrase ends with an open cadence, and the second phrase ends with a closed cadence.
4. Melodies often modulate to standard goal keys.
    - In major keys, the standard goal key is the dominant (V).
    - In minor keys, the standard goal keys are the mediant (III) or the dominant (v).
5. Repetition and imitation of rhythms and melodic lines or motives are common.
6. Melodic forms derived from the dance forms of the period are usually binary or rounded binary.

Dance Forms

Review the following dance forms from the 18th century. Play and study the melody for each example.

Allemande

Meter: 4/4 or 2/2

Tempo: *Allegretto, Moderato, Allegro moderato*

Characteristics: A one note upbeat, (usually a 16th note); often of flow of continuous running 16th notes throughout. Stately and dignified character.

Figure 11.32

Johann Sebastian Bach
Partita 1 BWV 825 (Allemande)

Bourrée

Meter: 2/4, 4/4, or 2/2

Tempo: *Vivace, Allegro vivace*

Characteristics: Usually begins with an upbeat (quarter note or 2 eighth notes). Quick duple time; rhythmic and bright with steady quarter notes.

Figure 11.33

Johann Sebastian Bach
Partita for Solo Violin BWV 1002 (Bourree)

Courante

Meter: 3/4, 3/2, or 6/4

Tempo: *Moderato* (French *courante*); *Allegro, Vivace* (Italian *corrente*)

Characteristics: Often begins with an upbeat. Light texture and rapid figures (*courante* means "running"). Italian *corrente* is in quick triple time (usually 3/4) with running passages; French *courante* is in moderate tempo (3/2 or 6/4) with shifts from triple to duple time (hemiola).

Figure 11.34

Johann Sebastian Bach
French Suite 2 BWV 813 (Courante)

Chapter 11: Counterpoint

Gavotte

Meter: 4/4 or 2/2

Tempo: *Allegro, Allegro moderato*

Characteristics: French dance; usually two quarter note upbeats, so the phrase begins and ends in the middle of the measure

Figure 11.35

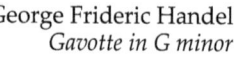

George Frideric Handel
Gavotte in G minor

Gigue

Meter: Compound time, often 6/8 or simple time in triplets

Tempo: *Allegro, Vivace, Presto*

Characteristics: Derived from the English word jig, but evolved differently in Italy and France: French *Gigue* is in compound time (often 6/8); Italian *Giga* is faster and has running notes.

Figure 11.36

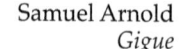

Samuel Arnold
Gigue

Minuet

Meter: 3/4 or 3/8

Tempo: *Andante, Moderato grazioso*

Characteristics: Graceful French dance; unhurried tempo; balanced phrases usually four measures long. May have an upbeat.

Figure 11.37

Christian Petzold
Menuet BWV Anh. 115

Sarabande

Meter: 3/2 or 3/4

Tempo: *Adagio, Lento*

Characteristics: Emphasis on second beat with long or accented notes. Can be chordal in texture.

Figure 11.38

Arcangelo Corelli
Sarabande

Other dance forms from this era that you may want to review are:

March
Polonaise
Passapied
Siciliana
Rigaudon

Planning a Melody

Here is a simple formula for planning and setting out a sixteen measure melody in a major key in binary(AB) form.

1. Plan out your melody on four systems of staff paper, with four measures in each system. (In the following example, notice the placement of clefs, key signatures, time signatures, bar lines, tempo markings and repeat signs.)
2. Choose cadences for each four measure phrase according to the form of the melody (in this case binary form).
3. Decide where the modulations will occur, and determine which keys will be involved.
4. Make a harmonic plan for the entire sixteen measure composition. The harmonic plan is a rough outline indicating the implied harmonies for your melody. These symbols do not have to reflect inversions or the exact structure of the bass part. They are intended to be a harmonic blueprint that will aid in creating a strong melody.

You can use these steps as a starting point for your melodies. Experiment on your own with different motives and patterns, following the basic structure. Use your imagination and study plenty of examples from the repertoire of 18th Century dances to improve the quality of your writing. Try to develop the ability to hear the notes you write down on paper. Remember also that music is meant to be heard, sing or play your melodies, and let your ear be your guide.

Figure 11.39

A Melody in Binary Form

A melody in binary form has two sections: A and B. In the worked example on the next page, both sections are eight measures long and consist of two four measure phrases.

Section A

The first two measures are in the tonic key. Complete the first phrase, ending in an authentic cadence. Use rhythmic or melodic motives from the given opening fragment to unify the music.

In the worked example, m. 3 is rhythmically based on motive B and the phrase ends with a half cadence in the tonic.

Write a second phrase that contains a modulation to the dominant and ends with an authentic cadence in that key. This is the traditional goal key for a major key composition. To create a smooth modulation, use a pivot chord and a logical harmonic progression. There is usually a repeat sign at the end of section A. Remember that cadences at the end of a section are more effective if scale degree $\hat{1}$ (the tonic) is in the soprano.

In the worked example, the second phrase repeats the opening measures exactly as originally presented. This is fine, since repetition is a common unifying feature in a composition. The phrase ends on the tonic of the new key, and the bass is decorated with an arpeggiation.

Here, we have written a simple bass part according to the implied harmony that was suggested for the original melodic plan.

Section B

The opening phrase of section B begins in the dominant key (the key in which section A ended) and ends with a half cadence in the tonic key.

In the worked example, mm. 9-10 are an exact transposition of mm. 1-2. This repetition is effective, but other techniques of motivic and rhythmic development may also be used. While this cadence is a little ambiguous (there is no return to the I chord in G major and no C naturals present), the chords do not form a cadence in D Major (ii-I), but they do form a half cadence in G major (iv- V).

The final phrase is in the tonic key, and uses rhythmic and motivic material from the opening phrase. This phrase ends with an authentic cadence. There is usually a repeat sign at the end of section B.

The worked example is derived from motive A. The melody ends on scale degree $\hat{1}$, providing a strong confirmation of the tonic key for this final cadence. Noticed also that the bass is again decorated with an arpeggiation.

Figure 11.40

Dance Type: Minuet

Phrase Endings

The melodies we are writing use two part phrase endings. Study the following arpeggiated bass lines. These are but a few of the many choices for phrase endings in these dance forms.

Figure 11.41

These endings are useful for a repeat at the end of section A. They occur after a modulation and lead the listener back to the tonic key at the beginning of the section.

Figure 11.42

C major leading back to the original key of A minor

F major leading back to the original key of D minor

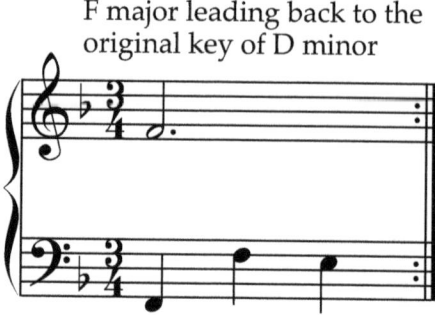

G major leading back to the original key of C major

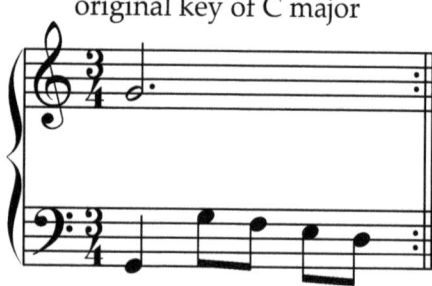

G major leading back to the original key of E minor

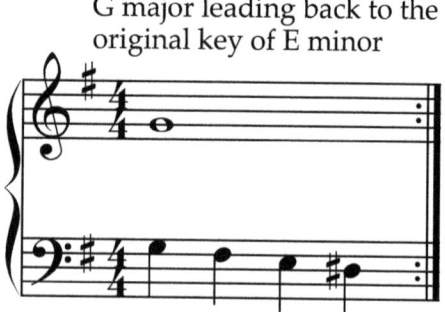

These are very effective endings, but if you choose to use them, you may also have to include first and second endings in your example. It depends on the key you choose at the beginning of section B. In Figure 11.43, the first ending leads back to the original key of G major, but not to section B which begins in D Major. Here, a second ending is required.

Figure 11.43

1. Each of the following opening fragments:
    (a)   Name the key.
    (b)   Name the type of 18th century dance that it represents.
    (c)   Continue it to create a 16 measure composition with four phrases, motivic unity, and a modulation to a traditional goal key.
    (d)   Mark the structural phrasing.
    (e)   Use binary form with repeat signs at appropriate points in the form. Name the form.
    (f)   For the first phrase, symbolize the implied harmony using functional chord symbols. At the end of this phrase name the key and cadence type.
    (g)   For the second phrase add a bass line and symbolize the implied harmony using functional chord symbols. At the end of this phrase name the key and cadence type.
    (h)   Add a bass part to the reaiming phrase endings to create two-part cadences. Name the key, provide functional chord symbols, and identify the type of cadence.

Dance type: _____

240   Chapter 11: Counterpoint

Dance type: _____

key:

Chapter 11: Counterpoint

A Binary Form Melody with an Upbeat

When the opening phrase of the binary form melody begins with an upbeat, each subsequent phrase should do the same. As a general (but not strict) rule, upbeats tend to use the same harmony as the earlier portion of the measure. Note that a change of harmony will sound stronger on a downbeat than on an upbeat.

In Figure 11.44, each phrase begins with a quarter note upbeat. This gives the melody rhythmic and harmonic unity. The upbeat to the B section is included in the repeat sign at the beginning of the third system.

Here are some other features to note in this example.

- The first phrase (mm. 1-4) ends with a half cadence.
- The second phrase (mm. 5-8) repeats the opening melodic fragment an octave lower.
- Section A ends with a perfect authentic cadence in the dominant key (D major). The final two notes of the melody (7-1) provide a strong confirmation of the new key.
- A simple bass part has been adddded to the second phrase in A.
- The B section starts with the repetition of the opening melodic fragment transposed into the dominant key.
- The third phrase (mm. 9-12) ends with a secondary dominant (V of vi) which adds tonal variety and color.
- The last phrase (mm.13-16) returns to the tonic key (G major) and ends with a perfect authentic cadence. Once again the melody ends on the tonic, giving a strong, final confirmation of the key.

Figure 11.44

Dance type: Minuet

2. Each of the following opening fragments:
   (a) Name the key.
   (b) Name the type of 18th century dance that it represents.
   (c) Continue it to create a 16 measure composition with four phrases, motivic unity, and a modulation to a traditional goal key.
   (d) Mark the structural phrasing.
   (e) Use binary form with repeat signs at appropriate points in the form. Name the form.
   (f) Add a bass part at each of the four phrase endings to create two-part cadences. Name the key, provide functional chord symbols, and identify the type of cadence.

Dance type:_____

Binary Form in Minor Keys

The tonal plan of melodies in minor keys often differs from that of melodies in major keys. Figure 11.45 will serve as a guide. Section A and section B are each eight measures long and divided into two four measure phrases.

Section A

The given two measure opening is in the tonic key of D minor. This first phrase (mm. 1-4) remains in D minor and ends with a half cadence that is decorated by a cadential six-four. Here, the quarter and eighth note motion from the opening fragment continues through the phrase, until the rhythm slows to half notes at the cadence.

The second phrase (mm. 5-8) uses material derived from the opening fragment. This phrase opens in the tonic key and modulates to the relative major (F Major). Section A ends with a perfect authentic cadence in the new key. Another option for melodies in a minor key is a modulation to the dominant minor (in this case, A minor). A simple bass part has been added to the second phrase of section A.

Section B

The third phrase (mm. 9-12) opens in F Major, the key in which section A ended. The melody incorporates material from the opening fragment, transposed into the new key. The phrase ends with a tonicization of chord iv. Note that other effective options for tonicization are chords VI and III. Chord III works particularly well with a melody that modulates to the dominant minor at the end of section A. Yet another option is to end the third phrase with a half cadence in the tonic key. The half cadence acts like a miniature dominant preparation, leading up to the return of the tonic in the fourth phrase.

The final phrase (mm. 13-16) is in the tonic key, and once again uses material derived from the opening fragment. The melody concludes with a perfect authentic cadence.

Figure 11.45

Dance type: March

3. Each of the following opening fragments:
   (a)   Name the key.
   (b)   Name the type of 18th century dance that it represents.
   (c)   Continue it to create a 16 measure composition with four phrases, motivic unity, and a modulation to a traditional goal key.
   (d)   Mark the structural phrasing.
   (e)   Use binary form with repeat signs at appropriate points in the form. Name the form.
   (f)   Add a bass part to the second phrase of Section A and at each of the four phrase endings to create two-part cadences. Name the key, provide functional chord symbols, and identify the type of cadence.

Dance type: _____

Chapter 11: Counterpoint

Dance type:_____

A Melody in Rounded Binary Form (A¹ BA²)

In rounded binary form, section A returns after section B. Figure 11.46 is 16 measures long. Section A¹ is eight measures long, and section B and A² are each four measures long.

Section A¹

The given opening is in the tonic key of F minor. The first phrase (mm. 1-4) ends in the tonic key with a half cadence decorated by a cadential six-four. The melody continues the stepwise eighth note motion from the opening fragment.

The second phrase (mm. 5-8) opens with a slight development of the first phrase and contains a modulation to the dominant minor (C minor). Section A¹ ends with a perfect authentic cadence in the new key. Note that the melody ends on the tonic. A simple bss part is added to the second phrase of A¹.

Section B

The third phrase (mm. 9-12) is entirely in C Minor (the key in which section A¹ ended) with an exact transposition of the opening fragment. This section ends with an authentic cadence in C Minor.

Section A²

The final phrase is a restatement of the opening phrase in section A¹. However, this phrase stays in the tonic key and ends with an authentic cadence.

Repeat Signs and Cadences

Notice that each half of the melody is repeated, in other words, section A¹ is repeated and then sections B and A² are repeated together. This pattern of repeats is common but not absolutely necessary. Rounded binary form is determined by the cadence at the end of the first A section and the return of A after the B section. As long as the cadence at the end of the A¹ section is an open cadence, that is, a half cadence or a cadence in any key other than the tonic, the form is rounded binary.

Figure 11.46

Dance type: Gigue

4. Each of the following opening fragments:
   - (a) Name the key.
   - (b) Name the type of 18th century dance that it represents.
   - (c) Continue it to create a 16 measure composition with four phrases, motivic unity, and a modulation to a traditional goal key.
   - (d) Mark the structural phrasing.
   - (e) Use rounded binary form with repeat signs at appropriate points in the form. Name the form.
   - (f) Add a bass part to the second phrase of A^1 and at each of the four phrase endings to create two-part cadences. Name the key, provide functional chord symbols, and identify the type of cadence.

Dance type:_____

key:

Dance type:_____

key:

Chapter 11: Counterpoint

5. Each of the following opening fragments:

   (a) Name the key.

   (b) Name the type of 18th century dance that it represents.

   (c) Continue it to create a 16 measure composition with four phrases, motivic unity, and a modulation to a traditional goal key.

   (d) Use rounded or simple or rounded binary form with repeat signs at appropriate points in the form. Name the form.

   (e) Mark the structural phrasing.

   (f) For the first phrase, symbolize the implied harmony using functional chord symbols. At the end of this phrase name the key and cadence type.

   (g) For the second phrase add a bass line and symbolize the implied harmony using functional chord symbols. At the end of this phrase name the key and cadence type.

   (h) For the third and fourth phrase endings: Add a bass line at the cadence, symbolize the implied harmony using functional chord symbols, and name the key and type of cadence.

Dance type:_____

Dance type:_____

www.ingramcontent.com/pod-product-compliance
Ingram Content Group UK Ltd.
Pitfield, Milton Keynes, MK11 3LW, UK
UKHW051302180426
11947UKWH00020B/1852